DATE DUE

DEMCO. INC. 38-2931

Our Emperors Have No Clothes

Also by Alan Weiss

Million Dollar Consulting

Making It Work

Managing for Peak Performance

The Innovation Formula (with Mike Robert)

Our Emperors Have No Clothes

BY

ALAN WEISS, PH.D.

Career Press
3 Tice Road
P.O. Box 687
Franklin Lakes, NJ 07417
1-800-Career-1
201-848-0310 (outside U.S.)
Fax: 201-848-1727

Our Emperors Have No Clothes
ISBN 1-56414-177-2, $21.99
Cover design by The Gottry Communications Group, Inc.
Text design by A Good Thing Inc.
Printed in the U.S.A. by Book-mart Press

To order this title by mail, please include price as noted above, $2.50 handling per order, and $1.00 for each book ordered. Send to: Career Press, Inc., 3 Tice Road, P.O. Box 687, Franklin Lakes, NJ 07417

Or call toll-free 1-800-CAREER-1 (Canada: 201-848-0310) to order using VISA or MasterCard, or for further information on books from Career Press.

Library of Congress Cataloging-in-Publication Data

Weiss, Alan 1946-
   Our emperors have no clothes/ by Alan Weiss.
   p. cm.
Includes index.
ISBN 1-56414-177-2 (hardcover)
   1. Management. 2. Leadership.
I. Title.
HD31.W433   1995
658.4'.092--dc20   95-185
                                                     CIP

This is dedicated to the one I love.
(with apologies to the Shirelles)

Note: The quotes used at the beginning of each of the four parts of this book are all excerpted from "The Emperor's New Clothes," from *Twelve Tales*, by Hans Christian Andersen, translated by Erik Bledgvad, McElderry Books, 1994.

Acknowledgments

No one can pontificate through a book like this, much less sell it to his agent and his publisher, without some solid experience and a host of first-hand observations. For that experience, and the opportunity to make those observations, I'm indebted to the clients of Summit Consulting Group, Inc., who have trusted my firm to be something more than the proverbial consultants called in to identify a problem—and who then stay to become part of it.

Particular thanks to clients and friends Marilyn Martiny of Hewlett-Packard; Steve Darien, Art Strohmer (retired), George Rizk, and another 50 fine people at Merck & Co; Fred Kerst of Calgon; Mike Magsig of Cologne Life Reinsurance; Mary Haymore of Allergan; Bill Kreykes of Rhode Island Hospital; Pat Scott formerly of GE and now with Professional Development Associates; Ron Gartner of Mercedes-Benz; Connie Bentley of Zenger-Miller; Mike Davis and Ed Steiger of Tastemaker; Mike Landry of Merck Frosst Canada, Ltd; Ed Baron, John Finneman, Bill Winter, and the rest of the gang at the American Press Institute; and Bill Chapin and Susan Maxman of the American Institute of Architects. Apologies to those I've inadvertently omitted.

I'm also in the debt of my friends who aren't clients, but who have helped me keep my ego in check through rigorous beatings, threats, and imprecations. These therapists include Jeff Herman, my literary agent; Susie DeWeese of Speakers Corner, who books many of my speeches; Lou Heckler, the unselfish professional who recommended me to her; the members of the New England Speakers Association, who made me their king; Bill Howe, headhunter extraordinaire; Bob Janson, David Whitsett, and Tom Walther, my consulting cabal; Ben Tregoe, who gave me my start—on his nickel—in this business; and Keith Darcy, ethicist.

My kids claim I never mention them. Danielle and Jason. There.

My love and thanks to my soulmate and wife of 27 years, Maria, who has always had the magic words: "Forget the mortgage—do what you have to do."

And finally, once again my thanks for the unerring editorial assistance of L. T. Weiss, who has now been with me through three books. May his kind go on forever.

Table of Contents

Introduction

My experiences in consulting demonstrate that the American worker, supervisor, and middle manager have received a bum rap for too long, and it's now time to set the record straight. Virtually all of the organizational bromides, models, aphorisms, and outright scams over the past decade have been aimed at increasing the productivity of the employee. But the fact is that quality improvement, continuous process improvement, empowerment, participative management, reengineering, downsizing, stewardship, servant leadership, doing more with less, grids, matrices, personality stereotyping, and all the other approaches guaranteed to create riches—for consultants—have only served to camouflage the most critical problem in American business.

Stupid management. Let's tell it like it is. The emperors have no clothes.

I've been in the consulting business for almost 25 years, and have run my own company for the last 10. During that period, I've traveled to 49 countries and 48 states, and visited in excess of 3,000 organizations, pubic and private, large and small, mostly successful, and occasionally desultory. I'm a highly productive, optimistic guy by almost any measure. And I tend to work with very profitable, blue-chip organizations.

There is ample evidence that enlightened leadership and brilliant management exist, which is the good news. However, they are notable by their relative rarity, which is the bad news. Too often I've seen the equivalent of "When morale improves, the beatings will stop" as official corporate policy. Captain Bligh would not be at all uncomfortable in a large part of organizational America. Compared to subordinates today, Spencer Christian had pretty decent job security. The greatest irony is that improved senior management is not capital intensive, and costs much less in the long run than does the tolerance of current ineptness. In my journeys through organizations, I found that many others felt the same way.

Thus, *Our Emperors Have No Clothes* was born. At first it was a book that simply detailed the excesses, boondoggles, profligacy, incompetence, and malfeasance that I observed in clients, prospects, vendors, suppliers, civic organizations, charities, other consulting firms, and the government. But I realized that it's too easy simply to carp, and my consultant's soul wouldn't let me proceed too far without offering some solutions. Not one of those solutions is vaguely related to rocket science or brain surgery. But then, no matter what you hear from the gurus or academics, management *seldom* is.

I offer here the obvious, which consultancy *usually* is. But the obvious has often been like the elephant in the room, which we politely refuse to recognize, although the sensory indications are impossible to miss. It's time we held senior managers to a standard representative of their remuneration. It's time employees stopped getting the blame for management mistakes and, much worse, getting the ax for management recovery. It's time to admit that the elephant is crushing us, and that it stinks.

We can no longer afford, nor tolerate, stupid management. But first, we have to call it what it is.

— Alan Weiss, Ph.D.
East Greenwich, Rhode Island

Part One

E x a m p l e s

"Many years ago, there lived an emperor who was so immensely fond of beautiful new clothes that he spent all his money on being splendidly dressed."

Chapter 1

Origins of Stupid Management
How Did These People Get That Way?

"Any fool can keep a rule. God gave him a brain to know when to break the rule."

—General Willard W. Scott

Do organizations really allow abysmally poor leaders to endure, let alone flourish? Shouldn't we conclude that our corporate Darwinism will ruthlessly eliminate the incompetent, especially when that ineptitude is reflected in the pockets of the shareholders? After all, capitalism is a cold system. It takes no prisoners, right?

Well, not quite. It takes a chosen few into very comfortable captivity, indeed. Take the case of Andrew Sigler who, at this writing, is the CEO of Champion International, and has been for more than 20 years. Over his tenure, Champion has generated a meager 8.6% annual return to its owners, which is worse than 90% of organizations of similar size, and far worse than its direct competitors in the paper industry. Although Champion stock has enjoyed a revival over recent years, it's still not within shouting distance of its 1987 high point.[1]

In 1993, Mr. Sigler earned $1,861,000, including a $220,000 bonus, in exchange for leading his company to a 2.7% annual rate of return over the prior 5 years. He was the 148th highest-paid CEO in the nation, ahead of such people as Josh Weston of Automatic Data Processing (20.2% annual rate of return), Philip Knight of Nike (44.8%), Harry Merlo of Louisiana-Pacific (37.5%), and the inestimable Warren Buffet of Berkshire Hathaway (28.3%). These gentlemen finished 55th, 2nd, 5th, and 13th, respectively, in ranking of five-year returns to shareholders.[2]

---

[1] See *Fortune*, June 13, 1994, p. 14: "The World's Worst?"

[2] *Fortune*, July 25, 1994, pp. 95–102: "CEO Pay."

Why am I picking on Mr. Sigler?

Mr. Sigler could have been any number of people in the example. Sanford I. Weill, CEO of Travelers Insurance, "ought to write out a check to his shareholders for $91 million as the most overpaid CEO in the country" according to a university math professor at California-Berkeley.[3] We have allowed our organizational pyramids to resemble heaven as one gets closer to the top. Past sins are forgiven, the world looks completely different, mere mortals do the dirty work, *and nothing unpleasant can ever happen to you.* If I keep getting rewarded despite my performance, how much better can heaven actually be? You've got a pass that will get me through the pearly gates? Sorry, I don't think so. I don't see how I could be as happy as I am behind the boardroom doors.

I know a woman named Margarette. She used to work as a sales representative for a large computer manufacturer. You all know people like her. She received a 2-week training program that combined an orientation to the company's products with a professional selling skills course, both of which were quite well done. She was then placed under the tutelage of a veteran district manager, received a couple of weeks of on-the-job training, was handed her car keys and a map to her territory, and told, "Go get 'em!" And so Margarette lugged her bag and dutifully visited her prospects, spending evenings studying the company literature and filing her reports.

Unfortunately, a combination of the increasing competition, economic uncertainty, consumer fickleness, and—sad to say—a basic lack of sales talent caused Margarette to miss her quota for her first quarter. Her district manager gave her some advice, accompanied her on a few calls, and provided some helpful feedback. Margarette talked to her colleagues, studied even harder, and worked more feverishly to make her second-quarter quota, which she missed by an even wider margin. In another 30 days, after less than 9 months on the job, she was terminated. The company considered it a failure on its part as well as Margarette's, and tried to understand what they had done wrong in the selection and training process to avoid similar, costly mistakes.

Margarette's plight should be very familiar to most of you. The more a job has a tangible, quantitative performance expectation, the easier it is to measure results and reach conclusions about progress. And the more the job has a direct impact on profitability and shareholder value, the more urgent it becomes to assess performance and make dispassionate decisions about competence. The sales force has traditionally been the most vivid example of these dynamics. No organization that I've ever seen can afford (a) poor information about the performance of its salespeople, (b) tolerance of poor

---

[3] See "Survey Finds CEO Pay Has Little to Do with Performance," citing Professor Graif Crystal, *Providence Journal,* Oct. 9, 1994, p. F18.

performers in sales jobs, and (c) ignorance about the criteria that determine whether one is likely to be successful in a sales position. In other words, organizations have to know:

1. What constitutes success in the position?
2. How will we know it if it happens?
3. What do we do with excellent performers and poor performers?

That kind of scrutiny seems to evaporate as we ascend the corporate ladder. I've seen underwriters held accountable for the risks they've accepted or rejected, reporters held accountable for the accuracy and timeliness of their stories, and bank branch managers held accountable for the profitability and new product sales of their branches. Few excuses are accepted from these performers. (One of my favorite general managers has a sign in his office, prominently displayed, which simply states "No Whining.")

However, when was the last time you saw an executive held to the success of the implementation of the strategic plan? When was the last time an executive vice president was fired because the costly "humongous total quality initiative" he or she personally sponsored turned out to be a flaming debacle? Down below, feet are held to the fire. Up above, the flames have died and the feet are up on desks.

Stupid management didn't just appear one day while the board was deliberating on what to have for lunch. It grew because our systems and procedures—let alone our rewards and incentives—encouraged it to grow. We threw a great deal of corporate fertilizer on it. Things stank, but we all agreed to ignore the smell.

Moreover, people tend to hire people just like themselves. Prospective employees "self-select" to a startling degree, choosing organizations that appeal to their own value systems. No one has been managing the process of holding top management responsible: Stupid managers hired others just like them, who rejoiced in the reward system operating so splendidly on their behalf.

Here is my genesis of the origins of stupid management.

1. Corporate hierarchies grow

As enterprises grew dramatically after World War II, more and more people were driven upwards, away from the product and the customer, to handle "administrative" needs. Legions of people developed, on payrolls that could easily afford them, whose job it was to manage *other people,* information, reporting, planning, training, and so forth. Not only did the specialties proliferate *but also the hierarchies within the specialties expanded*. It wasn't sufficient to have a training person, for example. The growing organization needed a training department, which required its own managers and support staff, as opposed to the original training person who *was the* support staff to the line operation.

What eventually developed were parallel hierarchies, which are something akin to parallel universes on *Star Trek*. If you think I'm being facetious, take a look at the corporate organization charts. Many of them now have entities called chief human resources officer, chief information systems officer, chief financial officer, chief operating officer, chief customer relations officer, and on and on. We've assumed that the most effective way to support the organization is to create parallel hierarchies, so that departments might support departments (as opposed to people supporting each other).

These profligate hierarchies, standing like ancient artifacts in the Sahara, have pushed regiments of senior officers farther and farther away from direct accountability with the customer, the product, and the service.

2. Hierarchies assume a static nature

There's a rather interesting and immutable fact about human behavior. None of us readily abandons behaviors that we perceive have accounted for our success. This is why incredible sums of money are wasted on training programs for key people who haven't the slightest intention of changing. Imagine providing a class in delegating or empowering others to a group of executives who got where they are precisely because they have rigidly controlled everything in sight, including, but not limited to, the lunch menu, for the past 25 years? I've actually seen ethics programs provided for wheelers and dealers who have been consistently and richly rewarded by their organizations for bringing in business that requires the absence of ethics.

Once someone has gained the corner office, company parking space, stock options, trips to corporate retreats, and assorted other perquisites, they are not about to get up in the morning with an attitude of "let's make some waves!" They are going to tend to stick a toe in the water and hope that the ripples can be controlled. Hierarchies protect themselves—if you don't believe me, just ask a woman or minority member trying to go where no woman or minority member has gone before. Thus, people who succeeded in ascending the pyramids set themselves to work adding mortar and improving the view. They became self-sustaining over generations of management.

3. Complexity arrives

During the 1980s, the game changed. Depending on whom you talk to or whose book you read, this was caused by:

- The computer revolution
- Technological breakthrough and miniaturization
- The Japanese (we will hear about them repeatedly as we progress)
- The communications revolution

- Ronald Reagan
- The accent on quality
- The accent on customer service
- Globalization
- The Boston Consulting Group
- The banking crisis
- The Soviet Union
- Increasingly diverse demographics
- Lee Iacocca
- The women's movement
- Bill Gates
- UFOs

I realize that some of the entries above may be redundant, especially the last two. But the point is that change does accelerate exponentially, and there will never be an occasion to look back at the, '80s as "the decade of change." The '90s will be even more dramatic, as will the decades that follow.

Hierarchies can't deal with change very well, particularly since they are oriented toward stasis. It is a myth that employees are the most resistant to change. Senior management resists change as aggressively and desperately as any group I've ever encountered. They are least prepared to deal with it (being furthest from the customer), are most threatened by it (it may change the hierarchy), and are in the best position to assiduously resist it (they have the corporate clout). Picture a Rottweiler watching you move toward its dinner.

But the complexity of the '80s presented some serious problems. It was clear that something was needed to guide the organization, since traditional methods weren't working, and long-established enterprises were going under. When a Pan American Airlines has to fold the tent, it's a sobering moment for all organizations. There can come a point when earnings are so bad (or nonexistent) that even somnolent shareholders might protest. Executives who were accustomed to managing in unexciting times with little interference from their boards were rudely awakened to the fact that their neat, tabbed, complicated strategic documents, locked inside all of those three-ring binders in everyone's bottom drawer, were not going to be the route out. And that leads to the final stage in our journey.

4. The embracing of management fads and gimmicks

For longer than anyone cares to admit, executives have been subscribing to the fad-of-the-month club. With more and more people engaged in work distant from the customer, and parallel hierarchies cementing themselves together just when complexity demanded nimbleness and agility, the alternatives for resolving increasingly onerous corporate difficulties were reduced to two:

1. Think our way out of it, which is why we're paid so much.
2. Throw money at it, which we can do because we're paid so much.

Aiding and abetting solution #2, which is the more expensive but far easier of the two, is our industry of consultants, professors, writers, celebrity executives, experts, advice-givers, media gurus, motivational speakers, and other entrepreneurial folk who can easily spot someone trying to fix something without getting dirty or sweaty, or even highly involved. (Now, I myself am a consultant, speaker, and author, and have made a fine living at it. There are many in this industry and in these professions who perform high-quality, legitimate, and important work. Now that I've acknowledged that, back to the arena.)

For the edification of the reader, I've provided Figure 1.1 to depict the synergistic relationships that develop as executives seek a magic potion to solve their problems, and the experts see money to be made.

In this dynamic, the following actions are occurring:

Position	Left Gear	Right Gear
1.	Executive seeks panacea.	Professor perfects "breakthrough."
2.	Symptoms of problem identified.	Solution marketed, seeking problem.
3.	Solution purchased.	Solution sold.
4.	Heavy investment in solution.	Heavy profit from solution.
5.	CEO shows board action is taken.	Professor publicizes client to others.

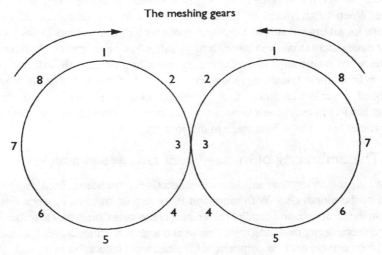

The meshing gears

Figure 1.1.

6.	Results are less than expected.	Professor: "implementation deficient."
7.	Approach is disavowed and abandoned.	Client is disavowed and abandoned.
8.	Regroup, seek new break-through.	Develop next breakthrough.

Lest you find this excessively cynical, let me remind you that some very situational, albeit valid, ideas have been transmogrified into management religions. Here are just a few of the approaches that may have been situational, occasionally applicable, dependent on the nature of the business, subject to executive egos and/or just plain gaseous, which have been embraced and abandoned over the recent past:

- Transactional analysis
- Left brain/right brain
- Total quality management
- Kroning[4]
- est
- A passion for excellence
- Time management
- Shareholder value
- Empowerment
- Reengineering

- Personality styles
- T-groups
- Continuous process improvement
- Statistical process improvement
- 1-minute management
- Customer service
- Strategic portfolios
- Return on assets (or equity)
- Downsizing[5]
- Restructuring

My apologies if I've omitted one of your favorites (or cast aspersions on your value system). My point is that even basically sound psychological approaches (transactional analysis) and logical business practices (customer service) were mixed with dubious psychobabble (est) and unproven tactics (downsizing) to create an alchemy of approaches designed to cure any ill. Hard thinking wasn't necessary, just hard cash.

Even the best of these approaches has failed, and the usual causes are lack of top-level support. What transpires isn't surprising, but it is alarming. The executives buy an expensive "solution" that the consultants help to implement, *and then another corporate hierarchy grows around the new program.* There are actually vice presidents of quality in many companies, and other

---

[4] If you'd care to learn how Pac Bell spent $40 million of the rate payers' money on New Age twaddle so bad that the California Public Utilities Commission had to step in, see *Success Magazine,* Oct. 1988, p. 96: "Let the Manager Beware: The Dangers of Mystical Management Advice," by Alan Weiss.

[5] See, for example, *The New York Times,* July 10, 1994, p. 21: "Questioning Productivity Beliefs."

people with titles like "director of TQM." Excuse me, but isn't quality *everyone's job?*

What's worse, I've encountered people who have decided that they will build, maintain, and ascend these new programmatic hierarchies, and will defend that career path with their lives. Consequently, there are otherwise sane people in organizations demanding that every decision be made only in conjunction with the application of the latest personality profile du jour, most of which aren't even validated instruments according to criteria published by the American Psychological Association. There are those who demand that employees and managers attend rigorously scheduled quality meetings, *even if it means canceling or postponing customer meetings.* Don't laugh; I've seen it firsthand. There is the now-case-study example of a new CEO at Florida Power and Light dismantling the very system that his predecessor had used to win the coveted Baldrige Award for Quality, because the new man realized that more attention was being paid—and resources devoted—to winning awards and conforming to award criteria than was directed to customer needs.

Exactly where is the cart and where is the horse? Not a bad question for executives to ponder.

And Then Came the Rules

So, executives moved from an affluent, growing period when any decision was a good decision and it was hard to go wrong, to one in which every major decision could have a profound impact on the success of the enterprise. They moved from guaranteed comfort to guaranteed discomfort, from normalcy to constant change, from a docile to an assertive workforce, and from leading to following. What hadn't changed were their abilities and tools. The best executives learned fast, innovated, took risks, and changed their behaviors. The rest tried to protect themselves. Unfortunately, it seems as if there are more of the latter than the former. And the majority has been assisted by those who would sell "easy" solutions and alliterative answers.

Unfortunately, I'm not discussing purely historical artifacts. The dynamics continue to operate much as they always have, except the results are more visible, forcing even comatose boards to occasionally consider some action. When GM's board decided—after agonizing soul searching—to relieve Ed Stempel of the CEO's post, the press reacted with front-page stories. In the hundreds of thousands of column inches devoted to the decision, only two small items were consistently missed:

1. The board acted as it was intended to act, in that boards have relatively few duties, one of which is to evaluate and act on executive performance.

2. The reason that things had moved to such a pitiful state was that the board had consistently failed to do anything about Stempel's predecessor, Roger Smith, who retired with full panoply even though his reign was so ludicrous that a documentary film about him won a foreign-film award.[6]

Or take the current plight of Goodrich under CEO John D. Ong. He moved the former tiremaker (How many of you thought they were still in that business?) into the PVC business, then sold that off and refocused on the chemical business. He can change course, it seems, as quickly as a fleeing rabbit. But he might be better off standing in the headlights for a while. His shareholders have reaped an underwhelming 1.4% return on equity annually since Ong became CEO in 1979, compared with the Standard & Poor's average of 14.4%. During that time, Goodrich's sales have dropped 3.5% per year, while the S&P index has grown at 5.4%. The stock is currently at 44; its recent high was 69 in 1989. *Business Week* quotes a former Goodrich executive as saying that the company "keeps getting fixed and fixed and fixed."[7]

As organizations have grown, they have created "rules" to govern themselves. These rules are often in the form of policies and procedures, operating manuals and guidelines, employee handbooks, value statements, missions, and so on. When I look around an organization and see yards of these books lining the walls, one thing becomes obvious: Management in these companies is trying to prevent judgment from being exercised. The more there are policies, the less executives are trusting their people. The fewer formal policies, the more latitude for judgment. If I allow you to exercise judgment, I have to trust that you will do the right thing, that your mistakes will be honest and constitute learning opportunities for you, and that your objectives are essentially congruent with mine. That is a leap of faith which relatively few executives are willing to negotiate.

I began my career in 1968 at Prudential Insurance, as a member of home office management in Newark, New Jersey. During those innocent times, Prudential would ring a bell at 10:30 and 2:30, which signaled morning and afternoon breaks. All of us—from hourly workers to midlevel managers—would take off to grab coffee, smoke a cigarette (still not a felony at that point), romance a coworker, and otherwise escape from the desks and

---

[6] The film was called *Roger and Me,* and showed in first-run, artsy movie houses around the country. The creator became an instant celebrity and later had a weekly television show called *TV Nation.*

[7] Statistics and citation from *Business Week,* July 18, 1994, p. 86: "Goodrich: From Tires to PVC to Chemicals to Aerospace."

phones that tethered us. Ten minutes later a second bell signaled the end of our freedom, and managers kept tabs on anyone who reported back too late.

Such abridgments of our "empowerment" wouldn't be tolerated today, of course, because this is a more enlightened time. Or is it?

These are some of the "rules" that, formally and informally, operate in organizations I've observed. Do any seem familiar to you? Whether written and formalized or enforced by an unspoken culture, they are equally inflexible:

- Men and women are expected to conform to certain dress codes, whether or not they interact with customers. This often extends to a man wearing his jacket whenever he leaves his desk, and to the height of the heels that women wear.
- Presentations to groups are made within strict parameters, including the format of the slides used, if and when questions are taken, hand-out material, and time limits.
- Certain company benefits are on the books but not to be used. For example, maternity leave may be 6 to 12 months, but women are expected to return to work in 2 months, and men are not expected to avail themselves of the benefit at all. Violating such mores means that you are not serious about your work.
- Some of the company values are for "show" only. For example, the organization may promote conservation by providing van pools, but employees are expected to work later than 5 p.m. despite the fact that the vans depart at that time.
- "Face time" is as important as the work itself, and being at work from, say, 7:30 a.m. to 7:30 p.m. is valuable, especially if your boss comes later and departs earlier. (One of my favorite incidents is the newly hired MBA graduate, with absolutely no assigned duties yet, arriving at 7:30 every morning. Even veterans at the game thought he was pushing it.)
- To advance in the organization, one must spend time in "selected" as-signments, some of which may be truly valuable (i.e., internationally, or in the sales force) and some of which are purely political (i.e., everyone at executive level has always spent time at headquarters, or everyone has to have worked in Bill's division).

How much freedom do organizations allow? How much opportunity is there for stupid management to reverse itself using new ideas, young blood, and outside influences? Not much.

In our survey work, we've found that the major factor cited as responsible for advancement in organizations, far above competence, experience, special projects, education, and even luck, is sponsorship. This is sometimes called *mentoring* or *championing*. Sponsorship is more than the traditional mentor, who may provide wisdom and feedback on one's performance, and serve as an outlet for difficult pressures. Sponsors aggressively support and promote their wards.

Sponsorship often begins at the time of hiring, when an executive takes personal responsibility for attracting, recruiting, and obtaining a highly regarded MBA candidate, crack salesperson, or technical specialist. It's not uncommon for these acquisitions to be a part of the executive's evaluation. Sometimes sponsorship begins somewhat later, when an executive spots a rising star from among the latest class of hires. It's a phenomenon that almost always takes place early in one's career. I've rarely heard of anyone being sponsored once they've been employed for several years, although there are exceptions when the company feels the need to promote minorities or women to compensate for past omissions.

Sponsors ensure that "their people" receive projects that will enable them to shine. Since the success of the person being sponsored is synonymous with the sponsor's own success, the individual is not permitted to fail. A "fail-safe" zone emerges, in which highly visible assignments and responsibilities are bestowed on people who receive a safety net as well. And those being sponsored learn how the game is played: They become primary adherents of the kinds of rules cited above. The system successfully reinforces itself.

Now, who is a sponsor most likely to choose as the "mentee"? The criteria are simple: Someone who is likely to shine, who will be willing to adhere to the rules, who will support the sponsor and represent the sponsor well. In other words, the sponsor chooses someone exactly like him. And it usually is a "him."

The power structure in most of our organizations remains predominantly white male. There is a significant risk in sponsoring someone who is not like you, and a white woman, minority male, or, especially, a minority woman represents high "risk." What if one of these people chooses to dress differently, or deliberately uses nonstandard English, or demands a holiday that is not on the approved list?[8] Sponsors support people like themselves, because it's more comfortable, it's informally supported by the organization, and there's less "risk."

The bottom line to all of this is that stupid management, like an amoeba, has a method of recreating itself. That's why, even in the face of poor operating results, board dissatisfaction, and shareholder unrest, changes at the top often have minimal impact when the vacancies are filled from within.

---

[8] Not only do many firms not allow Martin Luther King Day as a paid holiday, many do not even allow the Jewish holy days as paid holidays, even though Good Friday is allowed. The provision that one must apply "floating" days or personal days to these observances sends a clear message about acceptability.

Anyone with the initiative and strength to truly change the system *never would have endured in the system to that point*. Hence, the "farm team" is simply a mirror image of the major league franchise. It's no accident that some of the largest and most impressive organizations in the country—despite their cultures, products, and geographies—have had to go "outside" in order to procure the kind of top talent deemed necessary to take them into the future. These organizations have included Allied Signal, Merck & Co., Apple Computer, and United Airlines, to name a few. At this writing, it appears that Prudential will do so for the first time in more than a century.

Power and Powerlessness

While the origins of stupid management can be understood, its continuation is harder to rationalize. This is an age of rapid and mass communication, increasingly intelligent employees and consumers, more activist boards, tougher regulatory scrutiny, and tighter margins. Why do entire industries sometimes take a beating, as the auto industry and steel industries have, and yet fail to make transitions that seem obvious? Not one vacuum tube manufacturer successfully entered the transistor business.

The final point I want to make in this chapter pertains: Power does not corrupt, no matter what you might conclude from the aforementioned. *Powerlessness corrupts.* What we are witnessing today are essentially powerless organizations, in which employees have relatively little influence over the outcome of their work. Human beings cannot, like ants, work mindlessly in a community without individual power. Consequently, if real power is unavailable and unattainable, people in organizations will create artificial power, otherwise known as *bureaucracy*. Bureaucracy is the triumph of means over ends, the fixation on the input over the output, the emphasis on task rather than result. It is best summed up in the tacit explanation underlying any bureaucrat's response: "There is no reason for it, it's just our policy."

On a freezing cold February evening, I and one other passenger were on a 19-seat commuter plane bound from Boston to Quebec City. When we landed, the gate agent of the airline ushered us from a bitterly cold tarmac into a bitterly cold, deserted immigration area and told us to wait for the immigration agent. After a 10-minute wait that seemed like an hour, he appeared, and took his time arranging his desk and sorting through his colored pens. Finally, he turned to me and said, "Next!"

We went through the questions that are so vital to enter Canada from the U.S. (i.e., "Are you carrying any domestic farm animals in your luggage?"), after which he stamped my customs declaration and turned to the other, shivering passenger and said, "Next!"

After another round of questioning, the gate agent told us to wait in an area about 10 yards away for the customs agent. Some of you can guess what was about to happen: The immigration agent put away his papers, collected his pens, adjusted his uniform, walked 10 yards over to another desk and—*Voilà!*—he was the customs agent. Then he looked over at me. And said, "Next!"

I went into the stratosphere. "Are you talking to me?!" I yelled.

"Forms, please," he commanded.

"Why the hell didn't you just keep the forms when you first stamped them! Why are we freezing in here while you change desks?"

"Because this is the procedure," he meticulously informed me.

The other passenger told him that he left his forms with the first guy. I wish I'd have thought of that.

How many times a day do we deal with disempowered people who corrupt our systems and businesses? Most of us have our "favorites," whether in the division of motor vehicles, the local utility, or a department store's billing operation. Day in and day out, stupid management is exponentially multiplied by "procedures" that are solely in place to provide artificial power to those who have been denied real power.

After being treated poorly by Delta Airlines, I complained to the gate agent, who said she could do nothing, and who referred me to her supervisor, who told me he could do nothing. I then wrote to customer relations, which responded with a personal apology and the offer of 2,000 miles added to my frequent flyer account. I accepted with gratitude and a good feeling about Delta. But how much more effective would the relationship have been if that gate agent had the discretion, judgment, ability, and motivation to resolve the complaint on the spot? People rejoice when they are able to reach a top-level executive and have a complaint immediately resolved by someone with the clout to do so on the spot. We generally regard that experience as a positive one, which reinforces that the executives are really pro-consumer.

But just the opposite is true. If those executives were really pro-consumer and intelligent managers, they would surrender some of that clout and send it downward to those employees who actually deal with customers every day. *The fact that we have to laboriously climb up the corporate hierarchy to reach someone who will ultimately provide satisfaction is a major indicator of stupid management.* What a waste of everyone's time, from the consumer to the employee who can't be of help, and to the executive who is spending time resolving rather minor problems at an inflated salary level for such work.

So rather than provide employees with real power—which I define as the ability to make decisions that influence the outcome of their work—employees are largely *disempowered* and left to their own devices to create artificial power to give them some sense of control. "No, you can't substitute a side dish on this menu." "I'm sorry, but we don't handle exchanges during evening hours." "I'm not permitted to change anything over a $20 bill." "The only number you can call is the service number, even if it is constantly busy."

Not long ago I stayed in a Hyatt Regency Hotel that had a Hyatt Hotline advertised in the room. "For any problem, no matter how big or small, call the Hyatt Hotline. We're here to assist the business traveler with any need." I didn't have a room service menu. I quickly concluded that this was a job for the Hyatt Hotline. I anxiously dialed the number.

"Hello, Hyatt Hotline, how may we help you?"

"This is Alan Weiss in 703. I don't have a room service menu in the room."

"I'm sorry, we don't handle that. Try banquets. Good-bye."

What does that Hyatt Hotline handle, nuclear war?

Stupid management is much more pernicious and weedlike than it first appears. The systems and procedures that poor management implements are perpetuators of the status quo. What we see at lower levels, and often assign to poor attitudes and marginal performers, is simply the manifestation of stupid management at the top. Employees do not, by and large, enjoy confrontations, arguments, and insults. They generally receive their gratification from a job well done and a pleased customer. It's the system that mitigates against this.

There is a current rage for empowerment circulating about the land. At face value, this is a legitimate and positive technique. However, what actually transpires is an even more restrictive set of guidelines and procedures established by senior managers as "protection" against the empowerment. What results are employees who are given greater accountability with even less authority, more exposure to risk without the means to effectively alleviate it, and more decisions to be made without the skills and backing required to effectively make them. Empowerment is not abdication. It should be a collaborative effort to push real decision-making as far down into the organization's depths as possible. Unfortunately, it's all too often simply the latest vehicle used to throw some money at the problem and to create the impression that something is being done.

Where did stupid management come from, and how did people get that way? It grew from circumstances that became more complex and demanding while management styles remained simplistic and boards remained undemanding. It's nurtured by hierarchies that reproduce themselves, and by top-level people who hire in their own images. It's often hidden under the weight of tons of money being tossed into a myriad of programs designed to try to Band-Aid the symptoms while executives are absolved from grappling with the causes.

It's a product of our times that we've allowed to happen.

How to Clothe the Emperors, Part I

1. Boards must perform a minimum of three functions: Establish strategic goals, communicate those goals accurately to senior management, and evaluate senior management performance against those goals on a regular basis.

2. Support needs aren't automatically best met by different departments. Every manager in an organization should be a human resources manager. Support should be within the operation wherever possible. Support hierarchies should be eliminated. We don't need a chief human resources officer if management is doing its job.

3. CEOs specifically must be held accountable for what happens on their "watch." We should adhere more closely to the Japanese example. If people they chose for key positions are incompetent, then the CEOs have been incompetent.

4. No external program should be purchased (nor internally developed), no matter how lofty its goal, which does not tie in to the organization's strategic goals.

5. The only "awards" pursued by an organization should be bestowed by its customers. Customer focus groups and panels should be a regular component of an organization's operating philosophy.

6. Employees should be encouraged to use judgment, and be rewarded for the desired behaviors, not only "victories." Granting a refund on the spot to someone who was later shown not to have deserved it is laudatory behavior, nonetheless.

7. Organizations must carefully track bias in hiring, selection, and promotion. Diversity is neither legal requirement nor social nicety. It is inherently critical to creating a changing environment and escaping past stupidity.

8. Managers should be encouraged and rewarded for sponsoring people unlike themselves in appearance, background, viewpoints, gender, capabilities, etc.

9. Managers should be rewarded for how many people they develop, as evidenced by promotions of people who worked for them.

10. Power doesn't corrupt. Powerlessness corrupts. Give people real power.

Chapter 2

Examples from the Front I: Private Sector
Nonprofits That Aren't Supposed to Be That Way

"No man can climb out beyond the limitations of his own character."
—Robespierre

If individuals reacted to losing cash with the same aplomb that share-holders do when losing value, there would be a great many people sitting placidly around as the sheriff auctioned off the family home-stead. The *paterfamilias* would be addressing the media in the front yard by pointing out that, although it's been a bad year, the outfit is making superb progress toward its 5-year plan.

Organizations have developed all kinds of vision statements and mission statements, to the extent that they've often lost sight of what once was a quaint, uncomplicated goal: *to show a profit*. They have so much "vision" that they're blind. We've previously established that salespeople can be held rigorously to goals, and are developed (sometimes) or fired (usually) if they don't meet them. Senior management has not suffered a similar scrutiny. In fact, so-called 5-year plans become a series of 1-year plans, and accountability is repeat-edly shuffled until all the cards are on the floor.

The fact of the matter is that with all of the planning tools and strategic matrices, with all of the books and binders, with all of the reports and retreats, executives often don't have a clue as to what they're doing strategically. All of the structure and formats only serve as an attempt to create some shape amidst the ambiguity. Strategy is tough to formulate, and extremely difficult to execute. What is re-quired is nimbleness and speed. What it usually entails is tedium and ponderousness. There is absolutely nothing in most executives' ca-reer paths which prepares them to be strategists, or even to recognize a viable strategy if they tripped over it. If you don't believe that, then explain IBM, or Sears, or Braniff. Even the legendary Wal-Mart is starting to take its lumps. Organizations like Hewlett-Packard and Merck—which I believe may possibly be the two best-run, most talented organizations in the land—have endured their ups and downs as well.

It would shock employees, stupefy shareholders, and titillate the press to view the actual strategic work of most top managers. I know; I've seen it.

Once, while I attempted to work with the senior team at Clorox many years ago, the group entered into a debate as to which comes first: strategy, objectives, or goals. This is tantamount to viewing the chicken/egg debate as simple to resolve. While I patiently tried to explain that the terms weren't important but the intent to build a future for the business was, the vice presidents and CEO wouldn't relent. After we'd finally managed to put that one aside (objectives "won"), I ran them through an exercise to determine what their strategic strengths were, and what forces actually drove their business. The 15 people in the room privately came up with about 20 different responses and combinations, which is not unusual. That kind of result means that the top team hadn't really discussed or reached consensus on the key drivers of the business, and were probably making high-level decisions that were often nonsupportive or even contradictory.

The CEO nearly needed resuscitation when I posted those results. He read the group out thoroughly, demanding to know how they could ignore what was so blatantly obvious to him, and what he had so clearly communicated in the past, which they, apparently en masse, hadn't heard. In other words, the strategy was "clear" to the CEO, and he had never bothered to confirm this with (or perhaps even communicate it to) anyone else. And so the ship sailed merrily along. That afternoon, which had been dedicated to objective decision-making, was abruptly canceled.

Differences at the Top

It is rather common for a senior group to cite wildly different strategic strengths and weaknesses, and highly diverse forces moving the business. In most cases, there is a sobering silence when I explain what's going on, and the CEO says something like, "We'd better begin at square one." I then remind them that we should actually begin at square zero, where we at least have a common starting point.

Why the differences at the top? For these reasons:

- Strategy is usually viewed as an annual exercise at best, an event that creates a "product," and not as a process to be used to actually run the business.
- Senior people are myopic because very few organizations actually have "top management teams." They usually have a collection of top managers, each atop his or her own hierarchy, which comes together

for arbitrary reasons. So they don't function as a team but rather as a sort of United Nations, each ambassador representing a sovereign interest. And we all know how well that works.

- Because of the corporate hierarchies, managers seldom receive sufficient insight into other operations or the entire operation. Consequently, the top financial person is likely to say that the driving force of the business is profit and return, while the top marketing person is apt to say it's really market share, and the head of operations is likely to believe it's production capability. You get the picture. We're all at the center of our own universe.

- Executives actually spend an inordinate amount of their time on low-level, high-detail, tactical trivialities, because they've failed to empower people below them. They like handling things with tangible outcomes, and they believe that they are paid to take action continually. Of course, nothing could be farther from the truth. The Great American Management Myth is that senior people are paid to take action. In fact, *they should be paid to achieve results.*

- There are few honest-to-goodness strategists employed by organizations. The corporate planning area is not where you're likely to find one, since strategy and planning are about as alike as are Mary Tyler Moore and Madonna. As a result, many organizations are either forced to rely on external consultants or on internal people who aren't very effective at confronting management weaknesses (since their retirement plan keeps flashing in front of their eyes), or aren't very adept at true strategy (since it's only an annual event and daily practice isn't required). As for the consultants, they range from the excellent to the execrable, and even the best of them can't be on site continuously to make sure executives do what they're supposed to. If the former could do that, then we wouldn't need the latter. Are you beginning to see the problem?

There's also the massive ego involvement of executives which muddies up the already opaque strategic waters. The owner of a consulting firm for which I once labored as a general manager told me one day that we were going to New York to assist Burlington's CEO, William Klopman, annually rated by *Fortune* magazine as one of America's "10 toughest bosses" and often referred to as "the number one SOB." I was on another assignment, and asked why I was being pulled off for this 1-day affair, although I knew the answer as soon as I asked. "Well, I thought I'd sort of sit in the back in case I was needed, and you could run the meeting," said he, without eye contact.

In other words, he was Lee and I was Pickett. Klopman was the Union II Corps atop Seminary Ridge.

Klopman wasn't tough: he was vindictive and mean. He had run an operation that was purchased by Burlington, and then went on to become CEO, firing 22 of the other 24 general managers in short order. His top team that day consisted of six or eight people. Shortly into the meeting, I requested some financial numbers to post for consideration in our decision making. Klopman turned to his chief financial officer and said, "Well, what are they?"

"I, I don't have them right at hand," stammered the CFO, obviously unprepared for the direction the discussion had taken.

"Well get out of here and find them, you stupid %#*??%$," replied the boss. "Why the *()^^$?!!@ do you think I keep you around? This is the only &*%%$#? thing you're any good for, and you're not very good at it, either."

With that, the white-faced executive hurried around the boardroom table and out into the corridor. Klopman continued to excoriate him in absentia. We did nothing until his return in about 10 minutes, and I could only imagine what was happening in his wake as he sought out the missing numbers.

Two things occurred to me that day, in addition to the fact that when I headed my own firm I would choose my clients carefully and never be reluctant to turn down business I didn't like. One was that the "signal" in the organization was that ruthlessness was required for advancement, and that you pleased the boss at any cost. The second was truly saddening: What kind of people subject themselves voluntarily to such treatment on a daily basis? Who endures such humiliation in return for only money? I became convinced that the real inferiors around that table were the people reporting to Klopman, and that the organization was probably filled with such weakness. How does such a place set a cogent strategy when one person's whim decides all debates? The answer is simple: It doesn't.

Short-Term Palliatives

If you think about the complexity issue raised in the first chapter, you may come to the conclusion that strategy is more art than science and that all organizations will undergo disruption and battering, as well as exultation and success, that couldn't have been foreseen or predicted. And you'd be right. *The goal of strategy should be to mitigate the lows and exploit the highs.* Instead, it's all-too-often embraced as the corporate religion, with all of the attendant mysticism and unquestioning of the faith.

Elaborate sets of values and mission statements are short-term palliatives, meant to provide the semblance of control in the face of events that can't be controlled. Let's begin with a firm that is profitable, has a charismatic and respected CEO, and is one of the most sophisticated and complex in the world: General Electric.

Jack Welch is the CEO's CEO, and, one would think, if anyone can set strategy well, his team can. His vision is simple: GE wants to be number 1 or 2 in every market it enters, or it will not stay in the market. He believes in speed and "boundaryless" organizations, in which employees get things done despite departments and "turf." He pioneered the "work out" concept, in which employees get together with each other and with customers to get to the heart of problems and make expeditious decisions.

In fact, the people who *leave* his team are all-stars, as evidenced by the likes of a Lawrence Bossidy going to Allied Signal as CEO and becoming one of the best in the country over there. GE is so rich in talent and so proficient at developing talent that its "bench" is deep enough to allow first-rate people to depart without organizational disruption. While the Kidder Peabody fiasco is usually cited as the exception to GE's intelligent strategic intent, it's only one in a discouragingly long line. Take a gander at some of the more newsworthy events that have pelted GE during Welch's watch:

1985: GE pleads guilty to fraud for overcharges to the Air Force on the Minuteman Missile. The company pays $2 million in penalties, criminal and civil.

1989: Whistleblowers alert the government to the issuance of false time cards on projects. The civil suit is settled for $3.5 million.

1990: A conviction for defrauding the Defense Department on overcharges of battlefield computer systems, with $30 million in penalties paid.

1992: This time it's jet engines, the fraud is on the Pentagon, and it involves bribes in Israel. Fines total more than $69 million.

1993: NBC News, a GE subsidiary, apologizes to GM for misleading and staged stories on crash tests. GM's $1 million legal fees are paid by NBC.[1]

Over the course of 8 years, that's in excess of $105 million paid to settle fraudulent and illegal acts of major proportion. We're not talking about someone cheating on an expense account, and we're not talking about acts that could have been perpetrated by a single, misguided individual acting alone. My belief is that Jack Welch is more outraged than anyone. Yet, despite the company's values, strategy, and strong organizational talents, things went wrong in a major way.

I am told that Peter Lynch, of Fidelity Magellan fame[2] once said that the investor should pick the stock of a business that can be run by a fool or an idiot, because sooner or later it will be. I would certainly concur that, sooner or later, every business is either run by someone who doesn't understand strategic

---

[1] Material cited from *Fortune*, Sep. 5, 1994, p. 46: "A Litany of Sins."

[2] One of the most long-term successful and largest mutual funds in existence.

thinking, understands it but is faced with conditions that couldn't have been anticipated, or both.

Next example: The automakers. The U.S. "big three," currently in the throes of a glorious comeback, are stereotypical examples of how systemic, tangible practices undermine any attempt at a cogent, intangible strategy.[3] And they've all lost a pile of money in the not-too-distant past—stockholders' money.

While it's common to blame the fuel crisis, changing consumer values, the dual-income family, the Japanese work ethic, and the phases of the moon on the brutal beating domestic automakers received a couple of decades ago, there is at least one more mundane factor, often overlooked. At the time of the Japanese "invasion in force," the automakers had a system in place that many large companies shared: Top executives' retirement pay was based on a formula involving the last several years of profitability prior to retirement. In other words, the more you showed on the bottom line over the final few years, the richer your retirement package. You don't have to be a student of human behavior to answer the following question: Given that set of circumstances, and the fact that you control capital expenditures, do you invest heavily in long-term research and development, or do you cut all possible expenses to maximize short-term return?

The answer is as obvious as a ham sandwich. I'm taking care of my family, thank you very much.

I don't claim that this is the only reason for Ford, GM, and Chrysler being mugged, but it's certainly a contributing factor. Japanese executives had no such arrangement. Here's an observation by Harry Pearce, a GM executive vice president, commenting on another fatal flaw of that old compensation scheme: "Executives were thankful to get a big bonus but often didn't know why. If you want to design a system that's set up just to hand out gratuities to people you like, that's the way you'd set it up."[4]

Do you remember People Express Airlines? An entrepreneur named Donald Burr created a cheap, no-frills airline that had backpackers and business people sitting next to each other in classless but on-time service. Pilots sat in the cockpit one day and loaded baggage the next. Flight attendants today were reservationists tomorrow. Everyone worked insane hours, and the place made money. The investors hailed Burr's "vision." The trouble was, as

---

[3] Incidentally, don't believe the claims that the U.S. is now number 1 in auto production again, having taken over from the Japanese. While this is technically true, it's only because of the large manufacturing being done in the U.S. by Japanese auto firms. These folks just keep popping up, don't they?

[4] Cited in *Fortune*, Sep. 5, 1994, p. 18: "Now Hear This."

with many entrepreneurs, you had to be lucky as well as good, and Burr's luck didn't hold. Nor did his "vision."

He expanded like crazy, purchased a *union operation,* Frontier Airlines, and immediately went down the tubes faster than Jimmy Carter did after he confessed to having lust in his heart. People Express is gone, a lot of people were thrown out of work, even more people lost money, and another miracle burst. Burr didn't have a vision or a strategy, he simply had an *idea.* If he had had anything more than that, he wouldn't have made the moves he did, he would have been better prepared to deal with some of the events that transpired, and People Express wouldn't be represented today by Southwest Air, which is a company with a vision and a strategy. I suspect that Southwest will face the assault of larger rivals, such as United's shuttle, with confidence and a blistering counterattack.

Southwest sees itself as an inexpensive, no-frills, on-time airline. Its acts are consistent with that belief system. It turns its planes around in about 15 minutes, maximizing their time in the air. It doesn't enforce stupid protocols among its employees, who dress casually and sometimes act bizarrely, but get the job done. It uses solely Boeing 737 jets, which means that crew training is constant and crews interchangeable, and it can achieve enormous savings on maintenance and spare parts. *Strategy is never perfect. But you can judge an organization's strategic integrity by its consistency.* Consistency doesn't mean conservatism or aversion to risk. It simply means that innovation and risk-taking will be consistent with its strategy.

Profitable organizations are seldom that way without interruption, which usually occurs when the unanticipated arrives. Both Sears and IBM, not to mention Chrysler and Ford, regained productivity. But they had to be brought back to their senses by the same shocks that destroyed organizations with fewer resources, poorer shareholders, and less time. GM, Ford, IBM, and GE are currently numbers 1, 2, 3, and 10 in total R&D spending in this country.[5]

When I hear executives chant, mantralike, "vision, mission, values," I know I'm in for a long day. And the employees are never fooled, because they believe what they *see,* not what they read or hear. So do I.

When a Number Isn't Really a Number

I sat at a senior management meeting at the request of the CEO of a new client. He thought that I would obtain a quick view of the management team's workings and help him understand why the organization was consistently missing its projections.

---

[5] *Business Week,* June 27, 1994, p. 79: "R&D's Biggest U.S. Spenders."

Almost immediately, two presentations sent me reeling. The first was an opening report by the vice president of finance that went something like this:

"As you know, we have fallen behind our budget for the year by 12% and our PR by 4%. However, the most disturbing factor at the moment is that the current quarter's projection was off by slightly more than 20%. The good news is that we're ahead of last year's PR at this point by 2% and are just about on last year's budget track. The prior year's quarterly projection was off by almost 30%, but if you'll recall that was largely caused by the recasting of the financials after the first half. So, while we're not in terrible shape, we could be doing better, and I'm anxious to hear your next quarter's projections today, along with their comparisons to PR, since we only have 60 more days to make changes in the PR for the year."

Everyone sort of nodded their heads while the first presenting business chief prepared his slides. So I asked the CEO's secretary, who was sitting next to me keeping the minutes, to explain what had just happened.

"Well, the budget is usually established near the end of the first quarter, when we have some idea of what the year is *really* likely to become in terms of sales and expenses. Once we set the budget, our parent company uses it to track our progress, although it's a bit of a game since we haven't met the budget for the past 7 years. It's more or less a good-looking number that they can take to *their* board and represents what would be a strong year in terms of our contribution to income.

"The PR is the 'Projected Results.' That's the number we keep on a rolling basis that represents what we think we'll really produce, and it's established close to the half-year mark. We're allowed to 'massage' that number, but once we're into the fourth quarter we're not allowed to change it.

"The 'projection' is each business head's rolling forecast of the next 90 days, which is supposed to represent the latest intelligence from the field on what will occur during that time frame. However, the field is notoriously optimistic, and the numbers are always inflated and virtually never met in reality."

"Now, wait a minute," I begged. "What is this all based on? Isn't there a plan developed prior to the current year that details what the organization should be achieving?"

"You must be kidding," she said, suppressing a guffaw. "There is a plan created during the final quarter of the prior year, but it's not even vaguely used for comparison. It sits in everyone's operating manuals but is never heard from again. The plan is based upon the *prior year's plan, not the prior year's actual results*. It's worthless."

"Let me get this straight. Are you telling me that the year's plan isn't used at all because it's based on a prior year's fictional plan, and that the company creates a budget during the first quarter which is *supposed* to be the year's plan, but then adjusts that at the half with a projected result that is lower still than both the plan and the budget??"

"You got it."

"And then the projected result can still be changed up to the fourth quarter?"

"Yep. And guess what?"

"What?"

"We usually don't hit that number, either."

Now I was a bit groggy. Here was a company in which a number wasn't a number. It had systemic provisions, accepted by its parent, to continually change and massage its forecasts, so that the end of the year was a virtual crapshoot. No one was accountable. Everyone played the system. The projections were simply wild-assed, best-case guesses, because there was no consequence for missing a projection. The system continually bailed out the management, who weren't really managers at all. If they were living in the ocean they'd be plankton, drifting with the currents, without any means whatsoever of self-propulsion.

I want to apologize to the world's plankton. I meant no disrespect.

Now came the second presentation.

The vice president for U.S. sales and marketing took the floor and presented his numbers. He said, of course, that he couldn't be certain of any of this, but it was a reasonable expectation. As far as I could see, he was currently behind both his budget and PR (and, I assumed, nowhere within hailing distance of the mythical plan) and had missed the current quarter's projection by about 25%, but he was projecting a next quarter that would place him squarely back on his PR and, perhaps, his budget.

The vice president of finance was duly skeptical, though, if I were he, I would have been rolling in the aisle.

"Let me test your reasoning here," said the financial guy. "Why do you see less customer attrition in the next quarter, which explains a lot of your revenue increases?"

"Well," replied the field guy, "We're thinking that we've seen the worst of it. Customers appear to be more stable, and they're expressing interest in some longer-term discounts."

"What's changed to make that happen? Attrition last quarter was slightly worse than last year."

At this point, the CEO looked at me and then asked the presenter, point blank: "What are the causes of your attrition, and how are you eliminating them?"

"Well," stammered the VP, "we've had some plant closings that have bottomed out; the economy is improving in most of our territories; the competition seems to be rebounding; and we're introducing new products and services that should be highly attractive to our current customer base."

The CEO had exposed a classic problem with that one question. The field chief hadn't the slightest idea of what was causing his attrition. Classically, when you ask the field—the people suffering the attrition—about the causes, they site factors *external to themselves*. Thus, no one was citing "poor service," "reps changing accounts," "late delivery times," or "losing contact with the buyer" as reasons. Also, the competitions' rebound was cited as a reason to believe a general resurgence was in the offing. But in an industry such as this, where you grow almost solely by taking someone else's market share, the resurgence of the competition was not something to relish!

I listened to manager after manager cite why his numbers weren't absolutely solid, how key information was not available (imagine not knowing what the buying patterns of your largest customers are), and, in general, explain how they couldn't be held accountable for much more than cashing their pay checks each month.

When the CEO and I debriefed, he said, "Pitiful display, isn't it?"

"It is," I agreed, "and it's all your fault." The next 15 seconds, in my experience, dictate whether you never set foot in that office again or whether you're a regular visitor for many years.

The CEO's fault lay in the fact that he was too accommodating and too forgiving, and had allowed a system to develop with the parent which fostered such provisions. No one's feet were held to the fire. Systemically, the organization worked on a planning process that was fictional from the outset (based on a prior number that was never reached) and, therefore, not respected. This cast disrespect on the entire endeavor. Interpersonally, the CEO had allowed for a set of "avoiding behaviors" and excuses that made someone not in that room really responsible for the actual results, although who that someone was—the employees, the customers, the competition, the fates—no one was sure about.

These dynamics are common in our modern organizations. We have systems that are intrinsically counterproductive, behavioral sets and cultures that are created to avoid rather than affix accountability, or both. And those can occur in organizations in which people are actually trying to do their level best. Imagine what happens when you sprinkle in real ineptitude, runaway egos, and/or malice.

There are a finite number of factors that account for poor planning and ineffective strategy formulation within organizations. They are clear and definable, which means that they should also be preventable.

Historically, these and other blights on the planning process have created poor results that have, in turn, been blamed on the American worker. The bromides have included:

- Productivity is not as high as our foreign counterparts because of a "me first" attitude and an absence of loyalty to the company. (After all, why should massive layoffs make people disloyal?)

Checklist of Factors Mitigating Against Intelligent Planning and Results

- *Systems* are established which camouflage accountability by permitting dual sets of numbers, unverified assumptions, lack of close monitoring, poor feedback on actual performance, etc.
- *Cultures* are created which avoid confrontation, emphasize harmony over discord, place harshest scrutiny on lower levels, permit a "victimization" excuse ("If we had marketing support, we could've made those numbers"), and don't reflect actual performance in evaluations.[6]
- *Egos* of top people do not permit "failure" and preclude personal responsibility for poor results. What usually occurs in bad times is that the "books are cooked," by such devices as changing the fiscal year, selling assets, deferring expenses, taking credit for sales to be delivered in the next year, and/or brutalizing customs to accept what they don't need before they might need it.
- *Ineptitude* prevents even effective systems and cultures from performing up to potential, as when managers give artificially high performance ratings, financial planning is not understood because of an inability to grasp profit-and-loss statements and balance sheets, support systems aren't utilized correctly, and so on.

- Workers are not as quality conscious, and we provide inferior manufacturing and services. (If you believe that, compare our service mentality with that in Europe, where the typical hotel concierge believes that you are a guest only through his good graces.)
- Our work force isn't culturally diverse and reflects an "old boy" mentality that doesn't understand customers. (In reality, the U.S. work force is becoming one the most diverse in the world, even if we might have speeded the process up a bit. The Japanese culture is highly exclusionary, and European managers transferred to their American parent or subsidiary companies have a hard time understanding the premium we place on multiculturalism. The first thing many such managers try to do here is surround themselves with compatriots.)

---

[6] Consultants Coopers & Lybrand surveyed 250 companies, and while 75% described "company performance" as a key board issue, performance-based compensation for directors is used by less than 9%. See *The Wall Street Journal*, July 19, 1994, p. 1: "No Gander Sauce?"

In fact, the U.S. has regained the productivity lead, and we are far ahead of Japan in the service sector, largely because the Japanese tend to assign their surplus labor to the service sector.[7] The gross daily productivity per employed person in the U.S. is currently about $53,000, as compared to about $50,000 in France and $37,000 in both Japan and Britain.[8] It's not the worker—it's management that has been falling short.

Downsizing as the Holy Grail

This brings us to the final example for now from the world of the private sector. One of the worst of all of the fads and formulas to be implemented by top management is the great panacea called *downsizing* (or *rightsizing* for the politically correct and reality-avoiders). My observation is that executives, desperate to show their slowly awakening and uncharacteristically sentient boards some action in the face of poor results, have determined that quick, dramatic moves are the most "macho." (Forgive me, female readers, but most of these people right now are male, although many of the consultants leading downsizing efforts are women.)

So, with chests being pounded and charts of a slimmer organization unfurled, these strong men show the board that they will take the tough actions required to renew the bottom line. Of course, there are only three things obviously amiss here:

1. It was these same executives who allowed the organization to get as fat as it has, assuming that it is in that condition at all.
2. The tough work to be done involves making life tough for someone else, namely, the people being put out onto the street, and even that is usually directly handled by a hired gun, a lower-level manager in personnel, or the intercompany mail.
3. The bottom line is being renewed through expense reduction and not real productivity gains. *Unless you change the nature of the work itself, simply removing people does nothing except worsen productivity.*

---

[7] See *Business Week*, June 27, 1994, p. 44: "Is the Japanesse Dynamo Losing Juice?" by Christopher Farrell. My favorite example is at Narita Airport, where it's not unusual to find five baggage handlers standing around an automated luggage carousel making sure all the bags face the same direction.

[8] *Ibid.*

Those people who were let go *were doing something*. They weren't sitting around playing canasta or Super Mario Brothers; they were working. If the work wasn't necessary, then removing them should cause no disruption, but it almost always does.[9] Changing the nature of the work—whether one calls it reengineering, restructuring, reorganizations, or architectural occlusion—requires some actual planning, diligence, insight, and transition management. Simply throwing people out the door does not. Yet it's the latter, not the former, that most executives engage in when they pursue the Holy Grail of downsizing.

Why do I feel so cocky about this? Well, the studies have disclosed some interesting outcomes. A report from the Center for Economic Studies at our own beloved Census Bureau, covering 140,000 plants over 10 years, reveals that operations that increased employment (upsizers?) created as much productivity increase as did those that lowered employment.[10] Further, the Arthur D. Little consulting firm reports that only 16% of executives reported "progress in change" in their reengineering efforts, 45% were "partially satisfied," and 39% were "actively unhappy." Given the cost and disruption of reengineering, when 84% of the executives who ordered the interventions report less than adequate progress, there's reason to believe you're on to something, and it's rotten.

Management guru Peter Drucker says that "We are seeing way too many amputations before the diagnosis."[11] My experience is that the board and particularly the investors (especially institutional investors) are overjoyed at the short-term prospects to the extent that stock prices go up even before the first person is fired, such is the salivating that accompanies the mere announcement of downsizing. Senior management is instantly rewarded for the initiative. The problem is that the productivity of most organizations immediately plummets upon that same announcement. There is a very specific reason for this.

As shown in Figure 2.1, any enterprise can call upon no more than 100% of the skills and talents of its people. No one can really work at 110%, no

---

[9] When Nynex cut over 20,000 jobs beginning in 1984, it created an unexpected (by management) result: service complaints that have placed it at the bottom of New York's 40 phone companies. See *The Wall Street Journal*, June 7, 1994, p. 2: "Job-Cutting Medicine Fails to Remedy Productivity Ills at Many Companies," by Frederick Rose.

[10] These and the following statistics reported in *The New York Times*, July 10, 1994, p. 21: "Questioning Productivity Beliefs," by Barbara Presley Noble.

[11] *op. cit.*, Rose.

matter what her or his performance evaluations or what Anthony Robbins claims. Thus, the equation becomes one of where those talents are deployed: outwardly, toward the customer, product, and service, or inwardly, toward politics, turf, and self-preservation. In the healthiest organizations I've seen, as much as 90% of that talent can be focused externally, with only 10% consumed by the inevitable office politics, concerns about who will get the next promotion, and other esoterica. Companies like Federal Express, Hewlett-Packard, and Southwest Airlines seem habitually to function that way.

But I've also seen organizations that function in the reverse. I once worked for a consulting firm that was about 75% focused internally, meaning that the clients' fees were garnering just about a quarter of our actual potential. When you're treated rudely by a reservations clerk, or receive the wrong shipment, or can't get a rapid response from an organization, it's often because the employees are consumed by a more important priority—their own well-being.

When a downsizing—really a massive firing in any sane person's terms—is announced and implementation begun, productivity plummets for the indefinite future for these reasons:

- No one knows who will be next, so all employees keep their heads down and take no risks. These cutbacks seldom focus on solely poor performers or lowest seniority, so no one perceives himself as safe. Consequently, everyone "ducks."

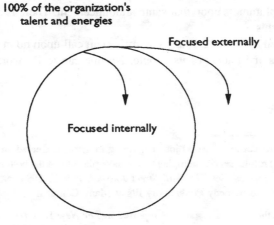

100% of the organization's talent and energies

Focused externally

Focused internally

Figure 2.1. The energy equation.

- Most intelligent people provide themselves with a backup, so that "paper hits the street." Résumés are released like ticker tape. *The people who will be the most successful at finding new jobs will be* (a) those who get there first, and (b) those who are the best performers. So the best people will strike quickly and will be seized by competitors. The best will tend to go; the mediocre will tend to remain.
- Those who do remain and are solid performers will feel guilty about their colleagues who have been let go. There is remorse, both on the part of the manager who had to fire subordinates, and on the part of employees, who wonder why it was the person next to them, who was a valued colleague and, often, a friend.
- No one ever believes it's "over," even when it truly is. Another quarter's bad results could spark more executive chest pounding and more investor bliss over reductions. Once it happens, no one feels "safe" for a long time, no matter what the company says or does.
- The contract of loyalty has been broken. Where close calls between family and work often were decided on behalf of the company (a half-day on Saturday won't kill me), those calls are now either made the other way or are begrudgingly made. (I'll have to put in an appearance on Saturday, but I'll sneak away Monday afternoon to make up for it.) The company no longer deserves "the benefit of the doubt," and employees look after themselves first.

The energy equation in Figure 2.1 goes into vertigo, and increasing amounts of talent and energy are absorbed internally, directed to one's own welfare, office gossip, undermining, and resentment. Downsizing isn't just a benign fad whose time will come and go; it's an abomination that has permitted weak management to escape the consequences of its own incompetence and that has penalized hundreds of thousands of blameless workers.

It is the *auto-da-fé* of the late 20th century, and many CEOs have become Torquemada.

How to Clothe the Emperors, Part 2

1. Boards must adopt performance-based compensation for all top executives and all board members.
2. Planning must be tied to strategy and strategic goals (there's a conceptual breakthrough) and must be completed and approved prior to the new fiscal year.
3. A plan is a plan and a number is a number. Performance is based on planned results without excuses or departures.
4. Any plans to downsize must include specific plans for the out-placement of all people affected, regardless of level, with appropriate compensation packages.
5. Any gains to the bottom line made through expense reductions which are not accompanied by revenue increases will not count toward any incentive compensation goals. No executive should be able to enrich him or herself by denying a living to employees.
6. No downsizing may be undertaken without a detailed plan to change the nature of the work itself, which explains how fewer employees will be able to support the key dimensions of the business and maintain service standards.
7. Executives are held accountable for what transpires on their watch. They are expected to resign—or are terminated—for preestablished transgressions, which should include fraud, financial manipulation, and the deliberate release of unsafe products.
8. Every executive involved in planning must have taken a company-approved program in strategic planning and financial management, and undergo a refresher course every 3 years.
9. Vision and mission statements must pertain to the pragmatic business goals of the company, and all top-level decisions must use them as a template.
10. No executive is hired from the outside who has thrived in a culture that violates or is not consistent with the tenets above.

Chapter 3

Examples from the Front II: Associations
The Confusion About Not-for-Profit and Surrender

"You should have seen it, sir, before the war."
— a former Confederate general in the late 1860s
describing the moon to Oscar Wilde

Trade associations are fabulous studies of an amalgam of lobbying, professional education, member representation, and stark amateurism. The best are cognizant of the fact that their members are both their "owners" and their "customers." The worst become oblivious to outside influence and create their own "silos"—hierarchies that are far more pernicious than their private-sector cousins.

If private-sector boards have been sleeping through executive ineptitude, public sector boards have been comatose. Even more appalling, the latter are filled with notables and heavyweights from the private sector, government, entertainment, philanthropy, and academia. Someone, somewhere, should have known better, but many board members apparently feel that attending three or four meetings a year, waltzing around at the prestigious and obligatory black-tie events, and cashing the five-figure annual stipend is more than enough work for any 12-month period.

How else can one explain the United Way fiasco, in which the executive director, William Armony, to be kind, piddled away millions, and to be candid, spent lavishly on his own perks money collected by volunteers to be distributed to charities? In comparison, when the NAACP found out that its relatively new executive director, Benjamin Chavis, secretly settled a harassment complaint by a former employee for an amount in excess of $300,000, they agonizingly deliberated for an entire day, and then fired him. It's not that boards can't do it; it's that some don't even try.

One of our major trade association clients has been the American Institute of Architects. While architects hold a fairly esteemed position in the public eye, they hold a very low position in their own eyes. It is one of the very few professions—and I believe the only one of its status—that has suffered a net decline in real income per professional over the past 10 years. Architects have seen their territory usurped by everyone from contractors who do their own design to homeowners performing their own work with the help of such amateur-builder havens as Home Depot.

About half the country's 100,000 registered architects belong to the AIA, which entitles them to place the initials "AIA" after their names. That particular designation only means that they are dues-paying members; it denotes no special certification or licensing. However, most consumers and many buyers believe that AIA implies some sort of approval (in actuality, individual states license architects through a testing process, which provides the designation RA: Registered Architect). That inference provides tremendous credibility and potential power to the organization.

Yet the organization has recognized that it must reorganize its structure and its efforts. It's not that it isn't profitable; it has shown a significant "profit" for a nonprofit, and its finances are the envy of other associations. The problem is its very success in that regard. *The profession of architecture could disappear tomorrow, yet the AIA could continue to operate very nicely for many years to come!* How is this possible? It's because the association had lost sight of what its purpose is and who its customer is.

The AIA, under its full-time executive director,[1] had become enamored of its sponsorship of architectural awards, maintenance of a historical property, prestige publications, and other status endeavors. The problem is that the vast preponderance of its constituency is solo-practitioner or small firm members, whose concerns tend to focus on the local zoning ordinances, educating people about the value that a professional architect brings to a

---

[1] For those of you unfamiliar with the workings of most trade associations, they are run day to day by a full-time professional staff, under the command of an executive director (or chief operating officer, or chief executive) whose salary can easily be in excess of a quarter-million dollars. The governance of the association is usually performed by a board elected directly or indirectly by the membership, under the aegis of a president and other officers. The officers and president are volunteers who are members of the association and, theoretically, guide the full-time executive team. Nontrade associations, such as the United Way or the Boy Scouts, often have outside directors, chosen for their ability or their name or their financial contributions.

project, and ferocious fee wars. The institute was intent on saluting the builders of cathedrals, while the membership was trying to scratch out a living designing residential additions and grocery stores.

So, where was the board? After all, the board is composed of members, so the real constituency should have been represented there, guiding the executives on what the focus should actually be.

The AIA board was, in my view, immense. It had close to 50 members (I believe the NAACP board has close to 90), which makes it half the size of the U.S. Senate, and whether that makes it half as good or twice as good as that august body, they're still in deep trouble. Accompanying the size problem was a complex set of directorships, committees, subcommittees, and procedures that made a receding glacier's pace seem breathless by comparison. In recommending to the board, my client, that it needed to reduce its size to something more manageable (which I believe to be about 24 directors at the outside), my investigations turned up the fact that no less than six other reports had recommended exactly the same thing. Two of these had come from other consultants, and four from internal studies issued by task forces created by the board and dating back over 10 years!

The optimist would say I was in good company. The pessimist recognizes that I had hit an immovable object.

The AIA directors, though members all, also loved the perks of the office. Why else would they take the time from their practices to assume the duties of an unpaid position? And that applied tenfold to the people who ran for office, since those responsibilities demanded far greater time. Not many of these people wanted to give up that perk during their watch and, thoughtfully, not many wanted to deny their potential successors the same rights.

Why do I frown on a large board? After all, there are examples of large boards being very effective, as several of the AIA members were not loath to share with me at every opportunity. The main problem is one of expediency. Large boards tend to be dysfunctionally democratic. They debate everything in full group. They micromanage. They get lost in process, procedure, and punctilio. (I sat at several meetings where vast amounts of time were lost debating parliamentary procedure and discussion rules, during which only the intercession of the assistant general counsel and parliamentarian prevented a complete meltdown.)

In this board's case, one of the main casualties was executive oversight. As noted earlier, all boards actually have three primary functions and, although there may be others that are defensible, if they perform these three well, the enterprise should be successful:

  1. Establish the strategic goals of the organization

2. Communicate the goals and performance expectations to senior management
3. Evaluate senior management against those goals regularly

These three "musts" apply to private and public boards alike, but are even more essential in public boards, which may have "nonprofessional" (i.e., member) representation and conflicting interests. *It's all too easy in the public sector to see roles reversed, with professional association management establishing the goals and directing the board's deliberations.*

Another contributing problem is that, while senior management remains constant, at least through the duration of their employment contract, and usually much longer, the board officers change annually and the directors change at regular intervals, as well. So the constancy resides in the paid staff, and the lack of continuity is with the board. At least in the private sector, boards tend to be less volatile.

Thus, the AIA board was unsure of what its role was and the position it should take with management. In addition, each new board administration would bring a new "theme" adopted by the incoming president, which might have nothing to do (and usually didn't) with preceding themes. This gave the full-time staff of 200 unending fits, since you can't turn an 18-wheeler of an association like this as if it were a Ferrari. The staff (few of whom were architects) listened politely, acted graciously, and then did what they thought made sense to them. The board listened politely, debated rigorously, made little real headway, and tried to emphasize to the staff what made sense in terms of the small consensus they could achieve. Meanwhile, the members sat out in Duluth and Dubuque wondering who was in charge. The only thing that they knew for sure was that they weren't.

At this writing, the AIA has taken several progressive steps. It has selected a new chief executive who knows the profession well and is a proven business professional with a fine track record. It's also created a closer link among its leaders, providing for a succession in which three successive presidents work closely together, to enhance continuity and cohesion. And it is attempting to utilize its annual convening of local leadership from around the country as a kind of advisory board or "house of delegates" to provide direct linkage with members. Finally, it's attempting to augment its local chapters, where most members claim they receive the real value-added of membership.

The board rejected our proposal to decrease its size.

The Myth of the Nonprofit

Associations, charitable institutions, and community organizations—from the Salvation Army to a school PTA—have often been seen as amateur operations with wonderful agendas, run by volunteers. So, we should "cut them some slack." Of course, one hears, there's bound to be some inefficiency, and even some waste, but that's more than made up for by the vast savings of the volunteer labor.

This might have been true 200 or so years ago when Betsy Ross and the Volunteer Flag Sewers of America were laboring over the Stars and Stripes, but it certainly hasn't applied in our lifetimes. Here are some examples at all levels:

- Trade associations are often well-run megabusinesses, from which the private sector could learn important lessons in management. Peter Drucker has frequently cited the Girl Scouts of America as one of the finest-run organizations of any type he has ever observed.[2]
- The operating budget of the AIA, noted above, is more than $60 million.
- The NAACP executive director, noted above, was initially able to settle a claim in excess of $300,000 without board knowledge or approval.
- The New England Chapter of the National Speakers Association, growing from 60 to 140 members in a little more than a year, found itself suddenly faced with managing a $100,000 budget, with systems and safeguards designed to handle a fraction of that.
- Aside from waste, actual embezzlement of funds at local chapter level is not uncommon in trade associations and is reported anecdotally by many officers at the national level (who have to "bail out" the subsidiary).
- Through lobbying efforts, public outreach, and member education, major nonprofits are among the most influential public entities in the country. The largest and most influential of all is the American Association of Retired People.
- Think about the energy equation discussed in Chapter 2.[3] Even in the local PTA or on the local hospital board, the time waste is tremendous when internal events take precedence over the customer, product, and service.
- One of the greatest errors of all community and local boards is that they equate board membership with fund raising. Board members are expected to contribute substantially to the cause, or be actively involved in fund-raising activities, or both. My advice to these boards has been consistent, though often unheeded: Local boards must provide governance. Fund raising is a different issue. Effective directors may or may

---

[2] One such early citation was in *Harvard Business Review*, July–Aug. 1989, p. 88: "What Business Can Learn From Non-Profits," by Peter Drucker.

[3] See p. 32.

not be effective fund-raisers, and effective fund-raisers may or may not be effective directors. But when you mix the two, governance always loses and fund raising overwhelms all else. In the best case with this admixture, you get a financially stable, poorly run organization.

Just because the organization is nonprofit—in this case, deliberately so— doesn't mean that all management intelligence and planning need cease at the lofty portals. The phenomenon is at its worst at the state and community levels, at which large donators, long-time supporters, the idle rich, the networking, and the unemployable gather to set and implement policy. Micromanagement isn't a threat in nonprofits; it's an operating policy. But nonprofit management doesn't require the surrender of common sense, of the search for innovation, or of a competitive-mindedness. Stupid management in nonprofits hurts the customers and volunteers no less than stupid management in for-profits hurts the customers and the employees.

The worst calamity in nonprofit management is a confusion (my kids would say they are clueless) about strategy and operational distinctions. Sit in on any number of management meetings, in any size operation, and you will find no distinctions between the "what" of direction and the "how" of implementation. Yet in that simple difference is a profound tool for management:

In Figure 3.1, we can see this relationship clearly.[4] The horizontal axis is strategic—what the organization is to be (typically the realm of "vision statements"). The vertical axis is tactical—how the organization will get there (often the "mission statements"). Just as I can't decide how to get somewhere until I know what the destination is, I can't assume that merely knowing the destination will propel me in that direction. I need to attend to both.

In the upper left is the organization that does both of these things well. It sets a clear and coherent direction and moves toward that goal expeditiously. An example might be The Salvation Army or many Little League organizations. In the upper right we have nonprofits that perform well on a daily basis (i.e., they raise money effectively, achieve high public awareness, etc.) but either don't have, or have lost sight of, a goal. The March of Dimes continued to collect money even after its original cause, polio, had been virtually eradicated. The

---

[4] As far as I know, this concept was first described in *Top Management Strategy: What It Is and How to Make It Work,* by Benjamin Tregoe and John Zimmerman, Simon & Schuster, 1980. For an explanation of applying these principles specifically to nonprofits, see *Best-Laid Plans: Turning Strategy into Action Throughout Your Organization,* by Alan Weiss, Las Brisas Research Press, 1994, especially Chap. 10, "Do Good and Good Will Follow: The Profitable World of the Non-Profit Organizations," pp. 183–96. [Originally published as *Making It Work,* Harper Business, 1990.]

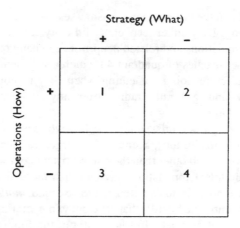

Figure 3.1. The strategic grid.

apparatus continued beyond the reason for its creation (remember the AIA can survive even if architecture doesn't). Another upper-right candidate is the United Way, which solicits and distributes hundreds of millions of dollars to a wide variety of charities but has been rocked by scandal at the highest levels and has been in frequent clashes with local organizations questioning its priorities.[5] The AIA I described above is also a quadrant-2 organization.

In the lower left we have an organization with clear goals but inefficient operations. Currently, the NAACP fits this description, having fired its executive director, facing a $3 million deficit, and actively (sometimes, acrimoniously) debating the best ways to meet its goals. Finally, in the lower right we have the organization that doesn't know where it's going, and isn't doing too well where it is. I'd place in this category the Pharmaceutical Manufacturer's Association at the time of Clinton's first health care assault. The PMA lost sight of its goals and didn't wage a very effective counterattack. That was left to individual drug companies, which created a highly effective, high-profile campaign about the need for research investment. Subsequently, the PMA was renamed the Pharmaceutical Manufacturer's and Research Association. Better late than never, but it was their members who led them out of quadrant 4.

---

[5] Ironically, the dismissed executive director told me once that "A clear statement of mission and 'buy in' by implementors of the strategy . . . is the major factor for us in successful implementation," *op. cit., Best-Laid Plans,* Weiss, p. 183.

The trouble is, in the private sector, businesses can't hang around in quadrant 4 for too long. They either recover, as did Chrysler, or they go under, as did Pan Am. Associations and related nonprofits can hang on by their fingernails in the nether reaches of quadrant 4 by increasing membership fees and dues, claiming they're doing something when they're not, changing their goals arbitrarily, and, generally, hiding from any scrutiny similar to Wall Street's or a regulatory agency's.

The term *nonprofit* is a misleading one for two reasons. First, it encompasses a myriad of institutions, agencies, and organizations, many of which have less to do with each other than they do with some of their private-sector cousins. A public television station may be much more similar to a nearby cable operation than it is to the Red Cross. Second, *nonprofit* implies to many (often including the board!) that efficiency in operating is secondary to effectiveness in meeting goals. In truth, without the former the latter can't happen on a sustained basis. While there might not be a "profit" in the sense of a return to the shareholders, there should be operational budgets that are met, debt paid off, productivity increased, and all those other bothersome measures that keep organizations from collapsing.

A brief digression about productivity: One of the stupidest of all management mistakes in those organizations that utilize volunteers is treating those volunteers as if they were cannon fodder and expendable. Every successful fund-raiser I've ever been a part of owed most of its success to the largely unseen workers who sacrificed inordinate amounts of time to make things happen. Because they're unpaid—and thought to be doing this for the commitment to the cause—they are regarded as being on the bottom of the food chain. This inevitably results in poor productivity.

Herein, a "bonus" list of preventing stupid management as it pertains to volunteers in the nonprofit sector is on page 43.

What's a Nonprofit to Do?

Let's examine some of the subgroups within nonprofits to see what their respective Achilles' heels may be.

The Private School. Private schools are usually run by a headmaster or headmistress chosen by the board of trustees. The board is invariably the *worst* body to make this selection, because it is composed of large financial contributors, local politicians, heads of public sector agencies, former headmasters, socially prominent locals, and others *who haven't a clue as to how to handle the selection process*. These groups should always go to an external source, such as an executive search firm, consulting firm, or even large private sector organization, and get *pro bono* assistance in the search and—most importantly—the interview process. I've personally seen local

How to Clothe the Emperors (with Volunteers), Part 2¹/₂

1. Treat those volunteers who are organizing others as you would your management team. Provide them with some simple perks, such as an office and phone on site.
2. Organize the volunteers into units and subunits with as much accountability pushed downward as possible. The smaller the working unit and the greater its accountability, the more likely that people will take their charge seriously.
3. Provide rewards for volunteers, in the form of plaques, prizes, a raffle, etc.
4. Allow volunteers time to socialize and network. Many will be drawn back in the future if they find they make valuable contacts and/or social acquaintances.
5. Publicize the volunteers. List all of their names in programs, ads, and publicity as much as possible. Place photos in the media, not just of the chairpeople and figureheads, but of everyone possible.
6. Send a personal "thank you" to *all* volunteers regularly. Those who are most neglected are people serving on long-term projects or who return year after year.
7. Involve the key volunteers in the decision-making process. Demonstrate that you take their opinions and advice seriously, *and then do take it seriously.*
8. Ensure that your volunteer force is diverse and reflects wide demographics, background, and styles. They will be more effective with the public.
9. Don't superimpose "last year's" structure on volunteers simply because it seemed to work. Allow for the possibility of this year's people "owning" their organization.
10. Join the volunteers periodically, and make sure all other key people in your hierarchy do as well. Don't let them serve you. Join them in serving your customers.

private schools, despite warnings from experts, engage in sloppy, political, superficial appointments of the people who will determine the educational challenges of their children, with disastrous results both educationally and financially.

The Community Help Organization. In this category we have specialized schools, soup kitchens, private shelters for battered women or substance
abuse, job training efforts, and similar entities *which were created through
the vision and efforts of a single person or small group.* The success of these
organizations contains the seeds for their demise. The entrepreneurial, dedicated founders usually excel in such areas as raising funds, organizing volunteers, and communicating the passion of the cause. However, they are seldom effective managers of people, planners, and financial administrators. As
the operation grows they need help, and they must modify their behaviors so
that the end result outweighs their personal ego investment. These are very
difficult dynamics to change, and often result in an effort's demise.

This occurs no less with groups and cliques. I spent a year not long ago
as a volunteer for the Samaritans, which is a suicide hot line utilizing a discussion technique called *befriending.* Suicide is a terrible problem in this
country, and the Samaritans, in this time of government cutback, are often
the only 24-hour help available. But the local effort had about the poorest
productivity I'd ever seen in any kind of organized enterprise. A small
coterie of "old-timers" ran the place with a religious passion for "befriending," a pseudo-therapeutic approach whose efficacy has never been proved.
Moreover, the staff became absorbed in the long-term callers who wove incredible tales of abuse, sexual dysfunction, and aberration, most of which
were patently false pranks played by the demented. There were many fine
volunteers in this outfit, but the staff wondered why attrition was so high,
assuming it was the stress of the work. Actually, the work was rewarding; it
was the stress of dealing with the staff that drove people out.

The Service Organization. These organizations generally combine a service goal with a social goal, and include everyone from the Elks and
Rotarians to the American Legion and Shriners. Some have elaborate rituals
and organization, and some are much more informal. The chronic problem
I've observed—and this applies to many other nonprofits which raise their
own funds locally—is an inordinate input into fund raising with a scant return for the efforts. *Volunteer time is worth money. You are better off trying
to solicit help (and money) once for a large amount than you are repeatedly
for small amounts.*

Have you ever been a member of a group that decided to hold a charity
golf match or local gambling night? They manage to raise $3,500, perhaps,
and consider it a successful affair. The problem is that the group has used 40
volunteers over a period of 2 months for a total of something like 640 person-
hours (2 hours a week per person for 8 weeks). At $5 an hour, for goodness
sake, the event broke even, not counting real out-of-pocket expenses for
rentals, publicity, phone, mailing, permits, etc. It was probably a loss on any
accountant's spreadsheet. And many of those people had talents and abilities

worth far more than $5 an hour: Think of the lawyers, doctors, consultants, accountants, teachers, realtors, merchants, and other professions usually comprising these volunteer ranks.

This is why *nonprofit* is such a pernicious term. At these events, *you want to create maximum profit, which means controlling expense and maximizing revenue.* If you were to approach those same 40 volunteers and successfully ask them for $100 each, you'd raise $4,000 clear profit immediately. Where is the tail and where is the dog? They not only need to be acting in sync, they also need to be connected!

The Charity. Whether humungous operations, such as the United Way and American Negro College Fund, or local operations, such as an effort to provide food for the homeless or support expensive medical operations, these efforts share some common problems from a management perspective.

First, their timing is often dreadful. They seek local support irrespective of whatever else is happening in the community. It's not unusual to have no solicitation for months and then have three causes ask for funds in the same week.

Second, they often don't separate themselves adequately from the scams. There are innumerable "police association" solicitations, or "antidrug handbook" advertisements sought over the phone and by mail by professional fund-raising outfits that keep most of what they raise. The "cause" is simply an excuse, and few dollars ever trickle down in the form of useful interventions. The pubic has become somewhat calloused by these cheats, and sometimes they are wittingly or unwittingly backed by legitimate outfits, such as the Police Benevolent Association.

Third, the charities don't create a personal, compelling approach, trying to throw a blanket over everyone rather than create a feeling of involvement. Two notable exceptions I've seen are the United Way and the American Heart Association, which, on the local level, solicit a volunteer in each neighborhood to approach his or her neighbors with a direct and personal message. The technique makes sense strategically. Unfortunately, it often fails in the execution, because the individual simply places notes in neighbors' mailboxes, which makes the solicitation as impersonal as it would have been coming directly from the organization.

The Local Theater Group. These groups are plagued by a "production capacity" driving force. In other words, they examine what they're good (or think they're good) at doing and then plan to do it. The afterthought, of course, is the marketing and the bottoms in the seats. These folks don't have a strategy; all they have is a tactic perfected by Rooney and Garland: "Let's put on a show!"

Local entertainment, recreation, and arts groups are invaluable assets to communities, but they must be as customer oriented as any large product manufacturer. The umpteenth rendition of *The Music Man* is not going to sell, no matter that Robert Preston himself has returned to play the lead. (OK, so I exaggerate a bit.) The community has to have a voice in the decision, through focus groups or surveys or response lines. Often, these endeavors are marked by the "vision" of a founder or founding group, which coincides with the public's preferences only accidentally and occasionally.

I've heard the plight "We're having trouble with our marketing" innumerable times from these organizations. Their trouble is that they have a solution in search of a need, a scratch in search of an itch. It's as if you're trying to mow my lawn when I don't have a yard. Invariably, these groups have figurehead boards of directors who are simply major contributors, so there's no guidance from that quarter.

Dirty Dancing

Every not-for-profit, irrespective of its intent or niche, needs a strategy that defines what it intends to be in its marketplace. Strategy is not a meretricious soul waiting around for a hidden tango. It's the music that an organization should publicly dance to.

One of the more egregiously stupid mistakes of nonprofit management is to deliberately eschew business people and professional expertise when forming their boards and advisory bodies. There seems to be a stigma attached, as if such people will compromise the aesthetic intent, or the operation will forever lose its amateur status and be forbidden to compete in the Olympics. Nonprofits, in fact, need such professionalism more than do their for-profit brethren, because the private-sector organizations have such ability inherent in their people; the nonprofits generally do not. Good advice has to come from some source, and nonprofits, sorry to say, usually do not attract business heavyweights as full-time employees.

Another error commonly committed is to believe one's own income projections. If someone says they'll think about a $5,000 contribution, or an organization says it will consider the group in its grant program, the money often goes right onto the balance sheet. As most of us in private business realize, money isn't good until:

1. The check is in your hands
2. The check clears the bank
3. You've spent or invested the money
4. Six months passes and no one has asked for it to be returned

Finally, nonprofits in my experience are notoriously poor trainers. They take on volunteers—or even staff members—with a cursory explanation of the basics of the operation and then turn them loose. There's virtually never any follow-up, and performance evaluations are rare. (When I suggested yearly performance evaluations to the Samaritans, including monitoring the counseling being provided on the phone, I was greeted with incredulity. "How can we do that?" asked the director of volunteers. "We'd be threatening our people and implying that we don't trust them."

"But aren't you really doing it to help the customer get quality service, and to aid the volunteer in his or her own learning and growth? Isn't it really a positive for everyone, including management, who would get feedback on the efficacy of the training and preparation?"

I was met with stony silence. Such approaches to feedback and in-service development, part of the religion of progressive organizations and embraced by the legal and the medical communities, for instance, are still anathema to many volunteer organizations. As a result, a vicious cycle is perpetuated, in which poor habits become ingrained *and serve as a role model for those who follow.* A great deal of the poor productivity within nonprofits is caused by a lack of development of workers, full-time and part-time, staff and volunteer. The notion of training a part-timer, to many in nonprofit management, is akin to throwing contributions into the river. Cannon fodder is used only when the part-timers are unavailable for the duty. Yet why have someone performing poorly for 5 hours a week when they could be performing well for 5 hours a week?

Training and development—which I prefer to term *organizational education*—is not a nonrenewable resource that must be nursed and apportioned. It's a cheap, renewable, always available resource that helps everyone perform better.

Why the Fuss?

Why even include a chapter on nonprofits? Isn't that a very specialized area with limited application to most people? Does stupid management in this area really matter?

Aside from the waste in the United Way and other examples, there are far greater implications than one might suspect. My estimate is that volunteerism in the United States is in excess of a $200-billion industry.[6] Those interested in nonprofit management had better be interested in planning, organizing, staffing, controlling, and all those other, wonderful management skills. Here

---

[6] The latest objective statistics I've seen place it at $150 billion in 1989, according to a Gallup Poll and reported in the *Providence Journal,* Oct. 9, 1989, p. 11: "New Management Posts Arise As Nation's Volunteers Abound," by Carol Kleiman.

are seven areas in which the best of the nonprofits perform quite well and have proved themselves capable of "competing" with any organization:

1. *Financial management.* The hard lesson seems to have been learned that without doing well yourself, you can't do well for others. The "bottom line" has become an object of intense interest because it now represents survival.

2. *Clarity of mission.* Because of the competition for the grant, contribution, and general funding, the best organizations have learned to be specific about their goals *and their impact on the environment and customer.*

3. *User-friendliness.* Every time I call the research library of the American Management Association, I get a rapid, accurate, and professional reply to my inquiry, no matter how esoteric it might be. Every time I call the phone company with a question about my rates, I am placed on hold, transferred, and confused. In non-profits, you're much more apt to be able to talk to someone who *knows,* because they can't afford fat staffs.

4. *Acceptance of advice.* Remember, I'm talking about the best examples here, and the best of these organizations *do* seek out help, because they feel more urgency and they have less ego involvement than their private counterparts.

5. *Lack of bias.* Nonprofits as a rule are probably far ahead of the private sector in establishing, maintaining, and rejoicing in a diverse workplace. They are more productive because of that diversity, and reflect their constituencies to far greater lengths.

6. *Flat organizations.* There is usually fairly open communication up and down, except in those operations that have allowed themselves to become bureaucratic. There should be and often is a minimum of management between volunteers and/or field workers and the top decision-makers.

7. *Community involvement.* For obvious reasons of good will and their fundamental missions, nonprofits are involved in collegial and collaborative community projects that generate good publicity and keep their cause in the public eye. The pharmaceutical manufacturers learned this lesson late, after Clinton's health broadside cast them as profiteers. Only belatedly were they able to recast that image as researchers and professionals enmeshed with the public welfare.

No one knows what the spirit of the land will be in the next decade, but it's quite possible it will be one of sharing, involvement, and mutual assistance. After all, there are some nonprofit organizations—including but not limited to such entities as CARE, the Red Cross, private schools, and the

Boy Scouts—which have endured and thrived through radically different cultural upheavals and societal changes. Nonprofits, even in their current profile, represent tremendous contributors to or detractors from the national economy. The point is not that they ought to be run well because it's an aesthetic nicety. The point is that they must be run well if they are to survive and make their vital contributions to the common weal.

We literally cannot afford anything less.

How to Clothe the Emperors, Part 3

1. Nonprofit boards should be kept to relatively small numbers (12 to 20), with external business people having strategic experience occupying at least half the seats.
2. The budget should be regarded as the "profit plan," and units and departments should be evaluated based on "profit performance."
3. One of the senior members of management should additionally carry accountability for education and development, for staff and volunteers.
4. No one within the organization, its membership, volunteers, or contributors should serve on the board without limit. The outside tenure limit should be 5 years.
5. All management personnel should receive mandatory education in management practices, and all internal board members should be educated in board governance. This can often be arranged for free through a local private-sector organization.
6. Fund-raisers should be evaluated for profit potential prior to launch, including an assessment of person-hours and significance of returns.
7. No matter how small the organization, an external financial audit must be conducted annually. These can often be secured *pro bono* from a local accounting firm if the budget is tight.
8. All people who are empowered to deposit and spend funds should be bonded, and anyone serving as an internal treasurer must have an accounting background.
9. Strategy formulation should be an ongoing process, facilitated by a skilled external, objective resource. Again, this can be done in collaboration with a private-sector firm.
10. Regular assessments of performance should be garnered from the customers, using their perspective to evaluate whether the institution's actions are meeting their needs.

Chapter 4

Examples from the Front III: Government
The Hall of Fame of Stupid Management

"Government has proved itself capable of doing only two things with great effectiveness. It can wage war. And it can inflate the currency."
—Peter Drucker

"If we had had good kings, we would still be monarchists."
—Lincoln Steffens

"No man's life, liberty, or property are safe while the legislature is in session."
—Gideon Tucker, New York State judge (1865)

Government agencies have taken it on the chin as examples of ineptitude. Anything vaguely smelling of governmental administration or even intervention becomes an avatar of inefficiency.

Yet the government has landed us on the moon, at damn near the exact time and place that it had promised, finishing no more over budget than had General Motors in trying to sell the Edsel with strikingly less success a decade earlier. The government, at the national level, has created an envious network of interstate highways, while allowing the railroad system to fall somewhat below that of, say, Upper Volta's. At the state level, while Rhode Island has been busy setting an intergalactic record by successfully indicting two consecutive chief justices of its supreme court (you just can't get help like you used to), the Carolinas have developed strong research-based economies and some of the most desirable living areas in the country. And although many of our cities are in such horrifying condition that the Japanese issue to tourists arriving here the equivalent of battlefield maps and survival tactics, municipalities such as Baltimore,

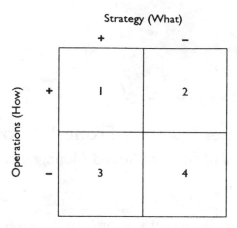

Figure 4.1. How does the postal service stack-up.

Pittsburgh, and Cleveland have revitalized themselves under impressive governmental and civic leadership.

In fact, there's even an enigma surrounding everybody's whipping target, the U.S. Postal Service (yeah, I know it's *quasi-governmental,* which is like trying to convince me that a Mercury is something other than a large Ford— it's a quasi-Ford). Here's a quick test to ensure that you're paying attention.

Let's revisit the strategic quadrants.

Quadrant 1 is an organization with a clear direction (the strategy, or "what") and an efficiency in its operations (the tactics, or "how"). In the private sector, this might be a Hewlett-Packard or a Federal Express. In quadrant 2, the organization operates well day to day but doesn't have a clear picture of its long-term identity or purpose, despite current profitability. Examples here would include the automakers prior to the Japanese invasion or many of today's successful health care providers, or even IBM.

In quadrant 3, we have an organization with a clear sense of its mission and future, but which is not operating well right now. This is typical of high-tech firms still trying to perfect their technologies, some of the pharmaceutical manufacturers, or McDonnell Douglas's aircraft business. Finally, quadrant 4 is the organization that doesn't know where it's going and doesn't know how to get there. Chrysler was here before its resurgence. Pan Am was here before its demise. USAir might be here today.

Where is the Postal Service? Think about it and choose a quadrant, but justify your choice based on your experience or other evidence.

There is no "right" answer, since the interpretation is subjective. But if you are representative at all of the more than 10,000 people I've asked this question as a keynote speaker and workshop leader, you've said one of the following:

Quadrant 4. The operation is hopeless. They regularly have to ask for rate increases to feed a bloated bureaucracy and huge, nonproductive, unionized labor force. The strategic weakness can be observed in their loss of market share to the likes of UPS and FedEx, and dreadful excursions into electronic mail and sales of clothing. Operationally, they could not make priority mail work as a guaranteed 2-day system; the mail is often late; and the lines at the counters are long enough to provide customers ample time to observe clerks doing absolutely nothing.

Quadrant 3. The place has a clear strategy and vision: It delivers the mail, despite rain, hail, and gloom of night. When you ignore the peripheral stuff, it's quite clear that it is funded, staffed, and perceived to have that goal as its *raison d'être*. But, operationally, it is all of the horrors described above. It's not unusual to get misdirected mail, or for first-class mail to make its trip at about the same rate you could have walked the letter to North Dakota.

Quadrant 2. The place is confused, as noted above. It hasn't a clue about its mission, which is why it cuts or reduces carriers and routes but does virtually nothing about the management overhead. It doesn't understand whether its competing with FedEx or in a very different kind of business. However, operationally it gets the job done. Nearly 98% of all mail gets to where it should be going within the service standards. And just where else in the world can you go and still mail a domestic letter for the equivalent of 32 cents across 3,000 miles?[1]

Quadrant 1. The postal service's blundering has become a convenient myth, along with the fact that all doctors are rich and dentists are always painful. For the reasons cited above, the place does an outstanding job with an insane volume of work, while fielding the second largest fleet of vehicles[2] on earth and a workforce of more than 600,000 people that, by the way, is notable for its diversity and equal opportunity. Its rate increases are no more unreasonable than are the price raises of its private-sector cousins.

This example causes as much acrimonious debate among my audiences as any I use. About 25% of each group places the postal service in each quadrant. We could equivocate by observing that "perception is reality" and leaving it at that, but once doesn't equivocate in a book with the title we're using.

---

[1] I'll tell you where: nowhere. In the 49 countries I've visited, there isn't one that has a less expensive service.

[2] Smaller than only the U.S. and Russian armies.

No, it seems to me that there's something else operating here, although I'll be the first to admit that when they find 4 kibillion pieces of mail undelivered in a restroom in Chicago's main post office, it does color one's thinking. And just when you think you've seen it all, another government bureaucrat steps to the fore and ketchup becomes a vegetable, people don't make errors but do "misspeak," and the *Congressional Record* is not a record of anything that is said in Congress but one of what the dear members of that body wish they had said, had they bothered to think before speaking.

The lowest common denominator in government seems to be somewhere below sentience. Incredibly, the populace has allowed public work to create values and measures that would be totally unacceptable even in the most stupidly managed private enterprise. We have actually come to believe in the necessity of—and even prize for its idiosyncrasies—stupidity in the public sector. Poorly conceived and managed public sector projects have become a self-fulfilling prophecy. There is, of course, no good reason for this to be the case. But if we lower our expectations and standards to a subterranean level, and provide no means to identify or punish pure lunacy, then we get what we deserve.

Governmental organizations create the silos and hierarchies described earlier, but do so with Kevlar-like strength. The leaders who emerge atop these structures not only have had their behaviors solidified by years of adhering to the system and its rules but also have had inordinate power that would be the envy of any private-sector megalomaniac. Remember the interesting case of Billy Mitchell who demonstrated he could sink no less than a battleship with no more than an airplane, right under the noses of all the battleship admirals? In the long term, of course, they named a bomber after him. In the short term, they court-martialed him and kept building battleships, which the Japanese then proved that they, too, could sink with their airplanes.[3]

The Worst Trait of Bureaucracies

The governmental silos become the worst bureaucracies of all. And the worst trait of any bureaucracy is that it effectively shuts down upward feedback. Everyone knew that the emperor had no clothes, but no one in the system wanted to risk the retirement plan and stock options. It took someone from outside the organization to point out the obvious.

So, too, do large governmental operations shut off feedback from the people who know the most: the employees who deal with the customers. Ask nearly any governmental worker how the job can be made more user-friendly

---

[3] Incompetence in the face of harsh reality is not any one ethnicity's trademark. The Japanese then proceeded to build their own battleships, including the two largest ever built, which we then proved that we could sink with *our* airplanes.

and more efficient, and he or she will most probably be able to tell you within 15 seconds. When I ask the postal clerks why the lines are so long, they inevitably tell me that there's never any contingency plan for the union-mandated breaks, sickness, vacation, or high volume. When there is, such as during the holidays when everyone knows there's a need, the system actually works better. Whenever I'm forced to make the world's most painful pilgrimage—a trip to the department of motor vehicles—I never stand in line or adhere to any of the thousands of instructions wallpapering the place in five languages. I always go to the director's office, tell a sob story to his secretary about my having only 20 minutes because I'm in the middle of a cure for acne over at DuPont, and she skillfully works the system so that I have my new registration or plates or car polish in half that time.

We have all become so inured with poor public systems that we have made it a science to outwit, outmaneuver, and circumvent them whenever possible. In some cases, that allows poor systems to perpetuate themselves and "underground" systems to work in parallel (the IRS comes to mind and, by the way, where would you place those folks on my chart?). In other cases, however, where such deviousness is impossible, we're simply left standing in line.

The leadership of most governmental operations is effectively walled off from the employees and the customers. Their primary goal is to perpetuate the system that got them where they are, and to do so religiously until retirement. It is absurd on the face of it to expect a private to tell a general how conditions ought to improve, but it's no less absurd to expect a civil service employee to tell a "super-rank" the same thing. The great problem, of course, is that *neither the general nor the department chief are smart enough to realize that they ought to be asking.* Everyone but Lord Raglan seemed to know that the Charge of the Light Brigade wouldn't work. Every Union soldier knew that Burnside's order to attack at Fredericksburg was suicidal; they pinned their names on their clothing so that their bodies could be identified afterwards. Similarly, highway department employees know that there will be more traffic disruption during repairs than the bosses anticipate, and people in state government realize that the new tax forms will be unworkable.

Why don't they say anything? Because no one is asking them.

As a frequent flyer, one of the scariest examples for me is the Air Traffic Control system (ATC). Prior to Ronald Reagan's mass firing of the controllers, one of the main points of conflict was labor/management relationships. Now, after a reconstituted system and elimination of the union (PATCO), ATC is still a hotbed of employee/management discontent. The only trouble with the myth of overworked air traffic controllers using outmoded technology to track too many aircraft in increasingly chaotic conditions, all the while munching on government-supplied antacid tablets, is that it's not a myth. These are the people charged with more lives each year, on a practical basis, than all the generals in all the armies in the world. Does the fact that they're at the bottom of one of the most entrenched, bureaucratic, slow-to-move silos in the country bother you? It scares the hell out of me.

In the private sector, it is increasingly common for an executive to realize that poor performers in any given area are not, in and of themselves, the problem. Their boss is the problem, for allowing that situation to develop and to endure. If nothing is done about their boss, it quickly becomes the executive who's the problem, for not doing anything about that person. As a consultant, I'm able to gain quick response when I point out this dynamic. The bottom line provides the rest of the motivation for the top manager to do something, instead of just bemoaning the poor help.

In the public sector, there's no such pressure. Senior people don't know what's going on half the time, and blame the civil service the other half. But the fact is, nothing beats superb management. Lousy organizations and mediocre people will perform fairly well when led and managed superbly, and excellent organizations and above-average people will fail when led and managed poorly.

True madness is sometimes defined as doing the same thing repeatedly while expecting different results. Why has the public sector gone mad?

The Madness Factors

A large part of the problem is that the public expects so little. We tend to whine that we're disempowered and that the "system" is immune to fixing, yet we turn out at the election booths in the lowest percentages of any democracy in the world. We get the kind of government we deserve, and here's why:

1. Public service does not pay well. I don't mean in comparison to professional athletes, I mean in comparison to vanilla, private-sector jobs. It does not, by dint of its structure and nature, attract the best and the brightest (although there are certainly some of them, drawn by sense of duty, serendipity, or the fates). The public sector draws neither the best college graduates nor the superb, retired executives.[4]

2. The public sector is the *only* part of the economy in which unionism has grown over the past decade.[5] Private-sector unions now claim only 11% of the workforce, the lowest mark in decades. In an age of work teams, results

---

[4] Some day, alien anthropologists will discover that our school teachers are paid as little as any profession in our society and will vaporize their translators, assuming that the translators read the documents incorrectly, since the interpretation is so illogical.

[5] By the year 2000, private-sector unionism is projected to fall to 7%, which is where it was 100 years ago. See *The Wall Street Journal*, Aug. 30, 1994, p. 1: "Unions' Outlook Remains Dim," citing Leo Troy of Rutgers University.

orientation, and empowerment, the unions' basic message has evaporated, and, where they exist, they tend to be impediments to rapid change. But in government, they are still seen as the working stiff's salvation—largely due to management ineptitude—and are braced not only to defeat management but to defeat the customer as well.

3. We set our expectations low, and they are met. We allow ourselves to be placed on hold for 23 minutes, then to grovel in order to have a clerk send a form to correct an error the clerk made in the first place. I recently called the post office and told them that my *Wall Street Journal* wasn't coming on time a few days a month. After the "it's not my job" shuffle, I wound up in a customer relations unit (itself a conceptual breakthrough for the government). There, a customer service specialist, no less, informed me that it was probably the *Journal*'s fault, that I'd have to fill out forms so they could track it, and I was rather presumptuous assuming it was the postal service's fault. Whereupon I asked him two questions:

- If one had the guarantee of *The Wall Street Journal,* an excellent and impressive operation, on the one hand, and the supposition of the postal service on the other, whom did he suggest I believe?
- What was the name of his direct manager?

His direct manager eventually called me long distance, apologized, guaranteed he'd find the cause of the problem, and fix it. And he did. My paper hasn't been late since. He was a potentially effective manager who was getting no feedback from a potentially horrible employee who was giving no feedback. If we set our expectations low enough, and do nothing when even they are not met, we will continue to plummet together.[6]

4. The public sector monitors itself. In the face of overwhelming public apathy, there is no one to watch governmental units *except other governmental units*. I don't know about you, but knowing that Congress has oversight responsibilities for the air traffic control system, let alone nuclear power, does not exactly enhance my sleep. There are no major equivalents of shareholders, competing organizations, or foreign threats to threaten the passivity of those on top of the hierarchies. The only watchdog of any consequence is

---

[6] Lowering standards is far from a public-sector monopoly. On a recent flight from San Francisco to Boston on United Airlines, the flight was delayed in leaving due to sloppy ground procedures. The ramp agent announced that we would have an "on-time departure at our new departure time," which was 15 minutes delayed! On a USAir flight to San Francisco, the pilot announced we would be 45 minutes late, since the aircraft was running behind all day. But he welcomed us to "an on-time arrival" in San Francisco, since the arrival matched the exact degree of lateness he had forecast! George Orwell, where are you when we need you?

the media, whose good work in this area is too often overshadowed by the excesses of sensationalism. In fact, there is something about the system that subverts even those who enter it with reform on their mind. Those swept into office on Bill Clinton's victory encouraged the press to write about the "new Congress" and the new reformers. Three months later, the press was writing about the new scandals and the new gridlock. How can a cabinet secretary accept gifts from the very organizations that he or she is expected to monitor? I don't know if it's arrogance, greed, sloth, or drugs. But I do know that part of it is arrant stupidity.

5. There is no such thing as bankruptcy. Take another look at Figure 4.1. What happens when a private-sector organization hits the bottom-right corner in quadrant 4? What happens is Braniff, Pan Am, Commodore Computer, and the U.S. merchant marine. They go broke and disappear.[7] Now what happens to a public-sector organization in such dire straits—like, say, the military's procurement budget, the social security administration, or the local school system? What happens is that they get more money thrown at them, almost always as a result of higher taxes. Think of this brilliant dynamic: Managers do a lousy job planning and executing their budgets and are rewarded with even larger budgets and more resources in order to dig a still deeper hole next year. No matter how badly one screws up a public mission—usually, but not always, short of outright criminal acts—he or she is not only unmolested but also rewarded. The consequences in public service simply do not match the performance goals.

6. There are too many ways around the system. My motor vehicles chicanery is a modest example. But I know when I cited it that you immediately thought of your own shenanigans with the IRS. One can remain perfectly legal in one's taxes, but depending on creativity and the right accountant, the amount owed on identical income can vary enormously. And one can remain perfectly illegal and stand a very good chance of not getting caught. If the populace truly paid the IRS what was owed and the "underground economy" was assessed along the way, there would be no budget deficit. In fact, there probably wouldn't be a family below the poverty level, every highway would be paved yearly, and school teachers would be paid what they're worth. Our ingenuity in circumventing government contributes to the mediocrity of government. We are all willing accomplices.

Do we simply get the kind of government we deserve, or is there a plot at work deep within CIA headquarters to ensure that the government retains

---

[7] Although, even here, government can be felt, since many such companies enter Chapter 11 bankruptcy, to emerge later as a reorganized concern whose shareholders have gone broke while top management hasn't.

redundancy, stupidity, and cupidity, despite the best intentions of the populace, in order to provide a home for so many otherwise unemployable civil servants? Unfortunately, it's the former, because the CIA couldn't do that as well as we have. (After all, it's a government agency.)

A brief example: A study was conducted by the people who do such things to measure the degree to which Americans understood their greatest competitive rival, the Japanese (here they are again). The Japanese, it seems, have a pretty good idea about our lifestyle and its pros and cons, which helps them to be effective marketers outside of their own shores. But what about us?

In the study,[8] young Americans were asked to name three famous Japanese people. The three most common responses were:

1. Yoko Ono
2. Bruce Lee
3. Godzilla

This is the absolute truth, but it gets even crazier. It seems that Yoko Ono is a U.S. citizen who hasn't lived in Japan in decades. Bruce Lee was an ethnic Chinese who lived and worked in Hong Kong. And Godzilla, despite his reigns of terror in Japan, was actually born in the Marshall Islands, a U.S. protectorate.

Government doesn't work because we've allowed it not to and haven't demanded much else from it. When there's an extraordinary call and brilliant leadership, we can launch into space, win a war against a primitive dictatorship, or vaccinate our populace against polio. When there's a tepid call and mediocre leadership, we can screw up the lens on a giant telescope, get kicked out of humanitarian aid missions by ragtag thugs, and allow disease to ravage society so long as it's restricted to certain parts of it.

What's really the difference between putting a George Schaeffer into office as mayor of Baltimore, who leads a revitalization of that city and, down the road, putting Marion Barry into office as mayor of Washington, D.C., who is arrested for cocaine possession when caught with his dealer, and is then supported in a bid for reelection when he returns from jail? Here are two cities that are so close geographically that they share the same airports, but so distant politically that they cherish values that are worlds apart. The difference, of course, is the voters.

You see, naked emperors in government are the most pernicious type of all, since the haberdasher is us.

The public sector can be saved, and I've tried to provide examples that demonstrate where and when that's happened. But what of the "why" and

---

[8] As reported in the *Providence Journal*, Mar. 30, 1994, p. E5.

the "how"? What is necessary to produce changes in the public sector that will create enlightened, rational, customer-centered service and responsiveness? Is such change even thinkable?

The Dynamics for Change

There is a reason that the public sector acts in the way that it does. If we examine a rational sequence of action, it looks like this:

Figure 4.2. Determinants of behavior.

Values are deeply held beliefs that form our attitudes. When the sociologists talk about "culture," whether national, local, organizational, or institutional, they are basically referring to a set of values that ultimately governs behaviors. Cultures change—often when leadership changes—because values change. Think about Germany during the '30s and '40s, or General Motors from the '50s to the '80s.

Values establish attitudes, and attitudes are reflected in our behaviors. Yet when we talk about "behavior modification" we usually jump right in at that bottom level. Which means we are legislating the changes; i.e., you will provide a consequence for me to behave in the way you desire (reward) and another for behaving in the way you do not desire (punishment). There are several problems with this carrot-and-stick approach.

First, my behavior will change only as long as the stick and carrot are present, and only as long as I truly believe you will use them. Parents' admonitions to children are readily ignored ("Don't you cross the street without looking, or I won't let you play outside again!" "Don't come back after 11 or you're grounded!") because the punishment is rarely invoked, much less maintained, and the rewards far outweigh the consequences. When you try to change my behavior through threat, you may get movement and compliance, but you will not get motivation or commitment. The great governmental example of this is the Volstead Act. We all know how well that worked.

No one's values were changed. Nobody believed that drinking was bad for them. Now contrast that with the antismoking movement, which has had a profound effect on American mores and health.

In the case of smoking, the population was educated. The government's position was one of enlightenment through fact and rational discourse (somewhat reflected in modern-day approaches to alcohol relative to dangers to pregnant women and their offspring).[9] To create a long-lived, intrinsic change in my behavior, you must appeal to the governor of my attitudes, which is my belief system. If I feel it's sophisticated and charming to smoke (just watch any Hollywood production from the '40s—you can't see the actors for the smoke), I will do so, despite the carrots and sticks. But if I feel it is not in my best interest because I may die from it, I may well cease the practice.

In general, values change because of appeals to my rational self-interest, while behaviors can be changed externally only through the application of power, be that power authority, financial, career, police, or otherwise. Even stopping "halfway," and trying to influence attitudes directly, doesn't work in the long term. These appeals are generally through peer pressure, or what the psychologists call *normative* pressure. In other words, don't be left out, be one of the crowd. Don't be a loner, conform. The advertising industry has often resorted to these kinds of "herd animal" appeals, citing statistics and authorities to influence the conformity in the American public.

So, the relationship between changing behavior and the potential interventions may be depicted in Figure 4.3.

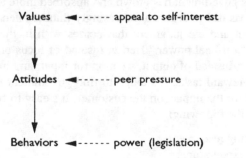

Figure 4.3. Interventions to change behavior.

---

[9] And legislation didn't work for smoking either, in that raising the tax per pack merely created more revenues and/or bootleg outlets, but no significant decrease in consumption.

To change behavior for the long term, we have to begin "upstream" with one's values, using self-interest as the leverage.

What has this to do with change in the management of our government? For one thing, we need new and different paradigms. We've learned that merely changing the office-holders doesn't necessarily change the system. When it does, the effects are strictly localized. We can have an excellent motor vehicles operation in one locale and a lousy one in another, because the leadership is different. The Department of the Interior may be run well, but there's no carryover to the Department of Transportation. Just as the government has been singularly unsuccessful at using power on the populace in most cases, the citizenry has not been successful trying to use power to change the government, whether at the ballot box, in public meetings, or by complaints to elected representatives.

There are three major keys that will open the doors required to let the mustiness out of our governmental machinery. None is easy or very pleasant to contemplate, but all change the basic values of the system.

First Key

The first step is the privatization of everything possible that makes even remote sense. Someone once said that government has two roles: Defend the coasts and deliver the mail. I'm thinking that only the first one continues to make sense.

Government suffers from a lack of top talent, and the inability to attract that talent. As government has grown and absorbed more and more "public" functions, it has had to draw on increasingly thinner talent pools. In the absence of talent and the judgment that comes with it, the bureaucracy has grown in its "artificial power." Hence, instead of focus on results, we have focus on rules; instead of output, we monitor input; and instead of celebrating ends, we reward tasks. It's tough to find government functionaries who are rewarded for the impact on the customer. It's easy to find those who are rewarded for the following:

- Conserving resources
- Cutting expenditures
- Finding those who are cheating the system
- Rejecting applications
- Adhering to policy and rule, despite inconvenience and loss
- Not questioning orders

If everything in our economy were left to free enterprise—as an extreme—jobs would either be filled by those who see an adequate return for their effort and capabilities or they would disappear. If the job were vital enough, the disappearance would not be tolerated by the public, and its remuneration would improve. When garbage collectors strike, the public responds through their elected officials. Some might complain that "sanitation engineers" aren't worth the $50,000 to $80,000 they earn in some major cities, but no one has found an acceptable way to get a distasteful job done cheaper. (It's interesting that the public tends to suffer through teachers strikes for much longer periods.)

The government can do a relatively good job in those areas requiring fairness for all citizens: law enforcement, foreign relations, control of the currency, etc. It usually does a terrible job at redressing social ills (welfare, housing) and enforcing morality (obscenity laws, controlled-substance policies). And it's plain dreadful at things that are within private-sector capabilities and have landed in the government domain out of default (transportation, construction).

In every place remotely possible, responsibilities from welfare administration to motor vehicle registration ought to be outsourced to the private sector, where they can be done more efficiently and managed with more talent. This will enable the second key.

Second Key

The size of government must be reduced at every level. The civil service rules must be changed to allow for the weeding out of nonperformers and moving performers out of nonperforming jobs.

In other words, government must be reengineered and downsized. The reengineering should focus it on the processes that service the public (i.e., collection and allocation of tax revenues, providing for public education, enforcing the law), and the downsizing can then focus on the fewer services that really need to be provided. Actually, more resources will be addressed toward fewer, but essential, services.

Government is as large and costly as it is primarily due to:

- Lifelong job guarantees
- Ineffective mechanisms to remove people
- Growth of rules over judgment, which requires administrators
- Lack of incentive for smaller government
- Inexhaustible revenue streams (tax, bond, and deficit financing)
- Acceptance of perquisites (staffs) in place of high compensation
- Proliferation of professional, bureaucrats despite conditions [10]

---

[10] As an example, although today's Armed Forces are far smaller that those in the field at the height of World War II, we actually have more flag officers (generals and admirals) today, in peacetime, than we did a half century ago.

We will never improve the proficiency of our public-sector decision making and implementation—we will never even make a dent in stupid management—unless we reduce the size of the monolith, enabling us to create the third key.

Third Key

We must create a public-service allure that is more than just that of patriotism and self-sacrifice. While these are noble objectives, they are overwhelmed by people in public service with all the wrong objectives: guaranteed employment, attractive retirement packages, lack of performance-based evaluation, inability to find work elsewhere, etc. Those with lofty goals and superb talents can still enter governmental service. We'll simply pay them better. In other words, we won't lose the stars by demanding higher talents in return for competitive incentives.

Years ago, I landed in Miami and debarked from a 747. Unfortunately, about a thousand people were doing the exact same thing from three similar aircraft. As we lined up at the immigration desks, a frenzied supervisor emerged and recognized that he was facing delays—and complaints—for the next 6 or 7 hours. He immediately made a wise decision (although one has to wonder why such things aren't anticipated, since the conditions I found myself in are hardly infrequent at Miami International). He instructed the eight agents on duty to check only passport photos for U.S. citizens, and forego all other procedures.

His minions loyally stood in front of their stations; a loudspeaker informed us to hold our passports, turned to the photo page, beside our faces, and we would simply walk through immigration. The system worked miraculously; the lines moved comfortably, until I reached the agent.

My passport picture was 7 years old and more typically resembled someone trying to dodge heavy artillery fire in the Balkans than a respected consultant. The agent held up a hand. Those behind me groaned.

He looked at the picture, then at me. He looked again, and back to me. Finally, after a third comparison, he looked me in the eye.

"Well, what do you think?" I asked.

"Close enough for government work," he said, and waved me through.

All too often, despite the rules, procedures, and scores of bureaucrats in place to enforce them, quality suffers anyway. Every attorney I've ever met in the Immigration and Naturalization Service, for example, has been so weak and incompetent that he or she would die in public service faster than quadraphonic sound in a record store. And many of them have displayed, in my presence, outright bigotry against those they're there to serve: people trying to legally enter this country.

The third key is to create compensation and incentive packages that compete with the private sector for the best and the brightest. Why do we operate under the assumption that government must accommodate itself with mediocre performers and rampant incompetence?

By privatizing, we be able to reduce the size of government and focus on truly essential, mass services. By reducing the size, we'll be able to pay more to attract the talent that will make the system a true servant of the customer—the people. Then the trick will be to ensure that the success does not create another stifling hierarchy.

How to Clothe the Emperors, Part 4

1. Vote for people who take positions that make sense, not for personalities.
2. Do not break the rules with the rationalization that everyone else is. If you collect unemployment and hold down a job, you deserve to be cheated by others.
3. Turn down fund-raising initiatives proposed by the legislature unless they contribute to the three keys mentioned before. These people are only bailing themselves out.
4. Follow your representatives' voting records, write them letters, and demand responses about their positions.
5. Attend local hearings for school boards, zoning, planning, finance, fire districts, etc.
6. When you find waste, incompetence, cheating, or rudeness, notify the media.
7. Become involved in grass roots efforts to effect reform.
8. Do not vote along party lines. Vote along self-interest lines to eradicate stupidity.
9. If you do have a private-sector choice, spend your money with the private sector (i.e., have your license renewed at an independent dealer, your car inspected at a gas station, your water provided by a private utility).
10. Strive for nothing less than a quadrant-1 government at every level.

Part Two

R o o t s

"With a whole crowd of selected gentlemen, the emperor visited the crafty swindlers, who were weaving away for all their worth, but without shred or thread."

Chapter 5

Lip Service to Change
Why We Should Believe Only What We See

"To many people, it is like a blind man in a dark room looking for a black cat that isn't there."

—Thomas A. Harris, on psychiatry from *I'm OK, You're OK*

I've always wanted to write a pragmatic pop-psychology book with the title *I'm OK, You Stink* because that's how most organizations operate.

A couple of summers ago, I took my dog, Trotsky,[1] for an early-morning walk along the nearby beach. Although he sniffed the usual detritus from the overnight tides, his interest was most drawn to a bland stretch of sand that looked exactly like all the other bland stretches of sand. Trotsky settled in and wouldn't move for 10 minutes, until satisfied that he had smelled everything worth sniffing.

It occurred to me that he had taken in a picture I would never know. He probably knew what animal had passed that way before him, whether it was healthy or ill, male or female, aggressive or scared, and in which direction it was headed. I could never know those things; Trotsky is equipped with sensory apparatus that we fragile humans don't possess. That's why dogs are so helpful as guards, investigators, herders, and companions.

But that's also why we need other people. What I miss, you might pick up, and what you overlook, I just may note. In organizations, one of the benefits of human interaction is precisely that sharing. (Which is why salespeople inevitably enjoy joint calls with trusted

---

[1] He is half German Shephard and half Siberian Husky, so I named him after the intellectual on his father's side. He looks exactly like a wolf, weighs 102 pounds, and suffers no fools gladly.

colleagues, and trainers like to work with experienced peers. You can learn so much more when another's antenna is also receiving.)

Yet most organizations don't work in this collegial, joint-dependency manner, despite the claims of self-directed teams, "boundarylessness," and flat hierarchies. What usually happens is that "I'm OK, You're Clearly Not" prevails. And while there are intense efforts made in most organizations to convince everyone that change and improvement are everywhere, they are usually egregiously transparent: signs in the cafeteria, stories in the house organ, plaques on office walls. There are consultants who specialize in "vision statements" and organization retreats, at which participants can rappel down mountains, ford streams, and put their physical well-being in each other's hands. The fact is, however, that most organizations eschew change culturally, resist it *from the top,* and no one I know rappels down the office façade or fords the parking lot.

Organizational Hypocrisy

No one in organizations really believes what he or she reads or hears. People only believe what they see. Show me a reward system, and I'll show you a value system. Senior management creates that which reflects its real values, and are helpless to do anything else, as though they are moths drawn to a light, or scalpers drawn to a Striesand concert. So while management may gleefully send people to outdoor experiences, claim that they are team centered, and talk the party line about commitment to quality, they can't help but reveal their real sentiments in their reward structure. It's sort of like sodium pentathol.

What the reward systems often say is, "Manage people brutally, but make your quotas, and you'll do just fine here." Or, "Meet your product goals, and I don't care about your subordinates, your interpersonal relations, or your expense account. Just help me meet my incentive numbers, and you'll be there with me."

You cannot espouse one set of values and expect them to be honored while rewarding another. Yet in our consulting practice we constantly observe harsh, dictatorial, and outright cruel management being promoted, recognized, and cited because key organizational financial goals were met. And we see honest, development-oriented, and supportive managers punished, transferred, and chastised because numbers weren't met. All of us trust what we see. What we see tells us what behaviors are required to do well and to prosper.

Why can't organizations make the change from the rigid, authoritarian hierarchies that disempower people to the more flexible, empowered operations that utilize people's talents and energies? Why do managers resist change when they claim they endorse it? And why do so many executives bemoan the fact that their senior team knows what has to be done but just can't execute it?

Part of the problem is in the misunderstanding of resistance to change. I don't believe that anyone really objects to a new tomorrow, with the comforts, challenges, and excitement that it brings. What people viscerally resist, however, is letting go of where they are.

Do you remember the playground equipment called "monkey bars"? The idea was to grasp each successive bar to propel yourself from one side to the other. When I first tried this, I immediately looked down, saw a drop of, oh, about 40 feet, and decided it would be prudent to tighten my grip on the first bar. After a while, my fingers and arms tired, and I dropped off, having gone nowhere at all but down.

After many such futile tries, I noticed that the kids who traveled across without a problem simply let go with one hand, reached out to grab the next bar, then repeated the process with the other hand. In other words, they had to let go in order to reach out. And they never looked down. The technique didn't require strength so much as it did momentum, and the only way to begin the momentum was to let go. Once you were in motion, it was far easier to maintain the motion.

Change in organizations is no different from traveling across those monkey bars. You have to let go in order to reach out. People in organizations don't fear change; they fear the "letting go." The other end of the monkey bars represented success for me, not threat or failure. It was letting go of my present hold that scared me. And, ironically, by not letting go I had to eventually release my grip anyway. You get tired just hanging on—more tired than if you were in motion toward a goal.

People in organizations need support in letting go. Yet what the executives, training programs, consultants, books, and programs du jour all try to do is to make them comfortable with the future. The executives, meanwhile, retain the old reward systems, old behaviors, and old styles because they,

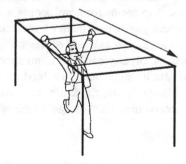

Figure 5.1. The monkey bars.

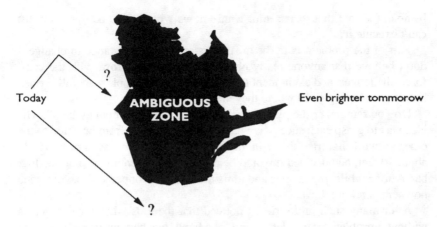

Today

AMBIGUOUS ZONE

Even brighter tommorow

Figure 5.2. The ambiguous zone.

more than anyone, are afraid of letting go. Their entire present existence, success, and self-esteem are wrapped up in the status quo. There may well indeed be an even brighter future with more honors, more money, and more self-actualization down the road, but they still don't want to let go. It's like trying to be in two places at once.

When organizations plan to change (and if they don't, change will force itself on them), they consider the future *but not the present*. Senior management generally makes no allowances for itself or its people to leave where they are. They simply focus on the new destination.

However, when people don't understand the nature of the transition ahead of them, and rightfully recognize it for an uncertain, uneasy, vaguely threatening period, they tend to hold on tighter to the bar they're on. Consequently, the organization builds no momentum to reach the future. And don't forget: No matter how secure the grip seems for now, people will eventually fall off the bar. You can't stay where you are, no matter how secure it seems.

It's management's job to resolve as much of the ambiguity as possible. In legitimate change efforts, ambiguity can't be eliminated. There's too much that can't be anticipated. But it can be acknowledged. I call this transient area the "ambiguous zone" (da da da da, da da da da), which is that area that must be traversed—the intervening bars—to get to the other side.[2] So long as

---

[2] For a nice discussion of the phenomenon, see *Managing Transitions: Making the Most of Change*, by Williams Bridges, Addison-Wesley, 1991. Bridges refers to the transient area as the "neutral zone."

I don't understand the nature of that ambiguity, I will be threatened by it, and so long as I am threatened, I will not loosen my grip on my secure present.

Typically, change focuses on outcomes, endings, new beginnings, you name it. But to affect a successful transition, we must first acknowledge and support "ending the old," or "terminating the present." Another way to view this is in Figure 5.3: Ending the present.

Why can't leadership help in this ending process? Why is it that in merely presenting the future without attempting to end the present, and without helping to minimize the ambiguity ahead, management willingly provides only lip service to real change? It's because they're as scared as anyone else:

- The values and rewards that guide the present organization must be changed today in order to help break with the present. They cannot simply be created "when we get there." People won't let go of the bar if the rewards are encouraging them to hold on. Yet it's the most senior people who are best treated by the current rewards and who determine the rewards. Consequently, they are least prone to change them until the new future is assured—which is a paradox. (We need to change these rewards to get to the future, but I'm going to wait until we're there before I change them.)
- It's easier to depict the future than it is to manage transitions through the ambiguous zone. Hence, most consulting approaches, training, fads, and support systems are oriented toward "visioning" and "breakthrough thinking" and "reengineering." It's relatively mundane to think about ending the present, and it's certainly discomfiting. I can paint you that picture, but I'm not so comfortable teaching you how to paint or, even worse, describing how to make paint. I can't begin to describe how many projects we've been asked to undertake to provide the "transition management" while ongoing "reengineering" or "rightsizing" or "change management" or something else is continuing. Some executive finally realized that no one is letting go; everyone is holding on to the bar.

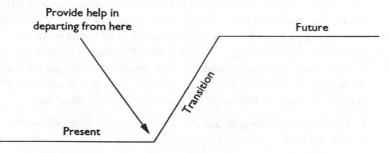

Figure 5.3. Ending the present.

- There is some bad news to convey. Inexorably, as change processes unfold, it becomes apparent that the present sets of skills, experiences, and behaviors in the organization will not be the ideal sets for the future. Some people will adjust easily, others will require development, some may have to accept less-demanding (and paying) jobs, and others will simply have to leave. In addition, vacancies will be filled by new players, possessing the new set of attributes, and they will alter the culture of the organization still more. The time to implement processes to deal with these realities is in the present. "Reskilling" workshops, outplacement help, counseling support, recruiting, and constant communications about what the company is doing are vital. It is far better that people be concerned about the real issues, and make intelligent decisions about them, than it is to be concerned about "grapevine" issues that will inevitably be even worse and cannot lead to intelligent decisions. Change is not intrinsically painful, but letting go of the present almost always is. Management has to stand up to its responsibility to candidly communicate and attend to these issues.
- The focus is too often on loss and people leaving. The focus needs to be on retention and people staying. The most important people to an organization that has undergone change are the people who are still there. At least two things have to happen: First, those who leave must be treated honestly and well, so that those who stay don't have "survivor guilt" and know that the organization has done its best to take care of colleagues. Second, if people are irrationally threatened they will immediately move to take care of themselves which, in a corporate environment, means "getting your paper out on the street." Who are the first employees to leave a threatening and ambiguous environment? Only the best people, who are smart enough to realize they are exposed, self-directed enough to take action sooner than later, and good enough to be attractive to prospective employers. Unless transitions are managed carefully, so that the people least apt to fit the future are the ones who voluntarily or involuntarily depart, the exact opposite will occur every time. Those people who are most relied on to make the new future successful are precisely the ones who aren't around to be a part of it. This isn't an accident of nature or an inevitable result of change. It's simply stupid; change management.
- Finally, there's a crass assumption made about skills and talents needed to help people adjust and to depart from the present. Management often assumes that any of the following can help with this transition:

1. Consultants assisting in the change, reengineering, or whatever
2. Internal human resources

3. Reading material, especially cute booklets, distributed to everyone
4. Task force of key managers
5. Time

In fact, special expertise is required to assist. If one viewed the process as art and science, the reengineering efforts and depictions of the future are mostly the latter, and the help with letting go is almost totally the former. I once heard a consultant from one of the big six accounting firms tell the client that the human support and transitions would be handled with their special project management techniques, closely approximating the templates and models that were used in the reengineering effort. I immediately knew I'd be around for a while. For while the executives in the room nodded pleasantly at the regimen of it all, they would soon find that processes respond well to flowcharts and critical paths, but people do not.

Finger-Pointing Time

When executives don't realize this, and don't have someone as enlightened as I am to explain it, they begin to seek out other reasons for people's refusing to let go. They assume, every time, that they are threatened by the future, not by leaving the present or by the ambiguous zone staring them in the face.

The response is not to look to themselves but to assume the "I'm OK, You're Deeply Troubled" posture and call for "involvement." This is the juncture during which task forces are formed, committees are convened, reports are compiled, and critical issues are weighed. And after all the forming, convening, compiling, and weighing, everyone agrees that the future is, indeed, the correct one, and that it needs to be better communicated, and that leadership has listened once again. After which, people tighten their grip still more. This is what I call "white-knuckle time," not to be confused at all with "Miller time."

At white-knuckle time (WKT), people begin to sense that management has become impatient with the lack of progress (into the ambiguous zone) and, from its lofty heights, clearly recognizes that it isn't the gods who have failed. After all, the task forces have achieved employee involvement; the reports have shown the vision to be pure; and the priorities have been established. Thus, the only thing that can be wrong is what we've known all along: Employees resist change. But it's time to take off the gloves. No more Mr. Nice Person. As an employee, I'm starting to stare downwards, and I'm seeing that 40-foot drop. *But I no longer have the strength in my arms to swing forward, even if I were so inclined.*

These futile responses to helping with transitions have a pernicious, subtle effect on organizational health: They suck the life right out of it.

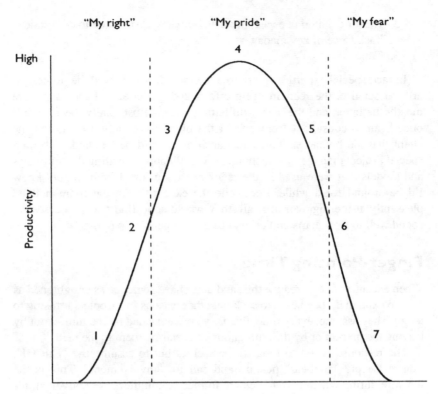

Figure 5.4. The stress curve.

Misguided efforts to "involve" employees, "take the organization's temperature," convene focus groups, survey the population, and, generally, focus me even more on the need to hang tight, sap my energy. Entire groups of people who were once at least neutral or ambivalent about change become unable to embrace it at all because; between doing their jobs and worrying about what's happening, they have no energy left. Even if I'm helped to understand (or forced to accept) that I must now reach out and grab the next wrung, I may not be successful doing it. I'm either near-paralyzed with fear, or I'm plain exhausted. As with everything pertaining to human life, we can depict this in a bell curve, as seen in Figure 5.4.[3]

---

[3] For more on the subject of stress and its role in employee comfort and discomfort, see *Danger in the Comfort Zone,* by Judith M. Bardwick, AMACOM, 1991. The diagram is adapted from that book.

On the low, left end of this curve, we have the people who believe that their job is an entitlement. Their stress levels are low, and so is their productivity. They are there to collect the paycheck, and they're doing you a favor by bothering to exert that much effort. At the "my right" positions you'll tend to hear these attitudes:

1. "Don't bother me. I don't owe you anything. You don't deserve anything."
2. "If I'm in the right mood, I'll do what the job minimally calls for, but don't ask for anything above and beyond that."

For perhaps a decade, a water treatment supervisor in Cranston, Rhode Island, ran a completely second, independent business out of his water treatment office. He was finally caught by accident. His response was, "Hey, I've been doing this for years, and no one has complained about the water treatment or my performance. What's the big deal?" He was right, of course. He had been under the supervision of stupid managers, and there was no stress level—challenges, performance evaluations, surprise visits—whatsoever. There are many people in these positions in government, but there are a surprising number in the private sector as well. The only trouble with early retirement is that too many people avail themselves of it while still on the payroll.

When stress increases within acceptable limits, it serves to get the old adrenaline streaming. We all need a certain amount of stress to perform well. We require a sense of urgency, of commitment, of obligation. We perform better at heightened levels of awareness. The people who claim that "I work best under pressure," or "I'm best when the deadline is approaching," are usually not kidding. In the newspaper business, this is a near-obligatory attribute.

So, in the "my pride" area we have people at the maximum of their productivity, operating within tolerable stress limits. This is the opposite of "distress"; the behaviorists sometimes refer to it as "eustress." Figure 5.5 shows the ideal productivity area. At these positions, the attitude is likely to be:

3. "I'll take some prudent risks and go beyond minimum expectations."
4. "I'll do whatever is necessary to get the job done within legal and ethical guidelines. Risks are part of the job, especially if the payoff is significant."
5. "I'll do whatever is necessary to get the job done, so long as I'm not overexposed. There is such a thing as being 'too visible.'"

People in the "my pride" area identify with their contribution to the work and take gratification from a job well done. The stress level is sufficient to keep them motivated, but not so strong as to scare them. In empowered organizations, people recognize and accept risk in return for justifiable benefits. They feel safe enough to do so without retribution. This is the classic "freedom to

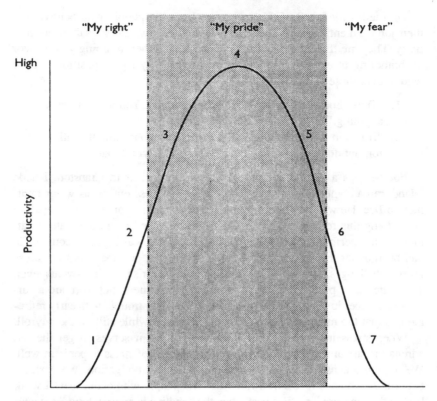

"My right" "My pride" "My fear"

Figure 5.5. Ideal productivity.

fail" mentality, which, in most organizations, translates as "You have the freedom to fail here. Once."

On the downside of the slope we have fear, because the stress has progressed to the point of being paralyzing. This is when people fear for their jobs, and visibility becomes a liability, not an asset. *A great many managers argue that fear is the real driver of performance.* This is arrant nonsense. Stress does drive performance, but only up to a point. Once it becomes fear, it inhibits performance. Those same managers begin to appreciate the middle positions but don't know when to stop turning the screws.

At positions in the fear zone, you encounter:

6. "I'll perform to the extent that I feel safe. I'll take no risks that expose me, and I'm going to be circumspect about what I do."

7. "I'm going to keep my head down and do nothing that draws any attention to me whatsoever. The less I do, the safer I am."

Note that you have the same behaviors manifest at position #7 that you do at position #1, but for very different reasons. This creates some frightening dynamics. For example, management sees people in position #1 and, rightfully, decides to increase the pressure on performance. However, they increase the pressure so much that the performers are driven straight across to position #7 without stopping anywhere in between. The result is that management concludes that "These are inferior people. They didn't perform when there was no pressure on them, and they won't perform under pressure either."

In the fear zone, people are afraid to act with initiative, to question, to take opposing positions and, in essence, to provide any value beyond the very basic nature of the work. And what drives people to that position rapidly? The threat of letting go, without the assurances that it's all right to do so.

Empty Tool Kits

These graphic, yet simple illustrations of why people tend to act the way they do are not the result of rocket scientists laboring through the night. They are simple tools, available from a plethora of sources, which should comprise the manager's "tool kit." All too often that tool kit is empty, or it has only the most basic of tools, such as a very large hammer and a paycheck.

This is not pop psychology. We're not pursuing the black cat. It's tough enough to be a manager these days without trying to be a psychologist, which is hard enough for the psychologists. But without a basic understanding of behaviors and motivations in the tool kit, organizations will be neither built nor repaired very well.

My father-in-law, who could fix a '62 Buick with an intuition that would be the envy of any psychic, used to tell me that "If you have the right tools, you can fix anything." He was scrupulous about keeping his tools in top condition, and he had a lot of them. Managers are using the wrong tools, and they're in shoddy condition.

The most popular instruments to understand employee behaviors and predispositions are the "personality tests" that are marketed under a variety of different names. Most of these are simplistic, and some are legal time bombs. Almost all attempt to "label" an employee, which, instead of helping management to understand behaviors, are used as a means to explain away behaviors. I can't tell you how many times I've heard managers who should know better say, "Well, what do you expect from a right-brainer. She'll never be able to deal with this much detail." In my opinion, you might as well cast a slur on someone's ancestry, because the speaker is committing an act of bigotry so insidious that a lawsuit should follow.

Have you ever heard, been the victim of, or been party to a conversation that included gems like these:

"Be careful, he's a driver, so he's going to make his decision without a lot of study of the facts."

"You're dealing with an INTJ, so don't expect a whole lot of sensitivity or intuiting."

"This person is a high 'I,' which means that he'll be quick to establish a relationship."

Managers have resorted to what amounts to horoscopes and crystal balls to try to understand behavior and, even then, instead of learning from them, use the results to explain why the individual *can't* perform. While we all have a set of behavioral predispositions that represent our highest comfort zones, we also have varying degrees of versatility, and it's that ability to modify behavior to suit the circumstances and the other performers that is the key. Instead of focusing on and building that versatility, managers tend to focus on a static "snapshot" of an individual's behaviors, on the crazy assumption that it never becomes a motion picture.

There are three major caveats in the area of understanding behavior and motivation.

Caveat 1. There are three components to our behaviors that are so variable and so changeable in their combinations that predicting behavior in any one situation is about as certain as predicting which number the ball will land on in roulette. Those three components are:

1. The biochemical, genetic inheritance that each of us receives from our parents, which they have inherited from their parents, and so on. Just as this affects physiological traits, it also affects psychological and behavioral traits.

2. The socialization and conditioning of our upbringing, including parents, friends, siblings, and others. Most psychologists believe that self-image is first formed by the age of 6. However, continued socialization occurs to varying degrees, based on one's circumstances.

3. The other performers and the environment in which we operate have profound affects on behavior. A highly assertive person may well become more amiable when confronted with a highly aggressive person. We act differently in front of our boss than we do in front of subordinates. We usually assume different roles at work, at home, in social situations, and in religious contexts. (Has your spouse ever said, "Excuse me, but you're not at the office now"?)

Given these three variables, and the permutations possible, predicting behavior makes weather forecasting seem like an exact science.

Caveat 2. Testing must be validated for it to be both accurate and reliable enough to apply to the workplace. The American Psychological Association has three general validation criteria that must be met for it to accept the use of a test:

1. Construct validity, which means that the test measures what it claims to measure.

2. Content validity, which means that what the test measures is actually important to the successful completion of the job in question.
3. Concurrent validity, which means that the test results will be highest among those actually performing in the desired manner in the job.

Without these three validity criteria, tests are not considered valid for use. Such validation studies are typically published in "refereed journals," such as the *Journal of Applied Psychology,* wherein independent sources (the referees) determine whether the validity studies are comprehensive and accurate. Most of the testing instruments that I see applied in the workplace do not meet these criteria.[4]

Caveat 3. Personality and behavioral clashes are some of the major causes of lack of performance and poor management on the job. Why do some executives move from one company to another, strikingly successful at the former, only to go down in flames at the latter? Their skills and abilities haven't changed. Their experiences remain intact. Obviously, they appeared to be excellent candidates in the interview process.

The difference is that their behavioral characteristics and preferred operating style simply do not match well with the new environment and new relationships. This can be investigated beforehand, but it seldom is. One report cites that these behavioral mismatches "largely account for the turnover rate for division heads and higher in U.S. corporations. In the past 5 years, that rate is 42% higher than the average in any previous 5-year period."[5]

The primary problem with the tendency to use pseudo-psychological methods and labeling practices to help explain behavior is that they violate our basic dictate: Believe what you see. Just as employees don't believe what they read or hear, managers shouldn't believe the results of a test (much less a nonvalid one) to explain away performance. They should focus on what they see and then pursue causes through an investigative, interactive process. Yes, that can be hard work. Yes, that's why managers are paid more money.

The traditional manager in this country has gained his or her status through two primary elements: the control of people and the control of information. Both of those elements have disappeared. In an age of downsizing

---

[4] If you find this surprising, you'll be shocked to know it's even worse elsewhere. In France, for example, almost all employers demand some form of graphology testing, which is a huge business in that country. Translation: People aren't hired without handwriting analysis, which is routinely used as a major factor in selection decisions. As a result, few applicants write letters in script, but businesses demand handwritten samples.

[5] See *The Wall Street Journal,* Aug. 29, 1994, p. 1: "The Latest Addition to Executive Suite Is Psychologist's Couch," by Amal Kumar Naj.

and lean operations, control of people is strictly limited. And when self-directed teams are a legitimate factor, the need for managers to control employees is minimal.

As for information, it is widely available through the desktop computer, personal computers, fax machines, voice mail, and any number of high-tech interventions. Organizations want employees to have as much information as possible with the least amount of interpretation and delay associated with it.

The emerging role for the manager is to perform as a team leader, a catalyst for performance, a leverage point that enables others to contribute exponentially. What other value-added is there to justify the position? That role is best met through the legitimate efforts to observe behavior, manage stress levels, create change, and help others to "let go" safely. That team leader role is one that helps people face and travel through the ambiguous zone.

It's too easy, and too dysfunctional, to give mere lip service to change. Employees will believe only what they see, and what they need to see is leadership that helps them perform at optimal levels.

How to Clothe the Emperors, Part Five

1. Help employees "cross the bar" by creating an environment in which it is okay to "let go."
2. Intelligently manage stress levels and demands so that employees feel invigorated and neither lethargic nor scared.
3. Set an example for using observed behavior. Don't jump "inside someone's head." Focus on what behaviors are appropriate or inappropriate.
4. Do not use any test instruments that are not validated, and use even those sparingly as one input to overall assessments.
5. Understand that education is superior to legislation and that real behavior change will come about as a result of appeals to rational self-interest, which may differ among various people.
6. Never use a label to characterize or describe someone, even if you feel it is a flattering one.
7. Understand that behavior cannot really be predicted, because of the variables involved in each situation. Versatility and judgment are the key attributes for success in most situations.
8. Don't use a "snapshot" of a person, when life is actually a motion picture. Look for growth, change, and evolution; don't create fixed images of others.
9. Provide guidance and honesty about ambiguous zones. Help people realize that the zones can't be eliminated, but they can be traversed.
10. View your position as one of support, not control; of helping others leverage their talents, not testing others' talents; and of empowering others, not disempowering others.

Chapter 6

Holier Than Thou
How the System Breeds Elitism

"When a top executive is selecting his key associates, there are only two qualities for which he should be willing to pay almost any price: taste and judgment. Almost everything else can be bought by the yard."
— John Gardner

On March 10, 1994, *The Wall Street Journal* featured the story of Fleet Bank's culmination of its "Fleet Focus" program. Fleet, the 15th largest bank in the nation, headquartered in Providence, Rhode Island, coming off a highly profitable year, had commissioned an ex-McKinsey consultant to lead a massive cost reduction study. Drafting 50 bank employees for full-time duty and another 200 for part-time assignments on the program, the consultant moved into an office adjoining that of Fleet CEO Terry Murray's and launched a draconian attack on bank practices and procedures.

This was no theoretical exercise. Under the rubric of "be healthy or be taken over," the bank's message was that survival itself was at stake. Officers and managers were expected ruthlessly to seek ways to cut costs, with jobs being a primary consideration. The result was an organizational holocaust; while no one marched to one's death, many marched to the unemployment line, having eliminated their own jobs. The *Journal* labeled it "suicide," and legends were quickly born about executives being applauded by Murray's team after recommending their departments be merged, and then dismissed by that same team as being incapable of leading the new unit. The market responded by increasing the stock price, and analysts gleefully moved Fleet from "sell" to "buy."

However, it was the final three paragraphs of the story's 22 column-inches that caught my eye. The bank's directors, it seemed, were to provide the final blessing for the changes at the annual March directors meeting at the Breakers in Florida. While some thought had been given to changing the venue to someplace slightly less lavish in view of the prevailing morale, the board had decided that the traditional meeting should not be disturbed, no matter what the cost or symbolism. Sometimes crassness reaches a level of obnoxiousness so gross that one scarcely knows where to begin with it. But let us try.

The Fleet board's refusal to deny itself its self-indulgent vacation, despite the obvious need for a symbolic "we're all in this together," is not unusual, though it is reprehensible. I had lunch with a senior vice president at the bank the next week. Her response was, "We're all talking about it, but we're not surprised." A branch manager with 20 years' service commented, "We all feel sad about it. It's terrible for morale." Meanwhile, newspapers noted that Fleet had installed bulletproof glass and a full-time security guard in the executive offices. Small wonder.

There is a consistent "holier-than-thou" attitude among business leadership which grows as stubbornly as any ragweed in the carefully tended gardens of participative management and total-quality whatever. In one of many excellent studies undertaken by Wyatt Consultants of Chicago, the success rate of quality improvement programs was assessed *by the same executives who contracted for them* as 44% effective for expense reduction, and 22% effective for productivity improvement. In other words, the preponderance of all quality efforts was deemed to be unsuccessful by the very people who paid for them. In my view, that failure rate says nothing about the quality of the programs or the motivation of the employees. It says everything about the commitment of leadership to become personally involved in their implementation and to serve as an exemplar for the effort.

What Do You Mean, "Eliminate It"?

Several years ago I was asked by a major utility to recommend cost-effective alternatives to improve communication. Senior executives found that, while the grapevine was alive and well, employees were continually citing frustration in attempts to be heard by their superiors. The executives were dismayed that they were constantly being surprised by employee problems and were thrust into reactive modes, rather than preventive ones. This was hardly a unique scenario, and the ensuing investigation was not open-heart surgery. However, the response was classic.

One of my core suggestions was to eliminate the executive dining room, which was a windowless concave located adjacent to the employee cafeteria. Not only was the top brass segregated, but they also were seen entering and leaving the place like it was some private club denied to the proletariat.

"What do you mean, 'eliminate it'?" asked the senior vice president for operations.

"I mean tear it down, remove the walls, get everyone in the same cafeteria line and at the same tables. Then, as that becomes the norm, you'll begin to hear what's on people's minds," said I, fastidiously.

"But that's a key executive perk."

"Well that key perk is one of the reasons that you're not hearing honest feedback, and that people feel afraid to approach you."

"You'll have to look elsewhere. I could never sell this to the executive team."

"Why don't you begin eating in the cafeteria yourself, and set the example? You're the number-2 officer in the place. I'm sure your colleagues would get the hint."

"I am not going to be the one who closed the executive dining room. And that's that."

It certainly is. These examples are not apocryphal. The two I've cited above represent the grand, organization-wide gesture, and the small, pragmatic adjustment. No matter. Naked emperors do not surrender any turf, possession, or privilege. They wrap themselves around their hard-won gains like some kind of exotic monkey, prehensile tail and all, refusing to give an inch unless pried off the branch or murdered. They don't pry off easily. We're going to have to kill them.

What is it about modern managers that create this holier-than-thou attitude, wherein "do as I say and not as I do" is an acceptable philosophy? I believe it has to do with the following: Corporate culture too often includes "rites of passage," which demand that one "pays dues" to achieve certain heights. Those dues can range from service abroad, to resuscitating poor-performing units, to spending 80% of the time on the road. The implicit—and often explicit—agreement is that once completed, those rites entitle the manager to a range of perquisites and privileges. When gained at such expense and investment, they are not easily surrendered.

This phenomenon, not incidentally, is often the excuse to bar rapid rise to women and minorities. While working on strategic direction in a major accounting firm, I inquired about the percentages of women and minorities among the 1,500 partners. The response was 6% and 4%, respectively, followed immediately by the disclaimer, "But you have to understand that it takes about 8 years to become a partner here, and those groups have only entered the system in the past 4 years or so."

"Ah, so it's a matter of climbing the ladder, as simple as that," I observed.

"That's right. The process is the same for everyone."

"Tell me, do you ever hire people directly as partners?"

"It's very rare. We call them 'direct hires.' "

"How many direct hires were made in the last year?"

"We hired 31 partners from the outside."

"And how many of those were white males?"

"Thirty."

Cultural rites of passage are used to exclude as well as to include, and they constitute psychological and temporal gains too important to cede.

Strategies Never Fail in Their Formulation

Executive actions are too hidden. It's relatively simple to check on the performance of a salesperson in an organization, but it's virtually impossible to do so for executives who delve into the intangible, the esoteric, and the incomprehensible. Corporate strategy is one such haven, wherein the executives perform Herculean feats of mental gymnastics, arriving at "environmental scans" and "future shareholder value" determinations with the agility of an acrobat. Once the elaborate documents are prepared, it's up to middle management to implement these grand schemes and dreams. This is basically akin to eating soup with your fingers.

Strategies never fail in their formulation, of course. How could they? They are aesthetically beautiful creations, with precise diagrams and projections, all arranged in tabbed, three-ring binders to demonstrate flexibility. Strategies fail in their execution, and how could they not? It generally requires the genius of a da Vinci, the wiliness of a Perot, and the patience of St. Francis to attempt to instantiate the vast conceptual work of the geniuses on the fourth floor.

Executives are judged on their ability to create the intangible, while employees are judged on their accomplishment of the tangible. Executives are measured on the basis of multiyear plans that change every year, while employees are measured based on current performance against quantitative goals.

There is a self-fulfilling elitism in organizations that executives subliminally accept. The elitism can take many forms, but it's always institutionalized and accepted by the culture, while reinforced through policy and procedure.

In a large pharmaceutical client, I've confronted management with what I call "Hay Point elitism." The Hay system, in place forever at some clients, is a compensation model that utilizes points based, presumably, on objective measures such as the number of people supervised, budget amounts managed, decision-making prerogatives, and other measures of accountability. (Let us blissfully ignore for the nonce the fact that today's workplace is no longer dependent on the number of bodies controlled or on independent budget authority. That's an issue we've touched on in the preceding chapter, and we'll discuss further in Artifice as Reality, Chapter 7.) The Hay system is one of many models that serve to replace the need for executives to use judgment.

I observed senior managers at my client respond to ideas and suggestions from subordinates based on their Hay Point designations. In other words, intelligence and creativity were deemed to be direct correlations of the Hay system.

"What do you think about that idea to organize around a national account focus?"

"Who came up with that, McGrath?"

"Yeah, I think so."

"McGrath's what, about a 750?"

"I think so."

"I don't know—sounds pretty farfetched to me."

"Wait a minute. That was Lutz, not McGrath. McGrath wanted to look at geographic territories. Lutz said that we'd be smart to look at key accounts. He's an executive director, so he must be around 1100."

"All right, that's more like it. Let's assign a task force to investigate that. Ask Lutz if he can head it."

When I broached this subject and provided such examples, there was nervous laughter in the room. Everyone recognized the system they had become sucked into. In other organizations, it can be title, or unit, or geographic office, or undergraduate school, or whether one has worked in a line operation. Whatever the measure or criterion, there are "official" standards by which worth and merit are based, and ideas are seldom analyzed for intrinsic value. It's the source that counts.

Executives are deliberately and comfortably isolated from the operation of the enterprise. Why does it make headlines each year when the Hyatt Hotel chain demands that its senior managers take the places of porters, registration clerks, and waiters? Because it's the grand, public exception, not the practical rule.

I'm not advocating that people at all levels change jobs on a daily basis (although PeopleExpress Airlines attempted this when pilots and flight crews took regular rotations behind the ticket counters and sorted baggage). But the much-vaunted "management by wandering around" has never come to pass. Either managers have cited the talk but never walked it, or they've wandered without knowing what they're looking for.

While being escorted through the operations of a New England insurance company by a veteran senior vice president, I noted that the employees were giving us a long and curious once-over. I remarked on this later to the vice president of human resources, who had arranged for my visit.

"Your people certainly aren't accustomed to outsiders wandering through the place, are they?" I asked.

"Oh, it wasn't you they were staring at. It was our executive who drew the attention."

"Why was that?"

"No one in those units had ever seen him before."

Some industries are better than others. In large retail stores, it's not unusual for senior managers to be wandering around, absorbing customers' reactions. Banks have tended to move branch management right out into the throngs on the floor, although I doubt you'll see their boss's boss hanging around. And sometimes the best of efforts are misplaced.

Flying to Atlanta, I noticed that a gentleman who flew in from Atlanta turned around and reboarded for the return. He sat across the aisle from me, and the flight attendants were very, well, attentive. I concluded he was a Delta executive testing the product, and I sent him a note. He invited himself over for a chat and carefully investigated my good and bad experiences with the airline. I was impressed, and he offered neither excuse nor panacea. He simply told me that he appreciated my business and explained how the organization was constantly trying to improve.

My only quibble: Why he was doing this in an eight-seat first class cabin and not in the back where most of the paying customers are known to hang out?

Finally, there is tremendous incompetence at the top, and the best place to hide is behind lofty ideals, stalwart phrases and heavy oak doors guarded by secretaries with the instincts of a Doberman. That incompetence isn't malicious or venal. It's an unfortunate but inevitable by-product of our organizational systems.

To this day and at this writing, most organizations have promoted people based on content expertise. The best underwriter becomes underwriting manager. The best photographer becomes photo editor. The best salesperson . . . well, you get the idea. This method of promotion based on prior success in a different job is what I call the "Slinky phenomenon," after the kid's toy that can climb to a higher level based solely on the momentum imparted by a controlling hand. It results in what a rather esteemed authority termed "The Peter Principle."

The problem, of course, is that the skills and behaviors required for a great salesperson do not necessarily lend themselves to great sales management. Outstanding accountants do not automatically become exceptional chief financial officers. Yet that's how the system has worked and continues to work, despite downsizing and fewer opportunities.

Senior managers want to promote the "tried and true." After all, that's how *they* ascended the hierarchy. So they find the only basis for objective assessment that they can, which is performance in the current job. And lest you think this is an abstract issue, consider this: Rarely has an outstanding ballplayer become a highly successful coach or manager in the major leagues of any sport. In fact, the great managers often boast of a ludicrously brief or ignoble professional career. The skills and behaviors needed to manage star ballplayers aren't necessarily to be found in star ballplayers. My observations are that the same holds true in organizational life.

One doesn't have to have been a great salesperson to lead and manage salespeople. (What about credibility? It usually arrives quickly enough once plans are exceeded, bonuses are paid, and proper recognition is bestowed on the troops.) Subsequent to banking's first wave of deregulation, the more innovative banks brought in marketing people from the retail industry to help organize and lead in the new competitive environment. *You can learn content.* It's much more difficult—and often impossible—for content experts to learn how to lead people.

The incompetence at the top, which frequently creates a default position of monastic inaccessibility, is a result of organizational cultures that reward content—knowing *things*—and ignore process—knowing *how.* Perhaps most importantly, the abilities to learn, to change, and to adapt are completely ignored, yet those are the attributes that are most critical to leadership in a tumultuous world.

An Embracing System

We have to change our institutions so that management is truly part of the enterprise and not removed from it. John Dewey once observed that:

> "Better it is for philosophy to err in active participation in the living struggles of its own age and times than to maintain an immense monastic impeccability. . . . Saints engage in introspection while burly sinners run the world."

The same holds true for our leaders. We need to discard the rubrics and the phrases that serve only to prevent us from thinking about the problem—matrix management, the virtual corporation, servant leadership, quality anything—and focus on the pragmatics of involving leadership in the day-to-day, tangible performance of the enterprise. They must be part of an embracing system that includes the customer, suppliers, the public, and employees.

"But wait," you say, "who will be responsible for the longer term, for the strategic view, for the proverbial 'big picture'?" I've never seen an organization that requires the big picture to be examined on a daily basis. There is plenty of time to do that in the twice-yearly retreats, while rappelling down mountains or behind conference room doors at monthly executive committee meetings. The fact is that the long-term objectives are only met by short-term performance, and if everyone is not engaged in bringing value-added to that performance, then why do we need them?

Some of you might have already figured this out, but for those of you who haven't, let's return to the Fleet example that opened this chapter. You'll note

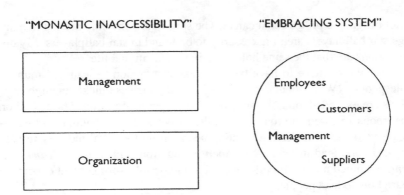

Fig 6.1. Inaccessibility or embrace?

that 250 executives and managers, from the highest level on down (CEO Murray was required to devote 50% of his time), were engaged from full-time to part-time commitment to the bank's cost reduction study over a period of a year. What were the ramifications of the loss of this volume of talent to the bank's normal operations? Surely Fleet sacrificed some of its day-to-day efficiency and discomfited its customers somewhat in order to dedicate this magnitude of management talent to the internal scrutiny.

Well, not exactly. I talked to one senior officer who told me that her boss had been assigned full-time to Fleet Focus. The unit compensated simply by dividing the departed executive's responsibilities among the three remaining subordinates, *two of whom were working the Focus effort part-time*. The result was continued, smooth performance for the unit, which met its business goals for the year. Customers didn't even notice. Did the reapportionment require some adjustments? Yes, there were some new demands made, some additional accountabilities assessed, and some more work invested. "But," said the officer, "not nearly as much as when the regulators are here and we have to comply with their audit requests."

Organizations must ask what value-added each position brings to the *ultimate customer or business objective*. In many cases, there are layers of management and control that bring no value whatsoever. Unless the customer perceives value sufficient to merit the cost, then only overhead is being added.

In Figure 6.2 below, the first sequence represents a computer that is manufactured by Apple, then sent directly to a retail store that sells, installs, and services the hardware and software. If each of these "stations" is given a value of 1, we could make the case that the consumer perceives a worth greater than the total (2) because of the simplicity and speed of the acquisition, minimum of people with whom to deal, ease of acquiring local help, etc. Let's say customer-perceived value is a 3.

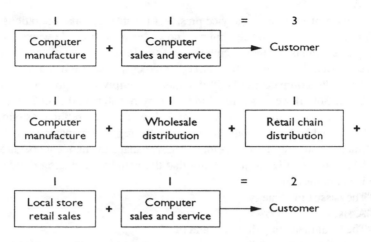

Fig. 6.2. Value added or deleted?

In the second sequence, the manufactured computer goes to a wholesaler, who supplies retail chains, which supply their local stores, which contract out for servicing and in-store sales. (Have you ever purchased a television set from a department store that provides a service contract to be fulfilled by a third party entirely?) In this case, the total value of each stop along the way is 5, but the customer may perceive only a value of 2 since there is significant delay and annoyance associated with trying to get help, finding appropriate software, obtaining repairs, and so on. ("Sorry, you'll have to call the manufacturer for that." "Our service firm will have to get back to you in the next 24 hours." "No, we can't guarantee repairs by next week.")

It's not the number of "stops" per se that represents a problem. It's their contribution to the customer's perceived value that determines the worth of his or her investment.

The same principle holds true for management. What value does a manager create in fulfilling his or her accountabilities? I'm convinced that the supervisors I see in the red jackets walking the airport concourses provide significant additional value as they coordinate flight arrivals and departures, attend to overbookings and missed flights, comfort the generally bewildered, and handle "one-off" situations, freeing the gate agents to handle the masses. I'm not at all convinced that myriad managers in most insurance companies provide much value at all. My claims are handled proficiently by a claims adjuster. (My insurer does not employ agents at all, removing one of the "stops" and thereby eliminating a major cost I've never found of value as the customer.) Why do we need "assistant managers," "second vice presidents," or "associate general managers"? The answer is simple. The customer doesn't. The organization culture does.

A couple of years ago, the vice president for international operations at a major client asked me to help him pare down his operation. He wanted to begin by analyzing how many secretaries and administrative people could be removed around the world without affecting the customer. He had a rough idea that he could eliminate $250,000 in expenses simply through that exercise.

"Look, Bob, if we're going to do this, why not start at the top?" I asked.

"You mean with the country managing directors?" he replied, astounded.

"No, with their bosses, *your* direct reports, the regional managing directors."

"But there are only four of them, and they manage the national operations."

"What *specifically* are they doing that the country managing director or you is not doing?"

"They assist in strategy."

"Assist whom?"

"The local managing directors and me."

"What else do they do?"

"They back up the local managers in case of turnover."

"Can't the local sales manager serve in that case?"

"Well, in fact they usually are the de facto executives, but without the same approval limits."

"What else do your direct reports do that impacts the customer?"

"My God." (Yes, that's a direct quote.)

The result was the elimination of Bob's four direct reports at a savings in excess of $450,000 per year. The secretaries are still there, providing value to the customers.

Why the Pedestal?

Executives have been bred to assume a holier-than-thou attitude. Our culture has heretofore demanded heroic leadership, which I believe to be a dying vestige of the World War II culture. (Bill Clinton is the first American President too young to have served in that war.) When military leaders reassummed civilian positions, their leadership was supposed to carry over. Militaristic, authoritarian organizations were a natural outgrowth. It's no accident that IBM and others adopted a "uniform" for success. I once worked with a Midwest food-processing company in which a junior member of the top management team addressed the president as "Mr. President." Compare this with the first-name basis that most modern firms have adapted with their younger workforces. It also was fairly common to continue to refer to people by their military rank in their civilian jobs. "Colonel, here are the reports. . . ."

That leadership aura produced a heroic ideal. The leader was to have all the answers and deliver his (always his) people from difficulties, prevailing over the competition (the enemy). For a long time, in a simpler and more innocent age, when James Dean was considered a rebel and the Beatles were radical, that posture could be maintained. Doctors were endorsing the "healthiest" cigarettes on television, and GM was telling the consumer what kind of car to buy. Oh, for the old days.

Like it or not, our current environment had better be one of post-heroic leadership. Success is too difficult and the route too complex to entrust one person's judgment and abilities. There are still a few holdout, large organizations in which the CEO continues to approve expenditures above $1,000 and sanctions every hire. But they are disappearing. (Contrast that with many hotel chains in which front-desk clerks have authority of up to $2,000 just to resolve a guest's complaint on the spot.) Post-heroic managers do the following:

- See themselves as a member of a team
- Judge their success by the team's success
- Eagerly entertain new ideas
- Provide processes and guidance, not answers
- Ensure that there is commitment among the implementors
- Align individual goals with organizational goals
- Gain leverage by working across boundaries and turf lines
- Focus on the customer first, employees second, and shareholders third
- Ensure that jobs are fulfilling and rewarding through feedback
- Focus on outcome and goals, not input and tasks
- Allow the freedom to fail
- Admit their mistakes and learn from them
- Continuously develop themselves and their people

Let's look at just one element of those accountabilities. Traditionally, I believe that senior managers had the view of the world depicted in Figure 6.3. They looked after themselves first, then saw to it that the stockholders were happy, then applied their attention to the employees. At the end of the line was the customer, lucky to be included at all. In this manner, senior management was able to cement itself into position, aided by somnolent boards that contained a great deal of cross-over conflicts of interest.[1]

Today, of course, the equation has been reversed. It's the customer first, then the employees, then the shareholders. If all of those people are happy, senior management will be taken care of. Just reverse the arrows in the illustration.

I could even make a case for employees coming first, because I've never seen an organization with unhappy employees and happy customers. But I won't split hairs about this. The point is to take care of business—the customer—and the rest will take care of itself.

---

[1] For example, you serve on my board's compensation committee, which designates my income, and I'll serve on yours.

Fig. 6.3. Old-style priorities.

"Holier than thou's" don't allow that to happen. And creating chaos for employees doesn't allow that to happen. How effective are Fleet employees going to be with their customers until the dust settles? One thing is certain: not as effective as they could be.

For more years than I care to think about, I had to listen to United Airlines flight attendants complaining about their management. I can attest to the fact that it impaired their performance. Will they be different with an employee-owned operation? Time will tell, but ingrained habits die hard.

Post-heroic leadership must view the value provided to the customer as the fundamental determinant in resource allocation and decision making. That value is based on the *customer's* perception, not the organization's. The

Fig. 6.4. New-style priorities.

quid pro quo for management is that, while customers readily look to cut prices, they don't readily accept cuts in value. Post-heroic leadership provides a value-driven organization, in which the leaders themselves are the last to reap the rewards.

If that sounds unselfish, egalitarian, far reaching, and innovative, welcome to the new paradigm. "Holier than thou" has to be replaced by "we're all in this together."

How to Clothe the Emperors, Part 6

1. Begin cost reductions and staff scrutiny at the top, not the bottom.
2. Apply value to jobs based on perceived value of the customer, not on "objective" criteria such as job points or seniority. (Which is basically as silly as saying, as does Mensa, that you are in the top 2% of the population in intelligence because you perform well on a given test. All that means is that you take that particular test well.)
3. Force managers to deal with customers daily, in some capacity.
4. Use 360-degree assessments of all managers (whereby peers, subordinates, superiors, and customers evaluate performance).
5. Remove the overwhelming focus on the trendy "long-term look," and make all managers responsible for some short-term results. Don't be afraid to ask, "What have you done for me lately?"
6. No one sets strategy without direct accountability for its implementation, using deadlines and performance criteria.
7. Promotions are based on careful assessments of skills and behaviors required for future success, and past success is considered only to the extent that the two are compatible.
8. Any position in which the incumbent manager can be removed for a period of 30 days without a net deleterious effect on customer or staff is, by definition, unnecessary.
9. All managers answer their own phones. If they're getting so many calls that they can't do their "work," then:
   (a) There is something wrong with the system.
   (b) Answering those calls *is* their priority work.
10. Seniority means nothing. It's performance that counts.

Chapter 7

Artifice as Reality
How Decisions Are Based on Myths, Not Reality

"When you're cold, don't expect sympathy from someone who's warm."
—Alexander Solzhenitsin
One Day in the Life of Ivan Denisovitch

"Someone who redoubles his efforts when he's forgotten his aim."
—Santayana's definition of a fanatic

The acceptance of myth and legend prevents management from the burden of having to make judgments, develop opinions, and take prudent risks. Myths in corporate life can range from the fairly innocuous—people in the Southeast don't like excessive sweetness—to the highly damaging—there is no market for a portable cassette player.

Particularly in prosperous times, management seldom takes the time or applies the insight to examine the fundamental assumptions being made about the business. "Let's do more of the same" is the reaction to positive developments. "Let's not do that anymore" is the reaction to negative developments. I can find people on the street at any hour who can make those decisions for minimum wage, and do it gladly.

Anyone can manage in good times. It takes brilliant leadership to manage in difficult times. And by the latter, I don't mean guiding the enterprise through a billion-dollar loss and claiming it would've been worse if it weren't for the economy. I mean making money during the bad times, preserving employees' jobs during tough periods, retaining valued customers when the competition attacks, and safeguarding cash flow when credit is tight.

If executives are to lead through turmoil and change, and through conditions that they cannot directly influence, they must have superb decision-making ability. There are two primary components to superb decision making, so pay attention. You might want to get out the highlighter:

Component #1: The head
Component #2: The gut

During my keynote speeches, I often ask for a volunteer from the audience, which may number anywhere from 100 to 2,000. Every time—not virtually every time, but every single time—there is a profound silence, followed by loss of eye contact. When I insist that I won't continue until I get one volunteer, and point out that I have an hour in the program and I've already been paid, there is nervous laughter and, eventually, a half-hearted arm is raised to break the standoff. The volunteer has just won a free book, accompanied to hearty applause.

These audiences are filled with *executives,* not blue-collar workers. In one particularly vivid example, I addressed the Key Executive Conference of the American Council of Life Insurance, which is the premiere event in that industry. Over 250 life insurance chief executives and chief operating officers attended,[1] and it took almost 90 seconds to get a volunteer. Remember, these were the top guns in their industry.

Why don't executives volunteer in that setting? Why are they afraid of the speaker whom they're paying to address them?

The fear is of the unknown. Those executives are making a visceral decision not to participate. Their gut is telling them that they're "safer" sitting this one out. (The psychology of group decision-making is interesting, in any case. The larger the group, the greater the likelihood that any one member of it will eschew the decision-making prerogative. The smaller the group, the more likely one will succumb to the need to be the *decision-maker.*) On those occasions with other groups, when I've tested my hypotheses by asking during a break to consider volunteering when I call for one later, I get many more hands, though still not the majority of the audience. In these instances, people have had the opportunity to *think about* my proposition, and some have decided that there might be something worthwhile about volunteering. That is, they've used their head.

There are two lessons to be learned here.

First, if high-ranking managers are afraid to "volunteer," then how likely is it that their subordinates—in the case of the insurance group, everyone

---

[1] Another problem, to be addressed later, was that at the time (1993) there were no minorities and exactly one woman among that group in front of me. When one executive asked me why it was difficult to relate to the current work force, I told him to look around the room.

from vice presidents on down—will volunteer on the job? How likely is it that anyone in the organization feels comfortable questioning a decision, trying to innovate, taking a risk, or speaking out?

Second, the reluctance to volunteer in what is, rationally, a highly safe environment (speakers do not humiliate their audiences if they intend to be invited back, for example, and the organizers do not countenance humiliating their customers) demonstrates how much decision-making suffers when only one of the two components is allowed to prevail.

You need both your head and your gut. The best leaders I've observed are *both* cerebral and visceral, analytic and intuitive, "thinking" and "feeling." These pairs are not mutually exclusive. Excellent decision-makers avail themselves of both assets.

Self-Fulfilling Prophesies and Other Scientific Marvels

A combination of proper analytic skills and "common sense" is required for an executive to be effective. Call it the place where art and science meet. When you have the overly scientific, you find yourself in Dr. Frankenstein's laboratory, which I did one day at a large consumer products company in California.

The organization was looking at a decline in business caused by a combination of more aggressive competition and their own failure to launch some new products that their plan had heavily relied on. So the employees were going to bear the brunt of management's failure in these two areas. A senior management meeting was to decide how best to downsize and to create several levels of contingency to react to various levels of revenue losses (and various degrees of shareholder ire). You see, it's simple to earn the big bucks: This management team was putting a hierarchy of firings in place to deal with a bad year, a horrible year, and a disastrous year. Imagine what would've happened if this talent and time had been devoted to trying to *improve* the year. My calculation was that they were spending time in a 3:1 ratio, with 3 times as much devoted to the contingencies as the correction.

A particularly officious young woman from staffing and planning was invited to the meeting to provide some of the details of implementing the phased reductions. As the session progressed, I became mesmerized by her high-tech language for what was, essentially, a high-touch problem. When asked at what point the second level of discharges would begin, for example, she replied:

> "Attrits from the prime round should have been in the outplace mode, off-site, if they were of grades 8 or higher. Other attrits would simply be gone. If profit levels for the second quarter fall below 85% of plan as determined

by this group, I will initiate secondary attrits. Human resources will inform and escort on the same day, which we advise be a Friday, if possible. Tertiary attrits will occur if profit falls below 75% of plan. Tertiary attrits will receive no outplace assistance, unless they are supergrade."

What this all meant, I deciphered, was that the people being let go were being referred to as "attrits" (short for *attrition*). This helped dehumanize the situation significantly. We could have been discussing reducing inventory or equipment leases. I'm not sure how the "attrits" reacted to all this, because I was soon out of there.[2]

This was a case of all head, all science. It was a pragmatic approach using computerlike precision to remove people as though they were merely expense items on the balance sheet. The result, needless to say, was disastrous for morale and did not address the underlying cause of the company's marketplace problems: nakedly stupid management. The reasoning and actions demonstrated in that room were indicative of the decisions and judgment applied outside of that room. The word that comes to mind is *execrable*.[3]

On the other side of the ledger, take the managers of a large research-based health care organization who believed that Asian employees were excellent technicians and researchers but did not have the "temperament" or "cultural instincts" to confront people. Consequently, Asians—as an entire class of people—were given all the opportunities they could handle, as long as they were in scientific and research areas and did not manage others.

Entire career paths were blocked by an unwritten and seldom-acknowledged myth that "Asians can't manage others." This visceral, irrational prejudice prevented many talented people from leveraging their abilities and drove still more out of the company. (Chapter 11 will deal with workplace diversity and the inability of executives to understand it.)

Another gut-level myth, without any basis in reality, is that certain schools produce the best talent, and that such talent should be pursued above all others. The results of this elitist mentality almost always are:

---

[2] I had been asked to consult on how to retain productivity while implementing these highly likely cuts. I told them that, if absolutely necessary, there should be only one cut, not rolling cuts, and a large investment had to be made in those who remained. Since that wasn't a strategy that fit with their philosophy of not spending a dime on people, we parted company rapidly thereafter.

[3] See the very public case of a man known as "Thrasher the Slasher," *Business Week*, May 9, 1994, p. 62: "He's Gutsy, Brilliant, and Carries an Ax." Robert Thrasher boasts of his success in cutting tens of thousands of people at Nynex, admits to his "pressure," yet can't remember a Sunday in 20 years when he hasn't worked. He is but one of many "mad scientists" of downsizing.

- Minorities suffer, because they are underrepresented in such schools, and management has the excuse that "we can't find any qualified minority candidates." For example, traditionally black colleges are always excluded from these "preferred" lists, yet these institutions are full of highly qualified, high-potential candidates. Management's position here is like saying that they're trying to find paper clips by looking in their coffee cups.
- Elitism comes home to roost, because these special candidates, often recruited and/or sponsored by an executive "mentor," can't be allowed to fail. No matter how awful they may truly be, there is too much money, too much credibility, and too much executive-level repute invested in each one. These hires will succeed because the organization won't permit them not to, irrespective of how badly they screw up.
- Degrees from other sources are devalued. Employees were once supported and admired, and then promoted, for obtaining a degree while on the job. The discipline, hard work, and commitment to job and to self-development were attributes that were viewed as important for promotion and higher levels of responsibility. No longer. Employees pursuing even MBAs from recognized, fine schools are told that their degrees will be worthless. Although the tuition refund system may reimburse the monetary expenditure, the hierarchy will never reimburse the effort. Inexplicably, the rigor and focus on earning a degree at night over several years have become "inferior" in the eyes of management.
- Good people leave. When they recognize that their degrees—despite their accomplishments, abilities, and potential—may well hold them back, they make the intelligent decision to leave while they are still marketable. Since the rules have apparently changed since they joined the company, there is no reason to continue to support the company. Typically, the greatest loss occurs among top-flight middle management and supervision, the very people who guide the company's day-to-day success.

The Good, the Bad, and the Very, Very Ugly

Since 1991, the top 25 downsizings as of this writing have resulted in excess of 624,000 people losing their jobs. That's just the top 25 over 4 years. In 1993 alone, 615,000 layoffs were *announced*. And in the first quarter of 1994, 192,000 had been disclosed. That last figure represents about 3,100 people a day losing their jobs.[4]

---

[4]*Ibid.*, p. 61.

Poor decisions are anathema to an organization's well-being in any case. But when they directly affect millions of people, their families, and their prospects (and their commensurate impact on the economic well-being of others), they are tantamount to criminal acts. No manager at any level should be permitted to cause human suffering on such a scale merely as an atonement for his or her poor decisions earlier. *Someone* was responsible for all those people being on board. *Someone* was responsible for formulating the plans that called for expansion, or growth, or increase, originally. And *someone* was responsible for the conditions that led us to where we are today: not making the money we had hoped to be making, with no clear strategy to change the situation, other than firing people.

Whenever you see large layoffs, meaning that they aren't done to remove incompetency and poor performers, you are seeing a *management failure,* not an employee failure, product failure, or service failure. You are observing the last refuge of the management scoundrel, unless, of course, the executive has decided to leave as well, committing ritual suicide as an example of his or her responsibility. Let me know the next time you read an article that describes how an executive announces a layoff that begins with his or her own resignation, *sans* golden parachute, with the same benefit package as those "attrits" are receiving. Better send it to me by certified mail, just to make sure. (Examples from Japan don't count.)

More often, the executives are hunted down and killed (or first tortured through loss of responsibilities or "votes of confidence") by a board finally driven to frenzy. The victims that easily come to mind are John Sculley of Apple (and Steven Jobs before him), Ken Olsen at Digital, Kay Whitmore at Kodak, and James Robinson at American Express. Every one of the people on that list was once seen as a brilliant, entrepreneurial, visionary leader, running one of the finest companies in the land. Methinks that the good times ended and that the relationship of the CEO to the good times was ephemeral, at best.

How do organizations plummet from the heights? It's because management is so blinded by the blaze of success that they don't see the precipice. Sears fell from the stereotypical exemplar of American virtue and success to a poor third behind Wal-Mart and K-Mart largely, I believe, because its ancient leadership (I mean in terms of viewpoint, not ancestry) lost touch with the customer. Tastes change. Demographics change. But these things are hard to see when you're insulated in an executive suite and the only people you see look exactly like you, think exactly like you, and talk exactly like you, and have done so for decades. As long as the profits roll in, why examine any threats to that glorious existence?

When the stuff finally hit the fan so hard that the blades were bent, the inevitable result were layoffs below, followed by some further bizarre decision-making, such as the jettisoning of the catalog operation, a differentiating and distinguishing feature of the company.

Decision-making must include the analytical: accumulation and evaluation of information, comparisons, market surveys, competitive assessments, etc. It must also include the visceral: beliefs and values, the purpose of our existence, our contribution to the outside environment, our responsibilities to customers and employees. The two are not antithetical. George Merck, when leading the great pharmaceutical company named after his family, stated once: "Do good and good will follow." He believed that the company had honestly tried always to do what was best for the patient and the physician, and that profits never failed to follow when that pursuit was realized. Merck, of course, is one of the superb American success stories, one of the most valuable organizations on the planet and, for one unprecedented stretch of 7 consecutive years,[5] was named "America's Most Admired Company" in the annual poll of executives by *Fortune* magazine. George Merck's aphorism continues to appear in Merck literature and is cited by Merck employees. The results have been cashed by the shareholders.

Another factor in decision-making is the change in the dynamic affecting the very nature of the organization. Figure 7.1 shows the old relationship: The enterprise attempted to control its sources of materials (i.e., parts suppliers),

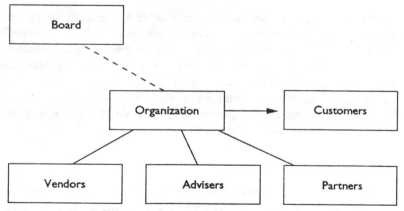

Fig. 7.1. The old relationships.

---

[5] 1986–1992, the only company to have held the "title" to that point, after IBM's 5-year run from the award's inception.

advisers (i.e., consultants and attorneys), and partners (i.e., brokers and agents), while being the sole face shown to the customer, who was a target. The board performed a largely ritualistic and rubber-stamp role, if that. The new dynamic is quite different. It can be portrayed in many ways, but here is one suggestion:

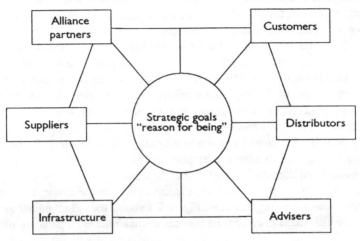

Fig. 7.2. An example of the new relationships.

There is no limit to the number or size of the interacting factors. However, the concept remains the same: Organizations have a "mission," a *raison d'être*. Those strategic goals are best met through a varied combination of partnerships and interactions, with customers and suppliers, for example, playing intrinsic roles. Information sources may be internal or external advisers, computers (management information systems), or the Internet. When viewed in this manner, decision-making must be different from the hierarchy depicted in Figure 7.1.

The Mythmakers

Some myths are based on actual occurrences that take on a mystical sense of direction for the company. Post-It Notes™ and their origins as a 3M scientist's unsuccessful work producing a temporary adhesive is one such example. GE based several television ads on the serendipitous discovery of Lexan.™ Fred Smith founded FedEx based on the hub-and-spoke premise of a college thesis—for which he received a "C," since the professor didn't feel the distribution aspects were workable.

These types of myths are factually based and are not so serendipitous. 3M, for example, demands that its researchers take 10% of company time and spend it on anything they choose. Their strategic goals call for them to achieve 25% of their revenues from products *that did not exist 5 years prior.* What do you think the emphasis is in a multibillion-dollar business that knows right now it needs to generate a quarter of its sales in 5 years from things that aren't around today?

So these "magical" discoveries are not so unusual after all, and they're not so much gifts from the gods as gifts developed by mortals who are inspired by the gods.[6]

But there are more nefarious and pernicious myths that are created out of smoke and mirrors. These are usually in the form of mission statements and values declarations. The fracture between what the organization claims it stands for, and how it acts, creates a sort of cognitive dissonance in decision making. Executives who construct and disseminate these false beliefs are the mythmakers.

In an operation that states "the customer comes first," you would expect punctilious attention to customer requests and feedback. But this isn't always the case. I was waiting to have lunch in a Ritz-Carlton in West Palm Beach, Florida. The waitress, I noted, did not take a single note as my wife and I gave her our order, nor did she at the adjacent table of four people. It was clear that the Ritz-Carlton training manual dictated that no notes be taken, I assume on the grounds that customers paying those rates demanded that the staff give them their undivided attention at all times.

Fifteen minutes later, our two tables were promptly served our meals. That was the good news. The bad news was that four of the six meals were incorrect. It was like the old Bob Newhart routine in which the airline pilot announces some mixed news: "I'm happy to inform you that we will be landing an hour early. However I'm not certain whether that will be in Miami or Buenos Aires."

Ritz-Carlton, in my observation, measures input, not output. The input is the taking of orders without notes, or the incessant "it's my pleasure" that every employee is conditioned to utter whenever someone makes a request or says "thank you." These are tasks, not results. And it's quite clear that it's really not always their pleasure. Behaviors speak louder than words. Results are more powerful than tasks, no matter how well-performed. What really pleases me is my meal served accurately and on time, and the help being unobtrusive. A simple "you're welcome" will do almost every time. (One of

---

[6] When my partner and I were writing our first book, *The Innovation Formula,* which highlighted 3M's innovation, an employee told us that one of their chemists accidentally spilled a formula she was preparing on her tennis sneakers. When, 2 weeks later, colleagues noticed that the portion of her sneakers with the spill was cleaner than the surrounding areas, Scotchguard™ was born!

their stated values is that "we're ladies and gentlemen serving ladies and gentlemen." I'd rather see something more mundane and pragmatic: "We're employees proud of delivering the results our guests require." The first statement focuses on who we are; the second focuses on why we're here.)

Organizations have to "walk their talk." At Nordstrom's, employees are encouraged to use their judgment at all times, and you get the feeling that they actually are doing so. (Even the vaunted Nordstrom's had problems when employees felt they were being asked to do one thing and rewarded for something quite different.) To balance the books on the Ritz-Carlton, they do permit their employees to spend up to $2,000 on the spot to resolve a guest problem.

The keys to effective decision-making in organizations are fairly simple, but often subsumed in the values, egos, platitudes and pomposity of the executive suite.

Primary Decision-Making Factors in Any Organization

1. What is the value-added that we provide to our customers?
2. What results, impact, or outcomes do our customers desire?
3. What are the resources available to meet our customer goals?
4. What are the constraints within which we must operate?
5. What must we accomplish, or we will have failed?
6. What alternatives are available to reach our goals?
7. What risks are inherent in our plans?
8. How will we maximize the outcome, minimize the input, and alleviate risk?
9. What will tell us if we are successful?
10. How will we replicate our success?

Ten steps. Simple as that. Add the bells and whistles that you prefer, but the essence remains the same, whether the decision involves the acquisition of another organization, or how to allocate staff for the next day's work.

Too often, no such template exists. Decisions are based on the mythological value system, or on the latest, most dire exigency, or on a pure-numbers basis. One has to believe that very few businesses are in operation *solely to make money.* All organizations (even nonprofits) must make money in order to survive and fulfill their reasons for existing. But those reasons for existing are rarely the mere acquisition of money and its dissemination to shareholders. Yet decisions are often based on little else.

In Figure 7.3 we've illustrated how the decision-making sequence might unfold. Once the customer's desires are known, alternatives to meet those desires are generated and fed into the system, which is constrained by the restraints and limitations that the enterprise faces. Those alternatives pass through a series of "filters," which are the "musts" to be accomplished (without which we fail),[7] the risks, the maximization of results, etc. At the conclusion, we have an alternative that maximizes output, minimizes input (resources are always scarce), alleviates risk commensurate with benefits expected, and enables us to monitor the actual salutary effects, so that they can be duplicated and improved upon.

Decision-making in this model is a combination of the analytical and the intuitive. The rational aspect is the systematic methodology and sequential basis to the process. One really can't afford to overlook risk, for example, no matter how alluring benefits may be. And alternatives are attractive only so long as they meet the must criteria, because without them, we are lost.

Musts generally "keep us within the lines." For instance, we must not spend more than $15,000, or we must deliver within 1 week, or the breakfast must be served hot. Without meeting these essentials, we are bankrupt, too late, or below customer expectations. Other needs are mere desires compared to the musts. It would be nice to spend as little as possible, to be ready as soon as possible, or to serve breakfast with no one at an adjoining table. But we won't fail if those goals aren't met, we'll fail if the musts aren't met.

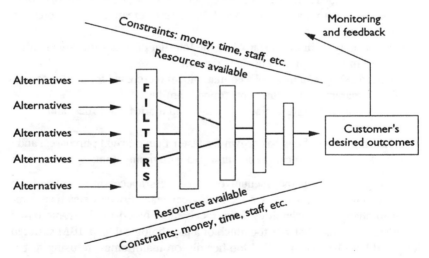

Fig. 7.3. A decision model.

---

[7] Many negotiations wind up in disasters because one of the parties has lost sight of its musts and, inadvertently, negotiates them away. Since a decision can't succeed if its musts are not met, that party is doomed to a failure of its own doing, not its adversary's.

The intuitive aspect enters when we help to define what the customer needs. (Remember that customers always know what they want, and providing what they need but didn't know they needed is the basis of value-added.) It's also important in generating the alternatives. We are often stuck in the rut of doing what we've always done, rather than examining the need to determine better ways to do things. Doing what we've always done is simple because it is the duplication of past tasks. Generating new alternatives is difficult, because we must focus on end results and "back into" better ways of getting there. This is where the creative, gut-level, innovative traits enter the fray.

The best time to examine new approaches is when you're doing well, which is exactly when most organizations settle into blissful complacency and pontificate that "thou shalt not mess with a sure thing." Yet creating from a point of desperation (market loss, complaints, poor quality, late deliveries) is extremely difficult. Creating new approaches from a position of strength is a day at the beach, because the focus is not on the past but on the future, and the organization's resources and repute are not embroiled in fixing past errors.

- Messenger services are dying because the fax machine is a better way.
- Answering services are disappearing voice mail is more efficient.
- Midlevel hotels are replacing room service with external vendors who can deliver from a variety of local restaurants, creating more choices at less cost.
- Video stores will disappear when the Internet provides for downloading of movies right into one's television.
- Catalog shopping has replaced many local merchants for dual-income, single-parent, and/or time-constrained families.
- Electronic aids have replaced paper-based diaries, card files, and calendars.
- Leasing automobiles has grown far faster than outright purchases, and the leasing of used cars is beginning to gain momentum.

No organization in the vacuum tube business successfully entered the transistor business. That was a technological leap. Frieden steadfastly refused to change its technology from mechanical-based to electronic-based calculators because that was too much of a psychological leap. IBM suffered long and hard because it relied too heavily on mainframes, refusing to believe the desktop computer revolution, and that was an arrogance problem.

Every day, organizations large and small are basing their decisions on past tasks, past alternatives, and what they already do well, rather than on changing customer needs, new methods, and what they are capable of doing well. Ironically, a "bandwagon effect" drives this condition, as illustrated in Figure 7.4. New ideas are an "uphill" climb for most enterprises, and they are shot down with fervor, usually under a barrage of "yes, buts." I was told once by the president of a bank that his was not a stifling culture. I instructed him to place a mark on a pad every time he heard a "yes, but" during the next day, whether on the phone, in a meeting, casually talking in the hall, or reading a memo. We reconvened at his office at 6 pm the following afternoon. His pad had 42 marks. Imagine: The president of the bank heard 42 "yes, buts" in one day. If you multiply that times his vice presidents, directors, managers, and staffers, that's probably thousands of "yes, buts" a week, hundreds of thousands a month, millions of reasons not to do things every year! By 7 pm, we were having drinks in a local bar, discussing how to fumigate the operation.

However, once the idea has gained some momentum—because of its sponsorship, its allure, its seemingly risk-free enticements, its benefit for key people—it becomes an unstoppable, headlong, careening descent down the other side of the hill. Just when people *should* be saying "yes, but" (i.e., let's look at some of the risks here), no one is. Ideas are killed before they have time to be explored, but they are not killed once they have any kind of motive power at all. The entire sequence is backwards.

Ideas are attacked—
"yes, but . . ."

Ideas are propelled—
"I'm on board"

Fig. 7.4. Uphill climb, frenzied descent.

Customers Are Not Like You and Me

No two customers are alike. One of the problems with blanket approaches to customer service, quality, improvement, and other iterations is that they tend to view a ubiquitous customer who can be described and indexed to within an inch of his or her existence. Customers, of course, are actually very different from each other because they have very different objectives, needs, and desired outcomes. It might be important for me to be seated immediately and then allowed to linger over coffee and a newspaper. However, you might prefer fast service so that you can come and go quickly. Someone else might prefer the widest possible menu selection. A fourth might look for convenient parking.

How does a company make decisions, then, when the outcomes may be very different for various constituencies? Part of the decision-making must accommodate the types of customers and the types of outcomes that will reflect on the resources being committed, the time invested, the risks assumed, and the standards accepted. The grid may look something like Figure 7.5.

In Figure 7.5, the organization has identified four different outcomes it will provide, with #4 being significantly more opulent and value-laden than #1. It has also delineated four types of customers, ranging from #4, who will invest heavily in perceived value, to #1, who requires only basic services and will generally pay the lowest price possible for the commodity sought. The company has deemed its market compatibility to be in providing results #2, #3, and #4 to customer #4, results #2 and 3 to customer #3, and result #2 to customer #2. It will not cater to customer #1 at all, nor will it provide result #1 at all.

It's the absence of thinking along the lines of this model that has doomed many of the airlines. Southwest Airlines has clearly determined its customers and the results (value) it is willing to provide. USAir has clearly not seen anything through its haze. You can't be all things to all people (i.e., luxury, first-class carrier and cut-rate fare carrier), and you can't even be most things to most people. Mercedes-Benz is appealing to a different customer with its "C" class cars, but it hasn't tried to compete with Yugo.

Some organizations may be very content and highly successful remaining in a single box in the grid. Others may be in only two or three, and still others may operate with much larger grids. However, the point is immutable: When making decisions based on customer need, have you determined who

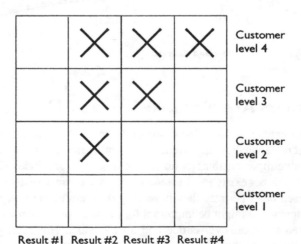

Result #1 Result #2 Result #3 Result #4

Fig. 7.5. Identifying market compatibility.

the customers are, and what the various results are that you can offer? Are you differentiating in the marketplace based on those factors ("niche" comes to mind)? And are your decisions made within the context of differing customer needs and differing results available?

Decision-making is a real-time, real-life discipline. You need your head and your gut. But you also need the tools.

How to Clothe the Emperors, Part 7

1. Every decision of import should be stated in terms of its desired *outcome*.
2. Decisions require analysis of resources and constraints that will circumscribe them.
3. Not all objectives are equal. The "musts" have to be separated because the decision will fail if they are not met.
4. No decision is without risk, and threats must be identified and ameliorated.
5. The customer's reaction and satisfaction must be monitored and measured, and used for further improvements in the decision's aftermath.
6. "Yes, buts . . . " should be stamped out with a vengeance when ideas are introduced.
7. Devil's advocate positions are required as the wagon starts to head down the hill with people clambering to get on board.
8. Decision-makers must recognize that customers differ, and their required results differ, and proactively decide which customers and which results make sense for the organization to pursue. Excellent decisions can be disastrous if they are made in inappropriate niches.
9. Decisions are based on reality, not myth. What the company *says* doesn't matter. What the company *does* matters.
10. Inaction is a decision in its own right: the decision to do nothing. One cannot escape risk through inaction. It will come and find you anyway.

Chapter 8

The Case of the Missing Values
Why "Ethical Management" Has Achieved Oxymoronic Status

"What is moral is what you feel good after. What is immoral is what you feel bad after."
> —Ernest Hemingway

"If winning does not matter, why does anyone bother to keep score?"
> —Adolph Rupp
> Legendary University of Kentucky basketball coach

In organizations, those who lie, cheat, and steal do so mainly because (choose only one of the following):

1. It is a world of cut-throat competition, and one must do everything possible to achieve an advantage.
2. Everyone is doing it, and people follow normative pressure.
3. The boss got there by doing it, so the "rules" are clear.
4. They are minorities and/or women, who see justification in compensating for past discriminatory treatment.
5. Organizations have lowered standards or are afraid, for legal reasons, to apply them, resulting in lower-quality employees.
6. They are ignorant of what is and is not ethical behavior.
7. It's easier than doing things the right way.
8. They seek to gain financially.
9. There is no more company loyalty, and all bonds are broken.
10. They want to help the company.
11. All of the above.
12. None of the above.

Well, what do you think? (Or did you read ahead to try to find the answer?) If you work in an organization, you have probably witnessed unethical behavior from time to time. Why was it perpetrated?

In my view, the answer is J. Most unethical actions stem from people seeking to help the company make its goals. They are committed to the goal of corporate well-being. Despite the "values statements" that festoon the annual reports, people react in a way in which *they believe management wants them to behave*. Every day employees face ethical dilemmas fostered and complicated by the people at the top.

In the interactive workshops my firm runs on ethical behavior, one of our case studies involves the following scenario. Decide what you would do in this case:

> You are interviewing a candidate for a position in your company. During the course of the interview, the candidate volunteers a confidential document from his or her present employer, a direct competitor of yours. What do you do?

The debate that rages in the workshops is not about the future of the candidate. Over 99% of respondents state that they would never hire this person, because an unethical act has been committed in offering the confidential company document. About two-thirds of the respondents recommend ending the interview immediately when the document is offered, and one-third recommend continuing it to a normal conclusion but without any intent of going further with the candidate. All feel that the candidate is highly likely to do the same thing to them as an employee.

Then the fun begins. Does one accept and/or read the document? Would you? Well, to my utter amazement and, frankly, to the astonishment of the CEOs who ask us to run the workshops, 40% of the groups not only declare they would accept and read the document but virtually all of that segment also claim that there is nothing wrong in so doing (and many state that they have done just that; the example is taken from an actual incident that is fairly common).

The debates among the groups have sometimes almost deteriorated to brawls. Those who advocate taking the document claim the following:

- It's not unethical, since it was offered.
- This is how competitive intelligence is gathered.
- The acquisition was unethical, but that was the action of the employee. The use of it subsequently is not unethical.
- We are paid and admonished, every day, to gather all the competitive information we can, in whatever manner we can.

Those who would not accept the document state:

- Once you accept it you are party to the act.

- You wouldn't want this done to you, so how can it be acceptable?
- Anything stamped "confidential" is clearly proprietary in the eyes of the owner.
- Competition can be effective while still played within the rules.

Some of the 60% against acceptance even claim they would call the employee's current company and warn management (although a portion of these people say they would do so only after checking with their legal department, and we all know where that would go).

In one workshop I conducted, I asked how many people in the room—all senior officers—had acquired competitive information in a similar fashion. Every one of the 20 people raised a hand, except the president. "Well," he sighed, "I appreciate your candor, but we'll have to change the culture. I would never countenance anything like this, and I don't want you sending that message to your people."

"Frank, do you know that marketing report that you get every month and that you make such a fuss about," asked the sales vice president. "How do you think we assemble it, with a crystal ball?"

The president had been countenancing the behavior; he just hadn't realized it. He was focused on the document in his hand, not on its pedigree.

The System Really Is Ethically Based

A senior vice president of human resources for a major insurance company once called us in to determine why there was so much cheating in his department on expense reports. "My people are supposed to be setting the example," he huffed, "and we're setting the wrong one." He suspected poor pay, inferior working conditions, a few rotten apples, confusion about the policies, and a host of other causes at work. We found the cause in a half-day of interviewing.

It seemed that the vice president was entitled to travel first class. Instead, he exchanged his tickets for coach, and pocketed the difference. He clearly felt this was a perquisite of his office. His people got the message loud and clear. They put in for meals they "could have eaten" but didn't, entertained each other instead of clients, and worked the system in any way possible. They weren't bad people. They were simply emulating their most visible exemplar.

The vice president listened carefully to our report. Then he threw us out.

Our free-enterprise system is based on some shockingly simple yet mandatory ethical criteria. You promise that you will provide a product or service of a certain quality and quantity at a certain time in a certain fashion. I promise to accept it in return for a certain payment rendered at a certain time in a certain manner. If either of us abrogates his or her responsibilities, the system breaks down. The reason that the former Communist block has such economic problems is not so much the lack of hard currency or lack of initiative, it's the lack of that history of ethical transaction. When cheating the other party is considered merely good business sense, and lying is admired as an excellent negotiating trait, individuals can get rich, but economies will not prosper.

Ethical management and behavior are not some niceties that will disappear in another few months. They are the basis of our capitalist system, which is the only system that's working worth a damn the last time I looked.[1]

The more pressure the organization places on its employees, the greater the likelihood that unethical acts will result in the name of that organization. In a study by London House a consulting firm, it was found that stress and ethical standards are linked. The more emotionally healthy and less stressed the respondent (as determined in a battery of tests), the higher that respondent tended to score on an ethics test.[2] Cause and effect aren't necessarily a "given" in such correlations, but the relationships seem more than casual.

There are two major types of ethical quandaries that organizations face: internal and external. The internal problems are created by conflicting pressures and unresolvable conflicts. For example, several years ago, United Airlines created a policy of customer satisfaction and urged its reservation agents to show customers every courtesy on the phone. In the case of airline reservations, this would include acquainting the caller with alternative fare options, restrictions, schedules, and so forth. Yet these very same employees were being measured based on calls per time unit. So the employees were encouraged to do one thing, but rewarded for doing the opposite (taking the least amount of time with a caller). I have seen the same phenomenon with telephone directory assistance operators, and people taking phone orders for catalog sales. When you encourage people to act in a certain way, then "hit" them for doing it and stop hitting them when they do the opposite, you will create, in this case, some very rude people on the phone. You will also produce some very stressed employees, who might not book the cheapest fare but will simply seek the quickest to book, despite the caller's request for the cheapest. Guess what happens when that passenger discovers he or she has been "had"?

These internal conflicts are most rife in the sales area. When "we are customer driven" is the watchword, but "make your numbers" is the real reward system, you get very questionable behavior. Customers will find material

---

[1] The trouble with capitalism, of course, is that it *creates* wealth wonderfully but *distributes* it so ineptly. But that's another story.

[2] See *The Wall Street Journal*, Apr. 11, 1991, p. B1: "Unethical Behavior, Stress Appear Linked."

they did not order on their loading docks. Or they will wait and wait for their "free" service while personnel are out on revenue-producing calls. Or returns will not be accepted and credited without lengthy delays and frustration. Show me a reward system and I'll show you a value system. If the reward calls for borderline behavior, borderline behavior is what you'll get.

One client asked us to conduct comprehensive focus groups throughout the organization to find the causes of discriminatory behavior and unethical actions that executives felt were all too common. We needn't have left the executive suite. Respondents all over the company, in virtually every function, told us the exact same thing: You can ruthlessly manage people here, but as long as you make your numbers and/or your product goals, you'll be richly rewarded. If you fail to meet those goals, no matter how well you manage people, you'll be punished. And if you meet your goals and manage people well, you'll be rewarded for meeting your goals. The effective management of people was never more than 5% of any manager's incentive compensation plan.

These internal conflicts are remedial. However, they are some of the most difficult to reconcile, because they require senior management recognizing that behaviors are determined by:

1. Their own actions and examples
2. How they reward people, financially and nonfinancially

What they'd prefer to do is remedy the situation without having to touch those two variables, and that's impossible.

On the external side, the conflicts are equally dismaying. When I was running a Latin American division of a consulting firm, I noted in my Venezuelan managing director's budget for the following year a small item labeled "commissions" in the amount of $17,500. "Jorge," I asked, "what is this amount for? We don't pay commissions to anyone."

"Well, it's a contingency in the event we have to pay third parties for assistance."

"What type of assistance, Jorge? We never contract out for consulting help."

"You know, cultural assistance, introductions, door opening, that sort of thing."

"In other words, this money is for bribes."

"Well, yes."

"Jorge, we don't engage in bribes. Anytime. Anyplace."

"Alan, grow up. It's the only way business is done here, especially in any government-run or government-licensed operation. Everyone else is doing it, and if we don't, we'll be at a competitive disadvantage. Forget making our plan for next year."

"My friend, we don't change our values based on the local government's degree of corruption, and if we can't get business without bribing people, then we'll leave the country. If you can't make your plan without bribery, tell me now, and I'll get somebody who can. But tell me now, and don't ever raise this issue again. By the way, if I ever determine that bribes have been used in our operation, anyone involved will be summarily fired and prosecuted."

Jorge made his plan the next year by doing very little business with the government and a lot of business with U.S. multinationals. He also expanded into Columbia and created a surprisingly vibrant market for us.

To me, this was a no-brainer. Where does Jorge's rationale stop? What if bribery is commonplace among furniture manufacturers in Georgia, or among fruit processors in Denver? Where does it end?

One of the schools of ethical thought is academically termed *deontological*. Aside from being a great word to work into cocktail conversation, its premise is refreshingly simple: Some acts are inherently ethical or unethical. Those who believe that animal experimentation, for example, is unethical no matter how much humans beings may benefit from it, are taking a deontological approach. The same would apply to those who oppose abortion or oppose capital punishment. Compare this to the utilitarian approach, which would hold that ethics depends on the greatest good for the greatest number, for example. Or to the teleologic approach,[3] which states that the outcome determines the ethics of the action. (You've seen Hemingway's approach cited at the beginning of the chapter, but let it be written that, to my knowledge, he never managed a sales force.)

I believed, deontologically, that bribery was unethical. I didn't care about the outcome (increased revenue for my division) or about the utility (someone will get that business, and it might as well be our company and the support of our employees' families). Some things are right and other things are wrong. Bribery is wrong. I don't care what the local culture dictates.[4] I don't care what was done before. It doesn't mean that I'll go out and shoot the people who engage in it, it simply means that I won't engage in it.

External conflicts also exist when there are demands that can't be reconciled among one's personal, professional, social, and civic lives. There are heartbreaking stories of police officers who, having produced 20 years of

---

[3] Going back to my undergraduate world history courses, I recollect that the Egyptians were among the first people to record use of bribes, usually to influence judges in their legal system. Regardless of culture and of financial outcome, bribes have generally been deemed unethical by all advanced cultures.

[4] I'm not certain, but I believe it was Dorothy Parker who observed, "If you teach a cannibal to use a fork, is that progress?"

decorated and lauded service, suddenly steal drugs or take a bribe because they can't meet the financial demands of a family illness. There are, of course, those who simply succumb to greed—Michael Milken needing $40 million garnered unethically because he couldn't be content with $30 million he earned honestly—but there are also those driven by overwhelming obligation to loved ones. (Or to a sense of obligation: There is a famous, old film of a Rice University football game in which an opponent is dashing down the sideline to score the decisive touchdown. A star Rice player *leaped off the bench and tackled the runner.* The score was awarded anyway and, after the game, the player tearfully admitted that he couldn't stand the pressure. He did it for Rice.)

And here's an interesting citation from the U.S. Army regulations:

"Men who take up arms against one another in public war do not cease on this account to be moral beings, responsible to one another and to God."

That passage is from the 1863 edition, during the height of the Civil War.

The Default Setting

Organizations have it tough these days, because they are in a position that they never expected to be in, aren't prepared to be in, and really shouldn't have to be in: purveyors of ethical standards. They are the victims of a confluence of social dynamics that include these developments:

- There has been a significant political move to the right over the past several decades. Deregulation has affected many major industries (i.e., airline and telephone). The arts, education, social services, and many other institutions formerly controlled or supported by government have been cast adrift or deemphasized. Who's really in charge of what today? Where are the sanctioning and approving bodies?
- Organizations have downsized significantly, as noted in earlier chapters, and decision-making has been pushed downward, without the frames of reference, experiences, and maturity that had been in place. How does one go about making some of these tough decisions?
- Our society, unfortunately, has emphasized legal remedies. Every social and business aspect, from parents' rights to copyrights, has been relegated to courts of law (note that they are never called "courts of justice"). Legal remedies preclude ethical remedies. How can I tell what's "right" without a legal precedent or opinion?
- Diversity of modern management groups has proliferated. As the white-male paradigm has been broken (or at least dented), the ease of finding someone "just like us" to work with has disappeared. We have become "moral strangers" in this regard, and the trust across ethnic

groups, racial groups, and even genders is relatively low.[5] The mere presence of women in the workplace alters traditional behaviors in many cases. How do I know what is appropriate and inappropriate?

- Traditional values have to be applied under current circumstances. The values may still be clear, but the conditions are increasingly complex. Our constitution allowed for slavery and denied women the vote. Morality's context changes as we have to deal with heart transplants, AIDS, abortion, electronic eavesdropping, and other aspects of progress. What am I to do when right and wrong don't seem so clear anymore?

- In an increasingly global economy, developing countries have differing mores. Global standards will be diverse. Who sets our standards and when do we apply them? Is that a business decision or a personal decision?

- The cynicism of youth is appalling. It's tough, however, to be ethical if the future isn't all that appealing. When graduation with even an advanced degree means a choice of menial jobs, when I'll never have it as good as my parents had it, when I'm looking at a lifestyle that has no appeal, why should I worry about what's right and wrong? It's every person for himself or herself.

Now consider the precarious role of modern organizations in that milieu. They have been cast as the molders of value by default, because:

1. The traditional family dinner table has disappeared. Growing up in the 50s and even the 60s, one heard two parents—a mother and a father—discussing life's vicissitudes. The answers weren't always right and the debate wasn't always objective, but ethical quandaries were explored. Dad didn't get the job because someone else knew someone. Mom thinks someone stole a cherished photograph at the last family reunion. You don't know what to do about the math test that someone stole and offered to you. The myth is that these discussions *solely* occurred on *Ozzie and Harriet* or *Donna Reed*. In one way, shape, or imperfect form or another, they occurred all the time when the family gathered.

The trouble is that the family doesn't gather any more. A larger and larger percentage of children are growing up in single-parent families. Those that aren't are usually in a dual-income family, with both parents engaged in

---

[5] For some of the best descriptions of these dynamics, see the works of Professor Joanne B. Ciulla, Ph.D., Distinguished Professor of Leadership and Ethics at the Jepson School of Leadership, University of Richmond. I heard her speak at the Leadership Group, Apr. 2, 1993, in New York.

careers.[6] Even those who enjoy the potential attention of a parent remaining at home are involved in dozens of extracurricular, after-school activities, from organized sports to drama, from 100-channel cable television to virtual-reality Nintendo. *The family does not provide the basics for values and ethics any more.*

2. Our religious institutions, once the bastions of morality and introspection, have come under attack themselves. Antiabortionists kill doctors in the name of God. An author is condemned to death by a religious leader because of his writings. Priests are accused and found guilty of sexual misconduct and molestation on a truly frightening scale. Ecumenism is observed intellectually but not in reality. America is simply not a place in which religious institutions have been successful in instilling Judeo-Christian ethics in the population at large.

If you don't believe that, just watch any church or synagogue parking lot after the service. The same people professing their love for mankind 5 minutes prior are now aggressively battling to gain an advantage in leaving the parking lot, thereby saving a precious 20 seconds that they won't know what to do with later, anyway. *The religious estate does not provide the basics for values and ethics any more.*

3. Our schools, once upon a time, taught such things and, more importantly, demonstrated them. Not only have many of our schools become battlefields but the teachers and administrators are often also among the combatants. Teacher strikes and school board politics overwhelm the real objective and the real customer: helping students learn. Our colleges and universities aren't much better. Donald McCabe, a professor at my alma mater, Rutgers, has studied university cheating for a long time, and documents that 67% of all college students cheat at some point in their schooling, and 41% of all undergraduates cheat on exams. These survey results come from the country's most prestigious colleges. The worst offenders? Business students, with 87% admitting to cheating at least once while in school. Honor codes (where exams are not monitored) tend to produce less cheating, but the basic conclusion is that character, more than circumstances, determines whether one cheats.[7]

---

[6] This statistic changes rapidly, but the last time I looked, as a sole bread-winner, married to my first wife, with two kids and a house in the suburbs, I was in less than 4% of the general population. I make no case for this as the "ideal" lifestyle, but it was once considered commonplace.

[7] See, for example, *People,* May 13, 1991, pp. 103-104: "Schools for Scandal: The dirty little secret of the campuses, says a study, is that most students cheat," by Eileen Garred et al.

After Syracuse University, my daughter's school, was hit with severe penalties by the NCAA for recruiting violations. I demanded of the chancellor to know who would be fired in addition to the head football coach. He wrote back that no one would be fired, including the head football coach, and that things "just got out of hand, without anyone really being to blame." At that point it became clear that we should have started the departures with him. *The schools are not providing the basics for values.*

4. The press and the media in general have, at worst, glorified the unethical and, at best, have vividly portrayed the crass nature of unethical acts. From Michael Milken to Pete Rose, we've seen the rich and famous exposed for the base nature of their actions. We've also been inundated with "tabloid" media, which blur the line between news and entertainment, reporting and acting, and truth and fiction. The proliferation of talk shows, seemingly serious discussions, has actually produced "professional guests" who change their story and their persona to fit the needs of the producers.

The major league baseball season was canceled in 1994, leaving us without a World Series for the first time in 90 years (when it was canceled due to payoffs) because of massive player and owner greed. No one seems to care all that much.

The press has expounded on the fact that Marion Barry, out of jail after serving time for narcotics use (and lying about it), was nominated as the shoe-in Democratic candidate for mayor of Washington, D.C., and Oliver North, one-time liar to Congress who escaped on a technicality, was in a close contest for governor of Virginia, having easily gained the Republican nomination (it's nice to see that these things are nonpartisan, isn't it?). "Just as Mr. Barry's supporters overlooked his drug conviction, Mr. North's supporters overlooked his admission that he lied to Congress . . . ," explains one article.[8] *The protection of the first amendment has not been the protection of our ethical principles.*

So the modern organization is left to provide some basis for ethical parameters among its employees, including those sitting in the executive suite. The old notions of right and wrong, the clear deontological positions, simply don't exist as they once did. Organizations are not poorly equipped to do this. They are unequipped to do this. It is like a symphony orchestra conductor who finds that the job calls not just for orchestration and leading but also for teaching how to read music.

It is no accident that our modern corporate world has so readily adapted to downsizing and rightsizing—throwing people out on the street. Aside from the considerations discussed in earlier chapters, there is also no moral imperative

---

[8] See *The New York Times,* Sep. 18, 1994, p. E3: "Blessed Are the Forgiven, for They Shall Run Again," by Richard L. Berke.

precluding it. Our "deskilling" of the work force—that is, breaking jobs down in fragmented, less sophisticated, less rewarding components—is really nothing more than Taylorism reincarnated from the 1920s.[9] We have become amoral out of ignorance, out of degeneration of our institutions, and our court of last resort—the organization—has not had the leadership or the tools to reclaim the situation. We are lost on the desert, and the only well has no bucket.

How to Build the Bucket

It's time we built a bucket so that we can at least get a drink. We can't quickly cure the social, educational, parental, media, religious, and economic ills that have led us here, but we can improve the organization's ability to deal with the ethical landscape and the players on it. After all, we know what's happening, so we should be smart enough to devise something to do about it instead of rending our garments and crying "Woe is us!"

There are three basic components of our ethical "toolbox":

1. Awareness that an act, issue, or circumstance is occurring that requires ethical considerations.
2. A skill set that allows us to do something about it, including the resources with which to act. This is the "can do."
3. A value system that tells us we ought to become involved and do something (prevent, reward, inhibit, discourage, etc.). This is the "want to do."

In this dynamic, 1 provides us with sentience, 2 with ability, and 3 with volition. Now, let's examine how these interrelate.

In Figure 8.1 you can see the four possible areas of interrelationships. They are as follows:

1. Would Do. Where awareness and values interact, I know that something requires my attention, and I believe that I should intervene in terms of encouraging or discouraging certain actions. However, I do not have the skills to do so. Consequently, I would do something if I could, but I'm not able. I can preach about it, decry it, and discuss the situation with others, but I'm not really able to influence the resultant behaviors very well. This is highly frustrating.

---

[9] Frederick Winslow Taylor was the father of "scientific management" and probably the first real management consultant. He evaluated manual labor by breaking it into constituent parts, timing each activity, and recommending faster ways to get things done. UPS continues to practice this today, dictating, for example, in which hand the truck driver should carry keys. See *Principles of Scientific Management*, Harper & Row, 1911.

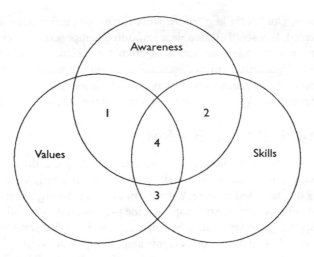

Figure 8.1. Dynamics controlling ethical actions.

One example would be a manager who sees unethical behavior among peers or superiors but doesn't have the clout to do anything about it. The best he or she can do is bring it to the attention of others who do have the skills to do something about it, thereby raising their awareness. Of course, they would also have to share the values, or they would be in area 2, "should do," but don't think it's necessary.

Another example is the manager who is in a position to do something but simply doesn't know *how*. Reports of sexual harassment have reached him (he's aware), and his value system tells him something must be done (he's willing). But the thought of discussing the subject with a long-term, highly regarded subordinate who is the object of the complaints is anathema to him. Similarly, there is no counseling program or human resource intervention available. He would do something if he could find a way, but he just can't determine what he can do.

Area 1 is remedial. It requires skills building and reinforcement, but it's really a matter of showing people how to use wood and leather straps to fashion a bucket.

2. Should Do. Where awareness and skills interact, I know that something has caught my attention, and I can certainly do something about it if I choose. But I don't feel I should. My values have not been brought into play significantly enough to rouse me to action. Someone else viewing the scene might feel that I should do something, but I don't feel that way.

An example here is the manager who knows that her subordinates are padding their expense accounts, supplying gifts to buyers, or leaving work early. She accepts it as part of the culture, something that she did and that others after her will undoubtedly do. If pressured, she might issue a memo and make some lip service pass at demonstrating that she has heard the concerns, but she will not take substantive action because she doesn't feel the need.

I believe that the "should do but won't" area has been exemplified by many of the stock-cheating scandals, in which huge commissions and paper profits were generated from bogus deals. Managers knew about what was going on but realized that some form of it had always taken place. They could have stopped it but felt no need to. It was part of the culture. The "should do" area produces tremendous escalations. If I cheat as a salesperson on my expenses to the tune of $25 a week, as a sales manager it may be $100. By the time I'm the vice president, the *process* and acceptance haven't changed, but the *content* and harm have, perhaps to the tune of $10,000. (Do not scoff. I've seen executives who easily add $50,000 a year to their compensation through unwritten "perquisites.")

"Should do but won't" sends all the wrong messages to the organization. People in this condition need to understand the need for the bucket to begin with.

3. Could Do. Where values and skills overlap, I am ready, willing, and able to take action. The problem is that I'm unaware that anything requiring action is going on. Call this one "blissful ignorance." But also call it "protecting the boss."

I ran into a human resources vice president at a hospital who was forever explaining to subordinates and peers that his job was to "manage the president." I asked him what on earth that entailed. He told me that he determined what news reached the CEO and what news didn't, so that the CEO could spend his time on truly high-priority matters and not be distracted by the trivial, which could be handled elsewhere.

"But isn't he smart enough to make that decision?" I asked. "And doesn't that make you the 'royal censor'?" I intoned. He claimed that only one person could really have the president's ear, and it would be him. Unfortunately, I had the other ear, and I managed to free-up both of them. The human resource guy was gone within a year.

Every day top executives are "protected" by those who feel that they shouldn't hear bad news. They are screened more effectively than a quarterback standing behind 2 tons of offensive linemen. The crime, though, is that they make little effort to free themselves. Any CEO or top manager can easily rid himself or herself of "yes people" and filters. Simply raise hell the first time you learn something has been withheld, and the message will be sent. Dan Rather, in one of television's most famous interrogations, asked Richard Nixon after the Watergate break-in was exposed, "But how much did you know, Mr. President, and when did you know it?" Nixon knew more than he was letting on, but it's an equal crime *not to know*. At that level, ignorance is never an excuse. You need to know where the water is.

4. Will Do. Only at point 4 do we have the basis for effective ethical actions, messages, and paradigms. I know what's happening, I believe something should be done about it, and I have the skills and resources to take care of it.

Those are not strictly executive attributes, although they should begin there. A truly "empowered" organization provides these three dynamics at all levels by:

- Sharing information openly and honestly and encouraging feedback
- Providing training, education, and development in ethical issues and dilemmas facing, or likely to face, the organization
- Establishing resources, internally (accessibility of top management, employee assistance programs, confidentiality) and externally (ombudsman, employee surveys, focus groups), to ensure that anyone can take action against ethical transgressions

This is not some Utopian dream. Many organizations do this very well. And they do it by treating their employees well first, because happy customers do not result from unhappy employees. Johnson & Johnson responded magnificently to the now-legendary Tylenol crisis, not because of effective "crisis management" but because they lived every day by a firm set of values in that organization, exemplified by CEO Jim Burke. Merck has produced the most admired field force in the pharmaceutical industry because top management has instituted tough medical and ethical guidelines that demand, for example, that competitors are never degraded and that side effects of Merck pharmaceuticals are always prominently discussed with doctors. Levi-Strauss has provided visible support and endorsement for a diverse workplace, in which all people are valued for their contributions, not their conformance. It's no accident that such companies are also immensely profitable.[10]

Organizational leaders must communicate their ethical standards through private, personal, internal channels, not just the "vision statements" and banners in the cafeteria. They must exemplify their behavior visibly and consistently.[11] They must insist on being informed of ethical transgressions. Protection is for endangered species, not leadership.

---

[10] For philanthropic examples, see *The New York Times,* Sep. 18, 1994, p. F11: "Do Business? Do Good? No. Do Both," by David Bollier.

[11] Here come the Japanese again, but their tradition of the executive resigning in the face of scandal or failure, because the buck stops there, is an admirable trait and strong message.

Finally, nothing less than a "zero-tolerance" policy is required. The risks of even minor "corner cutting" are simply too great in terms of potential escalation and exponential expansion. If there is less than a zero-tolerance policy for ethical violations, there will forever be enough loopholes to house a legion of lawyers. *And if we've left the ethics to the lawyers, all is lost.*

How to Clothe the Emperors, Part 8

1. Executives must create and nurture "pulse points" in the organization to establish alternative information streams to direct reports.
2. The organization must have a written policy on ethical violations and how they are to be reported, ensuring confidentiality when necessary.
3. Policies that intrinsically create conflict—i.e., provide service but we will pay you on the numbers only—must be eliminated.
4. Regularly—at least quarterly—senior management should devote time to discussing past, present, and future ethical conflicts and examine the skills, alerting systems, and preventive action in place to reconcile future issue.
5. Proved ethical violations should be dealt with firmly and publicly.
6. Unethical acts for the company's "good" are acts that degrade everyone. They should be dealt with as harshly as those done for personal gain.
7. A portion of executive compensation should be based on ethical conduct of that person's *division* or *department,* since the buck stops there.
8. Ethical training and awareness must be part of the organization's initial orientation program for new employees and regular training programs for existing employees.
9. All key executives should be required—and other managers requested—to invest time in community contributions, philanthropic work, civic support and similar activities, with company time provided for those engagements.
10. Never confuse legal issues and ethical issues, and never place the ethics oversight or monitoring responsibility in the legal department. What is unethical is often legal, and what is ethical is often illegal.

Part Three

Status

"The two Knights of the Loom each lifted an arm, as if they were holding something between them, and said, 'Look, here are the trousers...it feels as if one had nothing on at all; but that's just the beauty of it.'"

Chapter 9

Forces Perpetuating Stupid Management
The Invidious Nature of Reward Systems

"The only way to get rid of temptation is to yield to it."
—Oscar Wilde

"Everybody wants to go to Heaven, but nobody wants to die."
—Senator Walter Huddleston (D-KY)

The organizational elite particularly favor nautical analogies. They speak of "everyone rowing in the same direction," "carefully plotting our course," and "damn the torpedoes.'"[1] (Just to show that they also embrace aeronautic terminology, they readily speak of "golden parachutes," also.)

My favorite sea-going corporate aphorism, though, is that "this is a supertanker, and you can't just suddenly change its direction." Which means that the skipper will be ready to change his heading just as soon as he retires. "This isn't a speedboat, you know."

Well, I don't care whether it's a dinghy or the aircraft carrier *Nimitz*. Nothing turns in the water if the wheel is locked in one position, and there is no reward for plotting a new course or taking the wheel. Organizations don't change because the people who run them don't want to change, and they set up the ship's rules of engagement so that no one is motivated to change.

---

[1] Lest you think that this last phrase indicated bravery and risk taking, let me remind you that Admiral Farragut, who made the remark during the assault on Mobile Bay, was lashed to the mast of his flagship, *Hartford,* about 40 feet above the water line. It's not recorded what the sailors said who were below decks where the torpedoes (actually mines) were about to hit.

Show me a reward system and I'll show you a value system. Yes, I do tend to repeat this.

Here's the top-8 list (the publisher is on a budget and can't afford 10) of reasons why people act in ways that inhibit progress, maintain the status quo, and otherwise take on the heavy gait of brontosauruses.

Alan's Top 8 Reasons Why Employees Don't Change

1. People are rewarded for doing what's always been done

In most hierarchies there are rigid rules within the "silos," adherence to which constitutes success and failure. The reward is for continuance, not discontinuance; for compliance, not deviation.

Have you called United Airlines lately? It has taken great pleasure in recasting itself as an employee-owned airline. When you get the inevitable recorded message on the reservations lines, asking you to hold until after your departure date, you are now advised that "one of the new owners will be with you shortly." Well, okay, in that case the wait will be worth it; because these people will be quite anxious to help me. After all, they're no longer plebeian, low-paid functionaries who bad-mouth management every chance they get; they're now entrepreneurial, savvy owners, looking to create long-term business for their children to inherit. Right?

The reservationist told me that I couldn't use my free, first-class coupons for a trip to any major city prior to the year 2004, and then only with a connection and flying at night.

"In other words, you have plenty of seats available, but the few you've allotted to your awards program are already assigned," I pointed out.

"That's correct," she acknowledged, about to disconnect.

"Well, tell me, as an owner, do you think it's right that a customer such as I, traveling on full-fare, first-class tickets on your system, can't use the very awards intended for such patronage? How many of us are there? Why don't you do something about it?"

"Sir, I can't do anything about it. They make the rules and that's all there is to it. I'd change them if I could for you, but they know what's best for the system."

"There is no 'they' my friend. *You* are 'they.' You're an owner. You can change the rules."

"No, I would get in trouble for changing them, even if I thought I could. I am nothing here. I just follow orders."

"From whom?"

"From them."

Picture the difference over at Avis, an employee-owned company whose employees seem to believe it. Avis people are much more courteous than their wage-earning cousins at Hertz. At Hertz, the gold system puts your name in lights and you trudge from their bus to your car at the gold area. Hertz makes the classic mistake—which it has always made—of allowing so many people into its special programs that they cease to become special. As a result, really good customers go elsewhere, and they are presumably the ones the system was designed for in the first place.[2]

The Avis folks have a better idea. The bus takes you to your car, which is then pulled out for you by a friendly owner. He or she then asks if you need anything and if you know the way out of the lot. I've switched to Avis.

Finally, the role models in most organizations belie any lip service about change. When one looks at the corner office, company car, company condo, and all those other perquisites that make climbing the ladder so attractive, it becomes apparent that the incumbent's actions are the ones to emulate. And most of them will tell you, "Don't rock the boat." Most of us are very, very good at not rocking the boat, especially if you give me a car and a view for staying dead still.

2. People are penalized for trying something new

This is the converse of #1, and together they form a rather impressive force. Most organizations have highly developed immune systems that reject change with the invisible might of identical magnetic poles coming into proximity. Do what you will, you can't force them together for long. Your strength erodes.

There are legions of managers imprinted with reason #1 who have taken a sacred oath to enforce reason #2. If change happens, it won't be on their watch. They would have been proud to have been members of the duty watch of the *Titanic* that chill night. Above all, no changes. Damn the icebergs, full speed ahead.

The classic case here is that of salespeople trying to get anything out of "standard" practice by the home office. This is classic, because it's a case of eating your own foot because you're too stubborn to pay high prices at the corner market.

---

[2] Which is why it's often more comfortable to stay in an airport concourse at the departure gate than in one of the air clubs, which have become chaotic democracies, thanks to court rulings run amok. What was once a refuge for seasoned business travelers has become a raucous, low-class experience features babies being changed, drunks at the bar, and often not a seat to be found. Have you ever noticed that the "first class" line at airport ticket counters often moves much more slowly than the regular lines? What's the point?

Traditionally, salespeople are an entrepreneurial lot who will go to great lengths to obtain business. They work under a principle, often unfathomable in the accounting and shipping departments, that their goal is to achieve results, and no results are acceptable short of a customer remitting a check that clears the bank. Since only the customer can sign the check, it makes some vague sense to try to place that signer in a salutary mood. Modern-day consultants call this being "customer driven." Salespeople have always called it "getting a signature."

Ask virtually any salesperson what occurs when he or she attempts to provide payment terms, delivery times, product customization (note the cognate *customer* in that one), or any type of service outside of the sales manual, and you'll hear a common litany, despite the industry. In fact, you can be absolutely certain of four things:

1. The home office will deny or delay the request, jeopardizing the sale.
2. The salesperson will find a way around the obstacle and achieve what he or she wants "outside of the system."
3. Top management will issue all kinds of edicts in support of the home office folk—who are diligently following reason #1—while at the same time exhorting the field force to increase sales volume.
4. No matter who "wins" this one or how they do it, productivity will suffer and the customer won't be as happy as could be the case.

Salespeople are on the front line with the customer. They understand what changes are necessary in a changing market. Yet they're often regarded as nihilists, intent on destroying the system. And that is exactly what they should be doing.

Pitney Bowes has always driven me crazy. It holds a virtual monopoly on postage meters, and its service department has been about as responsive to us as a trained cat. That's right, there is no such thing. On top of that, we get a confusing array of bills indicating lease payments, warranty charges, local property tax, sewer connections, and all sorts of things that make no sense and are in unreadable formats, citing arcane agreements and serial numbers to the 19th position of *pi*.

After screaming for months, we were blessed with a visit from a woman who introduced herself as our new representative, Karen, and who, disturbingly, looked somewhat familiar. In the course of 45 minutes she cleared up all of our problems, simplified our billing, showed us that we had been overcharged, *and* sold us a newer, larger scale that we didn't need but I felt I owed her.

"Excuse me, but don't I know you?"

"I was wondering if you'd recognize me. I used to be a waitress at the restaurant down on the water where you and your wife were regulars."

"Of course—what are you doing here?!"

"It was a chance to make some more money and have greater freedom. But most of all, I see it as a quick route to management."

"How is that?"

"No one shows any initiative here. They all just follow the system. I've found that most of my customers are like you; they just want some decent service. I can do that because what's the worst that can happen to me? I can always be a waitress again. But that's unlikely."

"Why? Aren't you rocking the boat by helping us poor souls out?"

"I'm also bringing in major business. There's no way they can touch me."

Sure enough, our service was simplified and improved. Karen drops us personal notes, and I'm sure she's headed for great things in the meter business. The question, of course, is not how to find more Karens but how to change the organization's culture so that you don't have to be someone willing to bet your career every time you try to make a change.

3. Performance is not linked to reward, and vice versa

In one of my client focus groups, a participant said, "Management here is not paid to develop people. They are paid strictly to make the numbers."

"Oh, no," said another employee, "They aren't paid to make the numbers either, or we'd have exceeded our plan for the past 3 years. That's a myth. Managers are paid here for only one thing: to make each other look good. That's why they're paid so much, because that's the one thing they're very good at."

Digital Equipment (DEC), once the darling of the analysts, has fallen on hard times. Those hard times can be readily linked to a succession of executive miscalculations about the market and the customer preferences. For the fiscal year ending July 2, 1994, the company lost a staggering $2.1 billion, which is not easy to do. For that same period, the total pay for DEC's five top executives rose 70%.[3]

Now if you ask me, or any other sentient being, a 70% increase denotes incredibly excellent performance. Apparently not at DEC. What would a *decent* year have brought? Do those folks get 200% for breaking even? I don't even want to think about something as ridiculous as making a profit.

If you're wondering, the CEO, Robert Palmer, received stock options that on paper exceed his $900,000 salary. Departing sales vice president Edward Lucente and consulting chief Gresham Breback, Jr., had the misfortune of being cut in the downsizing—and went out to find new employment with $630,000 and $500,000 settlements, respectively.

---

[3] *Business Week,* Oct. 3, 1994, p. 6: "Payoffs At a Downsized DEC."

Most organizations do a horrid job at creating performance standards that have any measurable criteria attached. Even in the sales force, where quotas and volume are eminently measurable, there is often confusion about what constitutes new business vs. renewal business, who gets credit for what part of the sale, which territory is involved, and what the actual contribution to profit is. This last point is a killer; those organizations that do effectively measure sales and revenues often fail to measure margin and profit. The result is that you can be increasing business at the speed of sound while you're losing money doing so at the speed of light. In other words, you're rewarding your salespeople to drive you to the poorhouse.

Kepner-Tregoe is a training firm in Princeton, New Jersey, for which I once labored. It is the home of one of the great motivational programs of all time.

In order to enhance sales of its training programs to corporate clients, K-T's senior management decided to offer a promotional program. It would provide three new Cadillacs to the three top sales producers for the next year. Anyone could win them. Jut be one of the top three. Are you beginning to see the problem?

At the conclusion of the following year, the three winners were the same three people who had been the top producers the prior year. Nothing too unusual there. And they had produced about the same volume as they had the prior year. Therein was the firm's problem: no growth. However, now they had produced the same volume as the prior year *and* each had a $20,000 car for doing so. To sum this all up, K-T implemented a program that was able to generate the exact same amount of revenue as the prior year at an increased cost of $60,000. And these were people providing business training to major organizations!

I remember a meeting at which the managing director for South America announced that his team had generated revenues of $350,000, which was a 15% increase from the prior year. "What were the expenses?" asked a board member. "We spent $475,000," said the managing director, "and next year we will do even better!"

"If you do any better," intoned the board member, "we'll all lose our shirts."

Every job can have a performance objective that can be measured. If the job cannot, then it may well be a job not worth doing or paying for. And every performance objective can be linked to a reward commensurate with its contribution.

"Most job outputs are measurable," says consulting guru Bill Reddin. "Even St. Paul had clear key effectiveness areas, though Judgment Day does represent a long performance feedback loop."[4]

---

[4]*Effective Management by Objectives*, by W. J. Reddin, McGraw-Hill, 1971.

4. Executives assume that everyone wants what they want

I once worked for a president who told me that the finest hours of his life were after midnight, when he'd empty his briefcase in front of a fire and, with a glass of brandy, work through all of the gritty business problems facing the company.

"When did you sleep?"

"Sleep? Who needs sleep after that kind of invigorating night? Everyone should try it!"

Yes, and everyone should try slamming their fingers in the car door just to appreciate how much better off they are than someone who has done that by accident.

In most of the surveys we've done, and most of those you read in business literature, you'll find that executives *believe* that employees most treasure money, flexible hours, and incentives, and least care about having their ideas implemented, getting feedback, and how they are led. In fact, employees surveyed reply in just the opposite fashion.

At least one study has shown that over two-thirds of job satisfaction derives from leadership skills employed by superiors.[5] A population of 25,000 people in various businesses was studied, revealing that 69% of job satisfaction came from such leadership attributes as providing a vision, feedback on performance, recognition of talent, and a challenging environment. The stereotypical pay, incentives, and hours accounted for only 31% of job satisfaction.

"Blanket" motivational programs rarely work, because people are so different. The commonality, however, is that most people respond well to recognition of their contributions, investment in their personal and professional development, and feedback that demonstrates that someone is interested in them.

Executives live in a far different world. They often compare themselves to others based on their compensation and net worth. They disdain feedback and will actually work hard to avoid it. They generally do not believe in training and development for themselves, no matter how much things have changed in the environment. And their environment can be challenging only on their own terms: It's one thing to work all night on company business and prove to the board that you can handle anything, but the office routine had better be predictable, safe, and under control.

---

[5] See *Boardroom Reports,* Oct. 1, 1994, p. 15, citing Michael Leimbach, director of research, Wilson Learning Company, originally printed in *Sales & Marketing Management.*

Most executives feel that "vision" is a clever line or profound paragraph that can be shared with the troops, but the "real" strategy is too sensitive to circulate to the masses.

Years ago I worked with the Associated Press in New York. With the failure of UPI, it was leading a rather monopolistic life. Its executives were concerned, however, that people were not supporting the organization's direction. There seemed to be discontent in the ranks, especially at headquarters.

"Do you have a clearly articulated strategy detailing where you want to be in the next 5 years or so?" I asked.

"Absolutely," said the senior vice president. "It's right here."

He pulled from his bottom desk drawer a thick, three-ring binder.

"Has everyone seen it?" I continued.

"Yes, and of course, we all were party to it and agree on the direction completely."

"You all agree on the direction and you still have discontent?"

"Well, there's no discontent among the nine of us!"

"What do you mean, 'the nine of us'?"

"The nine of us on the executive committee who have seen this."

"You mean the employees have never seen that?"

"Are you crazy!? We could never let the employees see the organization's strategy!"

And for this I earn the big bucks.

5. Organizations measure safe, but stupid, things

Oscar Wilde once said, "A thing isn't necessarily true just because a man dies for it." Add to that, "A thing isn't necessarily important because it can be measured." A lot of human resource people are fond of saying that "if you can't measure it, it ain't important." When's the last time you measured how comfortable you were, how beautiful your kids are, or how safe you want to be on an airplane? We so mistrust our judgment (or others' judgment) that we insist on quantifying everything. *The result is that we've become very proficient at measuring the meaningless.*

Some years ago I was on the extension faculty of a GTE management development program conducted quarterly at its Connecticut headquarters. The company brought middle-management people together from its diverse operations (at the time, light bulbs to cellular communications) for a week's exposure to a variety of management techniques.

Now let it be known that these types of "immersion" programs are seldom very effective. They attempt a "blanket" approach to learning, despite one's job, locale, and individual needs. Consequently, there are some in the sessions who are bored, some who find the content irrelevant, others who aren't accustomed to classroom learning, and some who really benefit. It's a "throw dirt at the wall" approach, at best.

(A decade or so ago, large organizations created "universities" at which managers would learn both contemporary techniques and the company strategy. The most intense I was ever connected with was GE's at Crotonville, each of which lasted 6 weeks, used dormitory-like housing, and forbade participants to visit family during the entire program, no matter what holidays or family celebrations might have intervened. That program is "reduced" to a more manageable 2 weeks these days, but it's still one of the longer ones running. Many companies abandoned the attempt, went back to on-site training, and shuttered the "university.")

GTE opened its program about 12 years ago in a gorgeous facility erected for the purpose and costing many millions of dollars at a low point in company earnings. For quite a while, the inlaid carpets and fine wood finishes created some comment amid layoffs and freezes. But the program had some valid learning objectives and attracted a decent faculty (after all, they asked me, didn't they?), and I worked on it for about 6 years, off and on, as my schedule permitted.

Then one fine day, the top human resource people awoke to the fact that "customer service," "measurable results," and "quality guarantees" were all the rage, and they decided that they would guarantee the learning experience. If participants didn't like the program, as reflected on the abominable "smile sheets" one finds at the conclusion of nearly every corporate program under the guise of "feedback," there would be a refund. In fact, if the average rating fell below a certain ranking, the faculty member would be asked to rebate his or her fee.

Now there was just one problem with these lofty goals: The measure of training and development should be behavior change on the job. Thus, the *managers* of the participants might have been in a position to measure constructive changes and heightened productivity, assuming the course had content and techniques that contributed to such improvements. But the *participants,* whose ratings were to be used, were measuring only how much they enjoyed the week. The course wasn't created for them to enjoy; it was created to improve their performance. Sometimes the two are simply not equal. (I never "enjoyed" a final exam, trip to the dentist, or any health club workout machine I've ever laid eyes on.)

I was the highest-rated member of the entire faculty. But I told them that the measurement system was perverted, and even though there wasn't a remote chance that my programs would be rated poorly, I would not participate in the rebate because the basis for the measurement was groundless. If they wanted to measure performance back on the job, then count me in.

The great human resource intellect at GTE decided that I could partici-pate or leave. And so I left, with GTE measuring the wrong things (and still bragging about it) and losing its best faculty member because it didn't want to discuss the accurate but much harder issues of measuring performance, not attitude. I guess it accurately measured that I had the wrong attitude.

Organizations continue to measure things like sales calls, number of phone inquiries handled, hours spent on the job, amount of turnover, and other irrelevancies that constitute quantity not quality. They should be mea-suring amount of business, duration of customer business, number of calls until the inquiry is satisfied, output of the job, volume of customers who stay and of those who leave, and so on. They generally don't measure these things because they require tougher analyses and executive judgment. *A number isn't always a number.*

6. Rewards themselves can be nefarious

Although they usually don't realize it, organizations work on an atavistic Skinnerian behaviorism that translates to salary, incentive pay, and motiva-tional programs featuring gifts and rewards equaling the persuasion to work harder and smarter. In the most sophisticated environments, we see a sim-plistic philosophy of "do this, and you'll get that."

I once had a Pulitzer Prize–winning editor in one of my sessions at the American Press Institute who suffered badly from McLuhan's "mixed me-dia" effect: He mistakenly believed that the Pulitzer was a prize for knowing all things about all issues. He made it clear to anyone who would listen that motivation is quite a simple dynamic. "Simply pay more money, and people perform better. There's no more to it than that."

Well, there might be one more thing. If you pay an unhappy worker more money, what you will get is a richer, unhappy worker.

Behaviorism is either taken for granted in most environments or subject to the horrible pop psychology and stereotyping so rampant today. ("What do you expect from an INTJ?" "She's a left-brainer, so give her a list.") You cannot bribe people to do a good job, although you can bribe them, period.

Motivation can *only* be intrinsic. That is, you can't motivate me; I can only motivate myself. However, you can attempt to establish an environment that is conducive to that motivation. So you should pay me enough to get my mind out of my wallet and onto the business at hand. I won't work well if I'm defocused by the fact that I can't pay my mortgage or my kids' tuition, no matter how hard I work. But once I can pay it, paying me still more does not mean I'll pay someone else's mortgage or send other kids to college. Now hear this: Studies have found that there is no direct correlation or positive link between rewards and results from jobs that require higher-order thinking skills.[6]

We've already discussed that several priorities emerge in surveys of employees on motivation and gratification prior to the mention of pay, although employers usually rank it first. Rewards are often seen as converse punishments, "if you don't do this, you won' get this." Unless carefully constructed, rewards create "winners" and "losers," in that some people, for good reason, might not receive them. This can be especially severe if an individual is seen as "penalizing" a team's efforts.

Ironically, rewards are quite conservative, in that they will usually create "safe" attitudes so that the reward won' t be lost. "I'm going to go after only sure accounts, because if I pursue larger but tougher accounts, I'l risk not qualifying for the trip." The company might need those larger accounts, however, in the long term, but the reward is for the short term.

Once people are comfortable—they needn't be ecstatic—about their pay, management should focus on their individual gratifications and how to align them with the corporate objectives. This, of course, requires hard work and can't be done at the human resource department level. It must be done by the management team. In general, people require:

1. Rationale for why the job is important and how it contributes
2. Empowerment to make decisions that influence their results
3. Involvement with a team or support structure for mutual growth
4. Access to education and development for self-improvement
5. Trust and the security to make mistakes and continue to take risks

Stupid management asks how motivated people are. Intelligent management asks how people are motivated.

7. There are obstacles to performance that people trip over but don't discuss

The owner of a small, local firm once asked for my help with his organization. It had grown beyond the "mom and pop" stage, and he was frankly concerned about how well his structure was suited for international competition, rapid technological advance, and swift economic changes. Fair enough.

---

[6] For a fascinating discussion and synopsis of a talk on the subject, see *National Report on Human Resources,* American Society for Training and Development, Aug./Sep. 1994, p. 3: "Companies Won't Boost Performance by Offering Rewards," an interview of Alfie Kohn, author of *Punished by Rewards.*

Once I looked around, I discovered that he was his own worst nightmare. He had created patchwork reporting relationships that undercut his direct reports, kept people in the dark about strategy so that their decisions weren't coordinated, and generally intimidated the hell out of everyone. (There was a no-smoking policy, except in his office and his wife's, next door. No one quite knew what his wife did at the office, other than smoke.) Fortunately, I always demand payment in advance on these projects.

He was outraged at what I told him. In confidence, people had revealed how difficult it was to work under these conditions, but it was necessary only to observe and ask a few questions to reach the same conclusions. No one was ever willing or able to bring the owner's behavior up as a topic at the management meetings, so the team constantly pursued what I termed *ghosts:* ephemeral and evanescent reasons why things weren't better, rather than the temporal, corporeal reason sitting at the head of the table.

We parted company right after my report, he bitterly, and I with amusement. He had created a multimillion-dollar candy store, and he wasn't about to let anyone else stock the shelves or work the cash register.

Obstacles that people cannot or will not discuss are often referred to as "the elephant in the room." There's this huge, smelly creature that people have to maneuver around, hold their noses for, and keep out of its way lest they be crushed, and they all become conspirators to the silence. Occasionally, someone will acknowledge the elephant (i.e., "Let's be honest; we can't get this job done unless we get dedicated budget from the vice president."), which will either resolve the issue magnificently or create a second elephant. One of my favorite clients at Hewlett-Packard calls this act "putting the dead rat on the table." Enough for now with the animal analogies.

I've watched teams go through the motions for months on end when everyone knew their plans would never amount to a single result *unless* someone or something was included or excluded, but which no one had the courage to acknowledge openly. Sometimes this is another team member who is obstreperous, absent, or incompetent; sometimes it's the absence of funding. It could be the lack of buy-in from the actual decision-makers on the fourth floor; or it could be the knowledge that the company's financial situation could never support the model being created.

The result of all of this, no matter what the cause, is poor performance, because no one is committed and everyone is simply putting in his time. Nothing will change because no one expects it to. And the reward seems to be at best a fictitious creation, and at worst the blame for not moving something that couldn't be budged because an elephant was sitting on it.

Hannah Moore said, "Obstacles are those frightful things you see when you take your eyes off the goal." It's tough to see goals when the elephant is forcing you to shout across the table, take only shallow breaths, and watch where you walk.

8. Skills problems and attitude problems have nothing to do with each other

One of the great men in the management education business, Bob Mager, created a truly classic question, one that even naked managers can ask: Could they do the job if their lives depended on it?

Think about that one. If you put a gun to my head and asked if I'd now like to do the work, and I said, "Well, since you put it that way, okay," you've been dealing with an attitude problem. But if I said, "You might as well shoot me, the gun doesn't help," then you've got a real skills problem.

With skills deficiencies, the interventions include training, practice, feedback, and reinforcement. With attitude problems, the interventions require:

- Removing obstacles
- Removing punishments for desired performance
- Removing positive consequence for nonperformance
- Providing positive consequences for desired performance
- Providing punishments for nondesired performance or no performance

If I have a bad attitude, no amount of training, incentive, reward, or other encouragement is going to improve my performance until and unless the reasons for my attitude are identified and addressed. (One recourse is to get rid of my attitude, which is better than ignoring it and trying to "train" me.) Attitudes can result from personal matters gone awry, which are not job related and therefore not job remedial. They can also result from misconceptions (I thought I was in line for that job, and didn't get it.) or poor treatment (I was promised that job and didn't get it.).

As we established earlier, attitudes can't be seen. They are reflected in behavior, and it's that behavior that has attracted our attention. To delve deeper, we must understand if the behavior is due to attitudinal problems or to a simple inability to do the job, due to lack of tools, lack of understanding, or lack of competence. (Here, too, competence problems may result in my departure, which is still better than trying to "motivate" me.) Figure 9.1 shows an adaption of Mager's classic approach to this dynamic.[7]

It's not too much to expect that managers can ask these simple questions. And it's not too much to ask that they stop looking at rewards as a carrot-and-stick approach to performance.

The absence of money will defocus people. The presence of money does not highly focus them. It simply continues to remove discomfort. But no one

---

[7] Adapted from *Analyzing Performance Problems or You Really Oughta Wanna,* by Robert F. Mager and Peter Pipe, Pitman Learning, Inc., 1984. Used with permission.

excels through the absence of discomfort, or the consideration of how better off he is than the next guy. We excel because we reward ourselves through the accomplishment, results, and gratification of our work. Managers must strive to establish, maintain, and nurture such environments. Otherwise, they're just throwing money at the problem and haven't changed a thing.

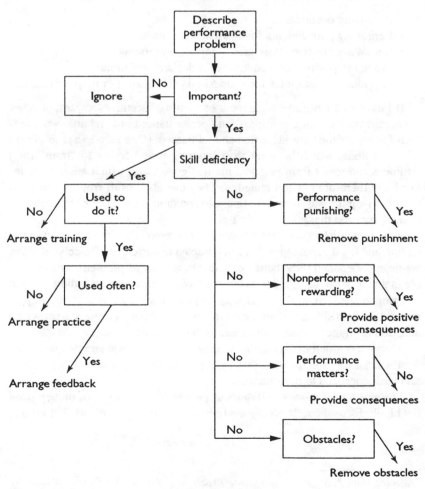

Figure 9.1. Performance analysis flowchart.

How to Clothe the Emperors, Part 9

1. Identify performance discrepancies and deviations based on behaviors that can be observed and described.
2. Identify whether the deviation is the result of attitude or skills deficiencies, and take appropriate actions to resolve either.
3. Do not implement blanket, broad-scale motivation programs, since they will not affect everyone the same.
4. Pay enough to resolve severe financial concerns. That is a starting point for any subsequent reward system.
5. Do not create "win/lose" incentive programs. If you must have incentive programs, create them so that everyone has a chance of succeeding.
7. Align individual and organizational goals so that the individual's intrinsic rewards create behaviors that generate organizational results.
8. Emphasize an environment in which individuals can be internally motivated. Do not confuse movement, which is external, with motivation, which is internal.
9. Measure results and output, not tasks and input.
10. Allow people to take risks, make mistakes, and learn from false starts. Reward behaviors, not "victories."

Chapter 10

Forces Confusing the Issues
The 11½ Great American Management Potholes

"That our national anthem is difficult to understand and hard to use
should not be surprising since it was written by a lawyer."
— letter to *The Wall Street Journal* about Francis Scott Key

We operate under some arcane and often astounding mythology in
our organizations.

I am forever being called in by management to reconcile the fact
that the cumulative performance ratings of managers are high, but the
organization's results are mediocre. But there's really no mystery.
The people are being measured on their *actions,* while the organization is being measured on its *results.* While the human resource
bureaucracy is assisting top management to measure meticulously
the numbers of people managed, spans of control, calls answered
per hour, meetings held with clients, and various other input, Wall
Street and shareholders are watching the bottom line and assessing
progress toward strategic business goals. Has the market share
increased? Is the return on equity growing? Has R&D investment
been commercialized?

You cannot measure and reward people on inputs if the business
goals are actually outputs (which they had better be). Tasks are irrelevant unless they produce the desired results. Actions are immaterial
if they don't produce desired outcomes.

Here are the potholes littering the organizational highways, causing
flattened earnings and damage to the machinery. They are in no particular order, because all of them are sitting out there awaiting the unwary
and unskilled driver.

Hazard #1: The Customer Is Paramount

We have seen the emergence of cultlike behavior that slavishly supports the notion that the customer can do no wrong. The apotheosis of this new religion was exemplified in Nordstrom's incredible act of customer faith: allowing people to return things for credit *that weren't even purchased in the store.* Customers are important, but they're supposed to be the lifeblood of the business, not the death knell. If enough customers returned goods that weren't purchased in the store, we'd no longer have an enterprise. Even the Salvation Army refuses some contributions.

As I've mentioned, I've never seen an organization with happy customers and unhappy employees. A focus on the customer is fine, but not to the exclusion of all else. I could make a case that the *employees* are actually the lifeblood of the business, and customers the external source of nourishment. (My problem, of course, is that the organism is sometimes brain dead at the top.) The more the employees of United Airlines were alienated by management, the lousier the cabin service became. The more pressure that UPS puts on its drivers for volume, the more lost and inaccurate deliveries we've experienced.

I know that the way I'm treated in any organization is a direct reflection of the way the employees are treated by management. The focus on customer service is fine, but not at the expense of employee motivation and initiative. The two are not mutually exclusive.

I have heard stories of customers who "buy" an outfit on their store credit card, wear it to an affair, and then return it for a refund. These customers should not be mindlessly supported. They should be thrown out of the store. Organizations should provide the best service to their best customers and not witlessly provide equal service and accommodation to everyone. The airlines seem to recognize this with their various recognition levels for frequent fliers. But note that even in these programs, customers attempt to abuse the system by selling their mileage, attempting to get mileage credit for the flights of others who fraudulently use their identification numbers, and demanding upgrades at the expense of full-fare passengers.

The customer isn't always right. Sometimes the customer is an outrageous pain in the butt. This is why employee empowerment is so important: Every employee should be empowered to kick unreasonable customers out.

Hazard #2: Problem-Solving Is the Key Attribute

In most organizations, an inordinate amount of management time is devoted to trying to restore conditions to previous levels of performance. When the magnitude of the problem is average, the approach is called *problem-solving.*

When the magnitude is high (viz., being reported in the newspapers), the approach is termed *crisis management.*

Problem-solving was first described by the Greeks about 2 millennia ago: You recognize that a problem exists (something is not happening in the manner you had expected), describe its characteristics (what, when, where, how), and hypothesize possible causes (why). You then test and apply corrective actions until the cause is removed and the problem goes away. This basic, analytical approach is as sound today as it was in antiquity, no matter what bells and whistles you attach to it. That's how problems are most rationally solved.

The problem (no pun intended) with this focus is that it inevitably restores performance to prior levels and expectations. In Figure 10.1, the top graphic shows such restoration. A person's performance, a piece of equipment, or a process is restored to prior levels of achievement. In the bottom graphic, however, the performance—which has been just fine—*is raised proactively to a new level.* In innovation, the performer decides to raise the bar. In problem-solving, a triggering, uncomfortable event (customer complaints, leaky roof, lost sale, misprinted letters) propels us into corrective action. In innovation, our judgment and knowledge of the environment motivate us to raise the standards.[1]

Both of these disciplines are important, but my anecdotal testing with clients and audiences consistently demonstrates that about 90% of management time is devoted to problem-solving, and only about 10% to innovation.

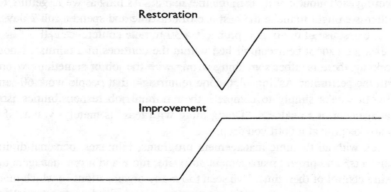

Figure 10.1. Problem solving vs. innovation.

---

[1] For a detailed comparison and discussion, see *The Innovation Formula: How Organizations Turn Change into Opportunity,* by Mike Robert and Alan Weiss (Ballinger: 1988).

Moreover, the great preponderance of organizational rewards are bestowed on the problem-solvers, not the innovators, because problem-solving is so much less ambiguous (we know it used to work), so much safer (how do we know we can achieve new standards?), and so much more gratifying (we're taking action and can see the results immediately).

No matter. Until our leaders understand that consciously raising the bar—proactively improving performance, with all the attendant risks and uncertainties—is at least as important as fixing what breaks, we will not demonstrate the exponential progress required in a rapidly changing business world. Instead of filling in the potholes, we should be devising alternative modes of travel.

Hazard #3: Time Is a Scarce Resource

Whenever someone says, "I'm sorry, but I just don't have the time," they are lying to you. What they actually mean is, "I don't intend to spend my time in the manner you are suggesting." Of course they *have* the time; they just don't want to use it with you.

Time is not the slippery, disappearing resource we often make it out to be. We control how we invest our time. But we often surrender that control, and sit at unproductive meetings, hold redundant discussions, and generally spin our wheels in the potholes of low-priority issues.

One of my clients calls meetings with widely dispersed team members on a regular basis because, "We should probably have at least one face-to-face meeting each month." And then the inevitable: "As long as we're getting together, we ought to make the best use of our time and spend a full 2 days."

The best use of our time is probably a 30-minute conference call.

If a job cannot be accomplished within the confines of a normal, 8-hour workday, there is either something wrong with the job or something wrong with the performer. Asking—let alone requiring—that people work 60- and 80-hour weeks simply to complete their normal job responsibilities isn't management, it's madness. "Doing more with less" is merely tyranny if it means keeping at it until you drop.

Yet, with all the time-management programs, Filofaxes, personal digital assistants,[2] and project management software, more and more managers are losing control of their time. I've seen too many organizations in which managers attend wall-to-wall meetings, morning to night, and no one can talk to customers because "they're all in meetings."

---

[2] That phrase, for the minicomputers that serve as notebooks, has always prompted me to envision people following me around using their fingers in place of my own.

Here are the reasons to invest or save your time. It's a conscious choice.

Invest to:	Save to:
• Develop subordinates	• Make decisions quickly
• Empower and involve others	• Show strong, personal leadership
• Learn and assimilate information	• Review what you already know
• Develop relationships	• Please others for the sake of it.
• Demonstrate concern with customers	• Ignore office politics and "turf"
• Create new standards of performance	• Review old standards of performance
• Safeguard high-quality issues	• Work on low-quality issues
• Establish commitment	• Proceed when others will follow you
• Provide for celebration/ motivation	• Bemoan a setback and whine
• Set strategy and direction	• Implement and take action

When the road is clear and visibility is excellent, drive fast. When there's fog and the road is unfamiliar, slow down.

Hazard #4: Refusing to Act Because "They" Won't Let You

I was addressing the 25 top officers of a major bank. They were pretty much in agreement about the institution's competitive position and the key actions needed to achieve the results called for by the strategy. However, the group kept finding reasons why the actions wouldn't be accepted. *They* would never stand for it. *They* would be hard to convince. There's no guarantee that *they* would buy in.

Finally, I pointed at the CEO. "Are you talking about him?" I asked. "Is it John who won't let you do these things?"

"Oh, no, John has been a strong supporter."

"Then I've got news for you. *You* are *they*. Or put it another way: There is no *they*."

If people at the top talk about the omnipotent, omnipresent *they* who won't allow something to happen, then people at the bottom have so many *they*'s that they're virtually paralyzed. We are all our own worst enemies and our largest roadblocks.

Talk to people in an employee-owned operation, and *they* will speak of *they*. Talk to the owner, and he or she will speak of *they*. The government talks of *they*, but so does the constituency. Who are *they*? Aliens? MTV? Or perhaps the Japanese, yet again?

They is us. We have created an imaginary friend (or enemy) who handily prevents us from taking risks, overcoming inertia, expressing outrage, changing the system, and improving on the status quo. We have to start admitting to our invisible sidekick and realizing that the device is an excuse, a self-imposed impediment to action.

No top manager worth the paycheck should allow any subordinate to escape accountability because *they* wouldn't allow something to happen, much less claim it as his or her own excuse. If we eliminated the *they* from organizational vocabularies, the corporate speed limit would increase by another 20 miles an hour. The result would not be reckless driving. *They* simply wouldn't be in the way any more.

Hazard #5: Walking on Water; Everyone Can Be Saved

Terminating employees is often the kindest thing a manager can do. Managers are not saviors. Not everyone can do every job, and not every job attribute is learnable. Behaviors can be modified only within finite ranges that, sometimes, are quite narrow. I'm not talking about downsizing, right-sizing, early-outs, or any other euphemism for throwing mass numbers of people out the door to salve the organization's wounds. I'm talking about the normal, daily process of removing those relatively few people who aren't measuring up.

One of the reasons that companies do get "fat" is that they don't continually remove the deadwood. I've been in organizations in which, on a scale of 1 to 5, virtually everyone receives the top 4 or 5 ratings. Yet the organization is performing at a mediocre 3. When I ask how this can be, I learn that the ratings are given to "keep morale up." If you don't believe it, take a look at the ratings the secretaries are receiving in your operation. They're probably universally high. They are given high ratings in lieu of the kind of pay those employees actually deserve.

One of my routine exercises with a top management team is to create a list of people who aren't bringing value to the organization, even though their job responsibilities are important, and should bring value. We then perform a triage: Who can contribute more if they are developed; who can contribute more if they are moved to less demanding work; and who cannot contribute more and should be terminated? Invariably, on the first pass, over 90% of those listed are placed in the "develop" category. I then ask the group to state specifically how that development will take place, who will provide it, and how they will know it's made a difference.

After everyone is done staring at the ceiling, I point out that in 6 months, we'd have the exact same list. The overwhelming likelihood is that, if any of those people could have contributed more through development, they already would have. The choice of further development is based on the reluctance of any senior manager to admit failure, to face the harshness of terminating someone, and to admit that he or she has been harboring such nonperformance for so long.

Yet the kindest thing that can be done for these employees is to deal with them honestly. They will continue to underperform, be undercompensated in their own eyes, and grow frustrated with their work. Moreover, they will constitute a great deal of the wind resistance that the vehicle is trying to overcome. Senior managers are paid to make hard decisions, not to generate creative excuses for poor performers.

Employees who had once performed adequately but who have fallen by the wayside can be those who:

- Technology has made obsolescent
- Have refused to develop past a certain plateau of performance
- Have had to change jobs due to restructuring
- Have been promoted beyond their abilities
- Were overrated in the first place, due to sloppy evaluations
- Have burned out through personal or professional stress
- Have developed interests that override their focus on the work
- Were pulled on the coattails of a now-departed superior
- Were hired under different market conditions
- Were hired on the basis of a track record elsewhere

If senior managers aren't meticulous in continually weeding out poor performers, the system will not do it for them (there is no *they*). And if they don't do it, their subordinates won't be encouraged to do it, because there is no role model and no obvious priority for doing so.

Employees who perform poorly do not constitute failure for their manager. But the unwillingness or inability to remove those people does constitute a failure to accept a primary accountability of the top jobs: removing people for their own good, as well as the organization's.

More people are done harm through inaction and lies than are done harm through honest critique and consequent removal. If you are frozen in the headlights of the oncoming truck, your fate is clear. It's better to hear the horn and get out of the way.

Hazard #6: There Is No Joy in Mudville

Our organizations have become dour places. There is no celebration, no rejoicing, no shared happiness over positive events. I remember talking to a national sales manager whose field force was in the midst of its greatest year. It had made the year's plan by late October, meaning that everything brought in over the final 2 months was gravy, adding to everyone's bonus and incentive compensation. Yet, the sales manager looked miserable.

"What on earth is bothering you?" I asked. "You should be on top of the world. On December 31 this entire company is going to look at you and your sales force as heroes."

"Yes," he said, "and on January 1, we'll all be bums again."

I don't know how many times I've heard executives deliver good news in stentorian tones and always with the admonition, "But we can't rest on our laurels. We have to work even harder from here." It's as if employees are children who believe that finding the prize in the crackerjack box means that their life's goals have been met, unless otherwise informed.

During bad times, executives walk around with appropriately glum expressions and send out the message that the holiday party will be curtailed, the annual awards banquet has been moved from West Palm Beach to the Cleveland Airport Marriott, and any office socializing that will detract from business (in other words, *any* office socializing) will not be received warmly. Everyone buckles down to the terrible truths of Being Behind Plan, and the place takes on the somber spirit of the third deck of rowers on an ancient Egyptian galley.

Conversely, however, when times are good, budgets are being surpassed and the world should be your oyster, there are warnings about the shellfish. Organizations have lost the ability to celebrate and pat their people on the back. There seems to be a fear that it might become a habit, or that it will be seen as a sign of lax management, or that, heaven forfend, a shareholder might hear about it.[3]

It's a lot easier to manage in Spartan times if one also manages appropriately in times of plenty. There is no momentum on a roller coaster that only wallows in the troughs. It's simply impossible to crest the next hill.

When was the last time people in organizations you belong to were encouraged to rejoice in their accomplishments, celebrate their talents, and party over their progress? I'd bet it's neither recent nor common. All organizational roads are two-way streets.

Hazard #7: Things Are Tight; Let's Cut Training

Despite years of acknowledging a fact of life as obvious as a ham sandwich, organizations continue to perform a knee-jerk reaction when confronted with poor results: They cut the training budget. No matter how intellectually

---

[3] I once heard that the definition of *Puritanism* was the dread fear that someone, somewhere, was enjoying himself.

astute the management, no matter how dedicated to "building for the future" and not "cutting the muscle along with the fat," emotionally they cannot help themselves.

If it's advertising, put a sexy woman in it, no matter what product; if it's an employee problem, form a task force and forget about it; and if it's a tight budget, cut training. There, that ought to do it.

Imagine a major league ball club in the midst of a very mediocre year. It was expected to be a contender but, midway through the season, it is mired in the bottom half of the division and is losing money at the gate. The answer is obvious, right?

"People, as the manager of this team, I've called this meeting to address our poor play and dismal results thus far in the season. Action is clearly called for, and I've decided what will best lift us from these doldrums of sloppy play, losing close ones to the competition, and not being in the proper condition to challenge the best clubs. We're going to close our workout room, fire the trainers, let the conditioning coach go, and, oh yes, reduce practice days to just two a month. There will be no more batting practice prior to games, and pitchers will no longer warm up between innings. I'm confident that this will put us in the shape we need to be in to raise our level of competitiveness for the remainder of the season. Oh, and if any of you want to practice on your own time, just be aware that we won't pay for it."

Now there's a team that's brilliantly managed. Yet that's exactly what happens when our corporate field generals cut the training budget. (There are variations of this lunacy. For example, many newspapers, when faced with hard times *will cut the promotional budget*. This is exactly what they preach to their advertisers *should not* be done when those bill payers fall on hard times, but do as I say, not as I do.)

Organizations cut the training budget for these reasons:

- Executives fail to see the payback of investments in their human assets. They tend to see human expenses, which need to be minimized.
- Training departments have notoriously poor reputations for being pie-in-the-sky operations, not business-related units. This is exacerbated when these functions adapt and preach the latest program du jour, such as servant right-brain total quality 1-minute empowerment.
- The budget is seldom committed and spent early in the year, and a "real" savings can be justified in recapturing the unexpended funds.
- In tough times, everyone should be "too busy to attend training sessions" anyway, so how can you spend money on programs no one can attend?
- "We can always reschedule it for next year." This assumes, of course, that the training and development has little to do with helping people perform better during this year's tough times. In other words, let's develop our people when they're already doing well. . . .

Organizations fall desperately behind the learning curve because training and education are perceived as ancillary activities, rather than as pragmatic catalysts to business results. When these support activities are erected in the separate silos we described in Chapter 1, they are more easily separated and jettisoned. This is why every manager should be a training manager, and why this support should be a normal part of any operation's daily activities. Both the vehicle and the roadway require constant attention for best performance.

Hazard #8: Always Promote the Best Performer

As we've noted, and as you read this paragraph, managers somewhere in the country are promoting their best salespeople to sales manager. The best photographers are becoming photo editors; the best underwriters are moving up to underwriting managers; and the best client service representative are being anointed client service supervisors. In many of those instances, two jobs are being ruined.

The best salespeople tend to be highly assertive, highly persuasive, and fairly impatient, and they accommodate detail to an average degree. These are relationship-builders who do not take rejection personally, who see every sale as a new challenge, and who are impatient to achieve their goals and set new standards. They know the details of their products and services, but just try to get them to send in an expense report or sales forecast on time and on the correct forms.

When you promote one of these hard-chargers to sales manager, you are asking that person to somewhat reduce his or her assertiveness—because that person now has to deal with other home office types, as well as provide counsel to the poorer performers in the sales force—and to raise the patience level and detail orientation. Now that individual is dependent on the performance of others and is responsible for following up with others for the very paperwork that he or she was remiss in completing not so long ago!

Success in the past does not guarantee success in the future. The behaviors required for one position do not automatically become applicable in the next, higher position. The successful homicide detective—hard driving, inquisitive, egocentric, skeptical, abrasive—would not tend to make a very good hostage negotiator ("I don't care who you have in there, we have guns and we're coming in. . . .").

One of the true no-brainers that executives engage in is the mindless promotion of people up the corporate ladder based purely on past performance, without so much as an inquiry into what the new job demands and how well equipped the candidate might be for it. Yet this is one of the key areas in which the big bucks of the big titles should really be earned. This is where the science lessens (here's what they've done) and the art increases (what are they capable of doing?).

If you mindlessly promote a top salesperson to sales manager, you've ruined at least two jobs, in that you've lost a stellar performer and created a lousy manager. And that's not even counting the damage done when a poor manager attempts to lead others, because he or she will continue to make poor people choices.

In selection, you can't look to the past and what's been accomplished. You have to look to the future and what needs to be done. You can't drive the car by using only the rear-view mirrors.

Hazard #9: Money Motivates

If throwing money at problems were the key to leading organizations, we wouldn't need business schools. Workout rooms equipped with large shovels would do the trick nicely. "Just shovel that money into this hole, people, and everything will be fine."

Money does not motivate. The absence of money will *demotivate,* but its presence will not improve morale. If you have unhappy people and you pay them more, you will then have wealthier, unhappy people.

Great truckloads of time are sent whizzing down corporate highways concerned about compensation plans, incentive pay, merit increases, banding, ratings, gain sharing, pay for performance, comparatios, steps, scales, discretionary awards, incentive trips, and all sorts of mazes that people need to negotiate for the next piece of cheese. The people at the top have lost sight of the fact that most people receive gratification from a job well done, and that not every shrug and moan must be acknowledged with a pay incentive. (Perhaps because the people at the top are so engrossed with stock options, deferred compensation, phantom stock, retirement plans, golden parachutes, and other perquisites, they've forgotten that there are other currencies in the realm.)

We've established in a prior chapter that people should be paid competitively and at a rate that allows for a relatively good life style. Beyond that, incentive should be rewarded for truly outstanding performance. However, there are alternatives to traditional incentive packages that reward people for a job well done and which remain—are enduring—far beyond the pay increase that's quickly spent and assimilated. They include:

- Enhanced decision-making latitude
- More contact with customers
- Training others
- Public recognition with other employees and/or customers
- A seat on high-visibility task forces or standing committees
- Choice of assignments
- Discretionary time off

- Credit in company literature or product guides
- Flex time
- Sabbaticals
- Courses, training, educational opportunities
- Community action representing the company
- Appearance in advertising
- Travel to overseas facilities
- Temporary assignments

The answer is often nonmonetary, assuming that people are paid a fair wage to begin with. In fact, it's the nonmonetary rewards that have a longer half-life, aren't dependent on forced distribution of limited incentive funds, and are attainable by large numbers of employees (i.e., you don't have to "lose" for me to "win"). Throwing money at people doesn't motivate them: it simply makes them scramble for the bills, and await the next time you toss the stuff. Both a Rolls-Royce and a Yugo get wet when it rains.

Hazard #10: You Have to Pay the Dues

As I write this, an exclusive private club in Detroit, previously a gathering place for auto industry executives, has rejected a General Motors executive for membership. The candidate is African-American. The club, which is immune to federal discrimination laws because of its private status, has delicately pointed out that it *already has one African-American member,* who is an executive at Chrysler. Well, there you are. What's all the fuss about?[*]

Organizations often insist that they are not discriminatory. People, no matter what their origins, gender, ethnicity, or race, must simply "pay the dues." This is one of the most egregiously narrow-minded and exclusionary precepts in the corporate lexicon, but it is one that is chanted as though it's a religious mantra.

"We have to get minorities (or women, or whomever) into the 'pipeline' so that they receive the experiences and seasoning required to move up into the executive ranks. It's really just a matter of time, but you can't expect us to place unprepared people in these roles simply because they're minorities."

That reasoning has just a few underlying sink holes:

1. Since the people in question were deliberately excluded in the past, doesn't remedial action providing for speedier inclusion now seem appropriate?

---

[*] To their credit, the two top-ranking GM members of the club immediately resigned. Whether other GM members will do so is still unclear. See *The New York Times,* October 23, 1994, p. 16: "G.M. President Quits Club After Black Is Barred," by Doron P. Levin.

2. Haven't there been white males who short-cut the process on occasion, because of their talents? Can't that apply to others? Sometimes the dues are waived.

3. Is there a law that says you can't make "heroic" efforts to find people who don't need the experience, who already have the seasoning, and can be brought in at those levels to show that you're serious about a diverse team?

In reality, I've found that sets of criteria for promotion are applied rigorously to minorities and to women, but aspects of them are often waived for white males. In one company, a college degree is absolutely required for jobs above a certain level, and no minority or woman gets in without them. But white males routinely draw exemptions because of mitigating circumstances. In another, white males receive the title and appropriate pay level immediately on promotion, but women and minorities are often placed in probationary periods that can last for months. I found one woman in a job for over a year without the proper title or pay level, while male counterparts routinely received both immediately when placed in the same position. In another, a job that had always been at director level when held by males was downgraded to associate director when a female was appointed, despite the fact that absolutely nothing had changed in its responsibilities or functions.

"I feel like I'm a swimmer," explained an African-American manager in one of my focus groups, "who not only has to perform every stroke in the book but has to do each one perfectly and longer than anyone else before it's recognized that I can swim. And even then, I'm told to 'take one more lap' just to make sure I wasn't lucky the first time." Let's demolish the toll roads.

Hazard #11: Talk the Talk

Not long ago I called our service contact number at MCI because some of our new 800 numbers were not receiving interstate calls as planned. Anyone can make a mistake and, although this was costing us money, I was confident that a switch had to be flipped somewhere, and that would be that.

After some endless and circuitous conversations with service representatives, I lost patience and asked for a service manager. After lengthy delays on "hold," and additional representatives asking me to repeat the entire story, I was told that all the managers were in a meeting.

"You mean they're meeting with *each other* and aren't available to talk to customers," asked I, incredulously.

"That's right," replied the rep, nonchalantly.

"Well, I'll tell you what. Let me have your executive offices."

"Why?"

"Because I'm going to speak to one of your executives, who will see how stupid this is, and who has the clout to correct it immediately."

"We don't give out that information."

"Just give me the city of your corporate office. I'll do the rest."

"We have many corporate offices."

"You only have one president! Where does he hang out?"

"I can't tell you that."

Any organization that trains its people to shield its executives—or, for that matter, which believes that internal meetings take precedence over customer problems—is not one where key players are "walking their talk." In every organization, two dynamics should always obtain:

1. Top management isn't needed to solve operational problems, because employees are empowered to resolve them at their level.
2. Irrespective of item 1, if a customer wants to talk to an executive, the customer can do that with no if's, and's, or but's about it.

I finally got through by calling back and patiently explaining that I wanted to write a complimentary letter about the excellent service I was receiving from the customer service people. The representative gave me everything but the CEO's personal physician in the next 16 seconds. "Talking the talk" is transparent, and even "walking the talk" is inadequate. Employees are asking that their leaders "walk the walk." Which leads to. . . .

Hazard #11½: Don't Believe Everything You Hear

It just might be a subordinate explaining how happy all the customers are, how well you manage, how good you look, and how beautifully you sing. Forget the radio; keep your eyes on the road.

How to Clothe the Emperors, Part 10

1. Encourage innovation, and the risk taking attendant to it. Do not reward problem solving if it merely continues fixing recurrent problems.
2. Reward results not tasks. The organization's performance as a whole should reflect the sum total of its individual performance reviews.
3. Customers are people, not gods. Educate employees to use discretion and judgment when interacting with customers. Happy customers without profit will lead to no customers at all.
4. Consciously invest time depending on urgency, subordinate development, commitment, and other required factors. Time is a controllable resource.
5. There is no "they." If something merits doing, then do it.
6. The kindest thing that can be done for some employees is to help them to leave. And that departure is always the kindest thing for the excellent performers who stay.
7. Celebrate good times, and the momentum will help you slog through bad times.
8. Training and development of people should be the last thing cut just before you close the doors for good. People are assets worth investing in.
9. Look for competence and talent in all people, and place those people in key positions as quickly as possible. No one walks in the 100-meter dash, but they don't walk in the mile either. The only "dues" worth collecting involve talent, not time.
10. Keep your money in your pocket. Help people find gratification and reward in the nature of the work itself, and then provide nonfinancial reward to as many people as possible. Share the true wealth.

Chapter 11

Forces of Light
The Five Irresistible Forces vs. the Immovable Objects

"Happiness must be beyond, or the fire will not burn as brightly as it might—the urge will not be great enough to make a great success."
— Theodore Dreiser
Jennie Gerhardt, 1911

"Many are stubborn in pursuit of the path they have chosen, few in pursuit of the goal."
— Nietzsche

Fortunately, there are trends and inescapable movements that are forcing remedial actions and prompting our emperors to reexamine their wardrobes. There is good news and there are positives, but the question remains as to whether our practices of management and our strategies will finally change to embrace tomorrow, or whether they will continue to try to perpetuate yesterday. Abraham Lincoln often emphasized what he considered the country's "last, best chance." If we don't take advantage of the opportunities being presented to us by the forces of society, economy, and technology, then we deserve what we get. And what we'll get will be described in Chapter 12.

There are many in our system who have seen the light. In a recent book about the resurgence of the U.S. automotive industry, many GM managers "realized as long as 10 years ago that GM was veering off course, but they were frozen out by hidebound bosses and peers."[1]

---

[1] Cited in *Business Week*, Oct. 10, 1994, p. 18: "When Detroit Stopped Spinning Its Wheels," by Kathleen Kerwin, reviewing *Comeback: The Fall & Rise of the American Automobile Industry*, by Paul Ingrasia and Joseph B. White (Simon & Schuster, 1984).

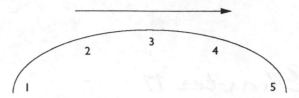

Figure 11.1. Trajectory of a fad.

There are key differences between fads and trends. Fads are short-lived and ephemeral, catching the public's fancy and then becoming common. In fact, their original cachet becomes their major liability as they quickly enter the public domain. Fads die when the question turns from "Where did you get that—I must have one" to "You mean you don't have one of these yet?" to "Are you still interested in that old stuff?"

Trends, however, are caused by socioeconomic and technological shifts. Trends are long-lived because their creation is due to an amalgam of forces that cannot be easily manipulated, directed, or forced "back into the box."

Fads are usually "things" that one buys and/or uses. Trends are movements that offer the ability to capitalize on their direction. The major problem with legitimate trends is that *they are often viewed as threats and not as opportunities by management.* Figures 11.1 above, and 11.2 (page 168) show the distinction in these cycles.

Point	Thrust	Typical Comments
1.	Opinion-makers notice	I've never seen anything like that
2.	Critical mass accepts	I've got to have one of these
3.	Badge of distinction	Have you ever seen one of these
4.	Mass possession	I had one when they weren't known yet
5.	Opinion-makers eschew	Old hat

In our society, fads have included Nehru Jackets, quadraphonic sound, pet rocks, hula hoops, hair styles, various diets and health regimens, computers "replacing books," meditation, est, and pyramid power. In management, fads have included:

- Outdoor team experiences
- Assessing personality styles
- Strategic matrices
- Shareholder value priorities
- Reengineering
- Downsizing
- Doing more with less

- Organizing around core competencies
- Outsourcing
- Peer review
- Customer-focused anything
- Empowering
- Corporate vision and mission
- Paperless office

- Quality anything
- Employee suggestion systems
- Telecommuting and teleconferencing replacing travel

Compare these fads to the trajectory in Figure 11.1. Some organizations have actually gone through all of them (and some seem to be recycling!). No matter that there may be some exceptional instances where these fads have had an impact; in most cases they are deemphasized in a year and gone in two. Management *must* accomplish the following goals if an enterprise is to be successful, fads or no fads:

1. Establish and clarify what the organization is to become
2. Organize and continually evolve to reach that goal
3. Acquire, retain, nurture, and reward the talent to reach the goal
4. Monitor the environment for opportunities and threats
5. Generate a profit that rewards the investors and supports the evolution of the business

Trends Are What You Make of Them

Trends are forces that develop both with and without our intervention. We shape technology, although we don't always appreciate what the resultant influence might be. Television was first proved feasible in the 1930s, but even when widely introduced in the 1950s few had foreseen that it would revolutionize America's leisure, creating institutions such as sitcoms and Ed Sullivan, and destroying institutions such as radio serials and Walter Winchell.

Social impact is often abetted by our educational institutions, the media, and the courts. But it is also often the result of slow-moving forces that suddenly take on immense proportions, such as immigration, value reassessments, and technological innovation.

Economic shifts are the most unpredictable. Despite claims to the contrary, they are largely uncontrolled by governmental and regulatory policy, and are often the result of societal perception and reaction. Both slumps and recoveries often take on a momentum of their own, apparently fueled only by inertia.

Figure 11.2 on the next page illustrates the trajectory of trends. Note that they are not intrinsically good or bad, short- or long-lived, large potential or small. They are forces that can be exploited and capitalized on, or feared and run from. The choice is ours.

Trends are what they seem to be: potential opportunities or potential threats, depending on one's point of view.

Trends in our society are not distinct from trends affecting our organizations, because the latter are an intrinsic part of the former. So, while fads such as Nehru jackets and quadraphonic sound had little organizational

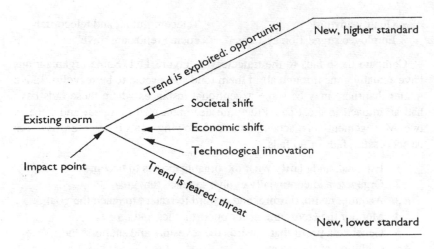

Figure 11.2. *Trajectory of trends.*

impact except for the few firms making those products, the following trends have a vast potential impact on our society and our enterprises:

- Vast information processing on an instantaneous basis
- Demographic shifts:
    aging population
    pluralistic and multicultural society
    internal population movements
    dual-income families
    increasing roles of women in business and society
- Instant global communications
- End of the Cold War, decline of ethnic clashes, rival superpowers
- Increase in modern illnesses, i.e., AIDS, stress, cancer
- Decline in unionism and collective bargaining
- Growth in community education and adult-learning options
- Growth of geopolitical markets and trading partners
- Continuing pressures on raw materials and resources

Following are the irresistible forces emerging from these trends which will provide opportunity—or threat—for the executive suite. The question is whether the "hidebound" management will win out and circle the wagons, or whether a more dynamic, confident management will embrace and exploit the trends for the betterment of the organization, its customers, its employees, and its shareholders.

Force #1: The Changing Accountability of Middle Management

Middle managers were once intended to administer people and information. The incumbents derived their power from the volume of each of these resources that they controlled. Traditional "turf" battles usually erupted over control concerns, and "body count" was the key indicator of power.

Today, everyone has access to information because of the speed, portability, miniaturization, and ease of use of technology. The personal computer has been joined by laptops, cellular phones, faxes, voice mail, and pagers, and accessibility in airplanes, cars, and briefcases. One is never out of touch.

In addition, people must work smarter, not harder. Leveraging resources is far more important than acquiring resources. Technology produces diminishing returns if, instead of doing more with fewer resources, people are forced to work harder to master the technology. So neither amounts of information nor numbers of people are paramount concerns anymore. It's rather a question of how much output can be generated with minimum input, while still providing adequate controls, personalized service where necessary, and human judgment.

Middle management will become the "high touch" of the "high tech" that Naisbitt was fond of talking about in his books about the future more than a decade ago.[2] This will require the abandonment of traditional, militaristic hierarchies and the creation or work teams in which team leaders are catalysts and facilitators, rather than controllers and managers. The problem is that middle management seldom receives the "people skills" required to lead effectively. Coaching and counseling will replace ordering and telling. Self-assessments will replace top-down reviews.

Current downsizing and layoffs at middle-management ranks have not resulted in the new organization dynamics. *Rather, we have a constant military hierarchy, but with larger spans of control*. But they are traditional hierarchies, nonetheless. Organizations cannot work smarter *unless they change both the nature of the work and the relationship of management to the performers*. Downsized organizations have usually resulted in a scaled-down version of the old one, attempting to produce larger amounts of work with fewer people, which is harder work, but not smarter work.

Figure 11.3 depicts just one form currently taking shape in some organizations. *Empowerment,* without the buzzword taint, simply means allowing performers to make the decisions that influence the outcome of their work

---

[2] For example, *Megatrends: Ten New Directions Transforming Our Lives,* by John Naisbitt (Warner Books, 1982).

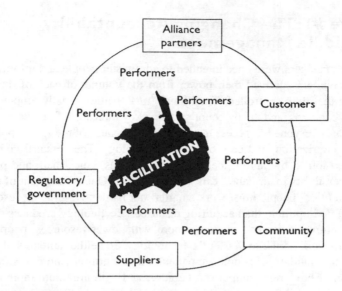

Figure 11.3. Middle management as facilitator.

with their constituencies. (This used to be called *delegation* in less-faddish times.) The facilitator helps them to do that: provides the skills needed, supplies feedback on effectiveness, resolves conflict among groups, and otherwise stays out of the way. How many of today's middle managers are adept at developing skills in others, supplying feedback and coaching, resolving conflict, and staying out of the way? Not many.

If senior management is willing to change dramatically the nature of the interactions, entrusting employees with the power to deal with their respective constituencies, and equipping managers to serve in the interstices, continually lubricating and improving the system, then the opportunities are vast for improved productivity, a restoration of the employer/employee compact (and resultant loyalty), and faster responsiveness to changing business conditions and environments. But if executives see such realignments as threatening to the traditional power sources and "silos," then we will continue to have smaller, less-efficient versions of the prior dinosaurs. (This is why, incidentally, organizations frequently hire consultants and contractors—many of whom are former employees recently laid off—in the wake of downsizing. This phenomenon isn't because of the conventional wisdom that the work is now being done without incurring fringe benefit costs and long-term commitments. It's because the nature of the work hasn't really changed, and the organization needs the same bodies that it always has needed. It's simply a human resources version of "doctoring the books.")

The old hierarchies will stand like monadnocks, eroding away in the elements as people work together in teams and collaborate on the surrounding plains.

Force #2: Vastly Different Demographics

Depending on various sources, exact dates tend to change, but the consensus is that sometime between the years 2000 and 2025, there will be no racial majority in the United States. Those termed *white* or *Caucasian* will be in the plurality but will be less than 50% of the overall population. Many people, descendants of mixed marriages, already have difficulty and resentment choosing an ethnicity or race on census forms. A high school principal in the South who banned interracial couples from the senior prom made headlines because his view was antediluvian, not because it represented the norm.[3]

While some bemoan the accent on "political correctness," the bureaucracy of the Americans with Disabilities Act, the legal hassles about which gay groups can march in which parades, the irony of Native Americans finally achieving affluence through the quintessential capitalism of big-time gambling, and even the "dress down" days that strip away business uniforms at least once a week in many organizations, the truth is inescapable: A combination of societal and demographic change, coupled with enabling legislation and key court decisions, has created very different customers, employees, suppliers, and competition.

The traditional interviewers and traditional managers in organizations have felt most comfortable hiring, selecting, promoting, nurturing, and mentoring those with whom they are most comfortable: people exactly like themselves. However, the very nature of those recruiters and managers is changing, and those who haven't changed are undergoing a shift in their paradigms. The best candidates may look nothing like them, have vastly different backgrounds, and share few of their social networks.

The "old boys network" still exists, and most studies will point out that white males earn proportionally more than nonwhite males and women in equivalent roles. But the times are changing. Look around most large organizations, and you're apt to see Asians, Hispanics, and African-Americans; women in senior positions; physically challenged people working alongside nonchallenged colleagues; homosexual workers with pictures of lovers on

---

[3] Not long after the protests arose and he was temporarily suspended, someone burned down the school. Immediately thereafter, the entire community—or at least the nonarsonists—collaborated to establish temporary facilities, and the whole episode has disappeared from the media.

their desks, sometimes with family benefits equal to heterosexual coworkers; and styles of dress that are anything but blue suits, white shirts, and wingtips.

Organizations have found, in opening their doors to this diversity, whether from true belief in its worth or from fear of government suit, that diverse peoples and viewpoints bring a practical business value to the workplace. In a time of innovation, global competition, and accelerating technologies, diversity isn't a humanitarian nicety so much as a pragmatic strategic need. There are studies being conducted at the moment which suggest that heterogeneous teams, for example, produce faster and more innovative results than do homogeneous teams.

The managers who are best able to find, embrace, and exploit these different talents will be those whose organizations best advance. Many of them will be clothed in very different outfits.

Force #3: Globalization and Strategic Thinking

Try to determine if a car is "made in America" today, and you'd better be prepared to engage in some intensive research. Your considerations will include parts that are made in Korea, Italy, Indonesia, and Mexico; whether or not Canada counts as American or North American; what percentages the government considers as determining origin; where assembly is done and who owns the assembly plant; and whether we're talking the nameplate or the actual product.

You could have a Buick that's actually quite foreign, and a Honda that's comfortably domestic. The question that matters, however, is: Does anyone really care so much any more?

There used to be a huge billboard in Connecticut, just across from the sprawling Sikorsky helicopter plant on the Merrit Parkway. The advertising was notable because it was a joint venture of local General Motors, Ford, and Chrysler dealers. Its message was, whatever you do and whatever you consider, "Buy American!" The sign always struck me as the very height of condescension and arrogance. It was Orwellian in its implicit belief that you could ask people to ignore quality, reject the best fit for their objectives, and turn away common sense, all in the name of blind faith. The billboard is gone. That kind of sentiment is going.

Even medium-sized organizations compete globally today. It's not uncommon to run into consultants who do nothing but help establish American business connections for smaller operations in the old Eastern Bloc, where such joint ventures are eagerly sought. Many U.S. Fortune 500 companies— Merck and Hewlett-Packard are good examples—derive about half their revenues and income from non-U.S. sales and operations. It's not unusual to find managers in American firms from Japan, Mexico, France, South Africa, and Australia, and to find U.S. managers in virtually every country in the world. Such is the interchange and interactions of global business and multi-national organizations.

Consequently, it's insufficient to think solely in terms of local markets, short-term goals, and extrapolations of current growth. Those are the dynamics of yesterday, when one could rely on unchanging conditions, responsiveness was key, problem solving was the critical discipline, and tactical issues were the only considerations. Since things won't change tomorrow, how can I maximize my profits today? If strategic thinking was done at all (and despite the executive retreats, business school gurus, and three-ring binders, it usually wasn't; most executive meetings almost instantly devolve into operational concerns), it was done once a year by an elite group of executives and "strategic planners," whatever they are.

Today, with constant change, varied forms of competition, international markets and customers, and an accent on service and support, all managers have to be able to think and act strategically at times, and senior managers had better spend most of their time in the "what," not the "how." The executives who survive—meaning that their organizations are not only prospering but also that their long-term prospects are compelling—will be those who share these traits:

- The ability to make rapid changes in direction
- Willingness to take risks and bear short-term Wall Street criticism
- Relationship building with the board of directors
- Leadership that clearly transmits the values of the organization
- Willingness to admit to and take the responsibility for errors
- Trust in others; managing tactically only by exception
- Subordination of ego in finding alliance partners and allies
- Strategic thinking and implementation on a daily basis

There are no objects so immovable that they can withstand the irresistible forces of global change.

Force #4: Technological Whizbang

A great deal of technology has been overly hyped. Amidst projections of a "checkless society" created from computer banking and electronic transfers, National Check Writers, the largest source of bank checks, has had banner years. The "paperless office" certainly hasn't put copy-machine-makers out of business, and a great many computers do nothing but tirelessly disgorge paper. More and more huge bookstores are opening, vast supermarkets of tomes, which leads me to believe that people are still reading the old-fashioned way.

On the other hand, as the economists are fond of saying, try to find a conventional typewriter in an office. Think about how often one says "fax it" or "FedEx™ it" during a typical workday. See how long you can go without seeing someone using a cellular phone or car phone. How many channels come across your cable box, as compared to your television of 10 years ago? How long can you travel through an airport or on a plane without seeing someone pounding the keys of a laptop?

Technology has changed our society and our businesses. While it might not be in any of our children's lifetimes that the United States will have a railroad system that will surpass, say, Burundi's, it will probably be in the next few years that we'll see dramatic new applications of our communications and information technologies. For example, in the next 5 years you will probably have access to:

- One personal phone number, that stays with you wherever you go
- Combination fax, copier, answering machine, printer, computer setups
- Video telephones on a common, cost-effective basis
- Fax capability to and from airplanes[4]
- Vast storehouses of information on an instantaneous basis
- Comprehensive computer handwriting recognition

Senior managers will have to embrace this technology and its likely advances as a primary factor in their business decisions. Those most comfortable with the technology, who have the most affinity for it, are generally not the people currently occupying the 40th-floor offices. Those most comfortable have only fairly recently entered the workforce.

Many years ago I was asked to conduct a survey of the ways in which technology was affecting Marine Midland Bank's New York City headquarters. I began with what was called the Office of the President, under the assumption that what was happening at the top would be influencing what I'd see further down. One of my early visits brought me to the elaborately appointed office of a sector (executive) vice president who, to my astonishment, had a monitor and keyboard on his credenza. It looked about as comfortable as a Lamborghini among the Amish.

"I'm impressed, John," I said, "to see a computer in your office. Are you a fan of this technology?"

"Absolutely. We have to face the fact that it's a tremendous time-saver, and we can't be afraid of it."

"Do you use it often?"

---

[4] GTE Airfone has launched a service whereby you can be called on the plane, from the ground. I tried it and, while convoluted, it works.

"Daily."

"Would you mind demonstrating how you use it?" I stood up to watch him demonstrate his expertise when, to my surprise, he began by pushing a buzzer next to the keyboard. I had never seen a computer start up from a buzzer.

Immediately after he pushed the button, the office door opened, producing his secretary, Nancy.

"Nancy, I believe you know Dr. Weiss. Would you mind demonstrating how we use the computer?"

Nancy then sat down at the credenza, and launched the programs that "we" used. John's ideas of computer literacy was having Nancy run the machine while he moved his lips.

Insurance quotes that used to take a week being calculated and approved at the home office are now produced by the sales agent via laptop and printer right in the prospect's home, greatly enhancing the ability to close the sale immediately. Auto dealers who once had to ask potential customers to envision the colors and options that weren't on the lot can now demonstrate them in optimal conditions using CD-ROM. Client service representatives who were once slaves to missing files and voluminous paperwork now display a customer's records on a screen and can immediately resolve problems during a single call.

The technological fads come and go, but the trends are unmistakable: faster service, more comprehensive support, instantaneous information, immediate satisfaction, sharper competitive edge. The senior managers who resist this force will be skewered by it.

Force #5: The Educated Customer

Customers are becoming downright ornery. They're demanding to know what things are made of, what support they'll get, the person who's in charge, and what the firm stands for. Who on earth do they think they are?

It's not difficult for a prospective auto buyer to use one of any number of services that, for a fee generally less than $50, will detail the exact cost to the dealer of any car, including the buyer's specific options. The CEO of any publicly held company and most private ones is easily found. Any charge card item can be disputed prior to payment, meaning that a shoddy piece of merchandise, undelivered service, or lousy meal may not be paid for—the ultimate buyer feedback. There is a legion of governmental agencies with departments dedicated solely to fielding consumer complaints (just a tad of irony there). And, naturally, the courts are clogged with every conceivable claim, lien, litigation, suit, and case filed by aggrieved and damaged consumers.[5]

---

[5] Two of the more bizarre incidents involved the woman who successfully sued McDonald's because its coffee was too hot, scalding her when it spilled. Note that

People at the top of organizational life have to start acting smarter if, for no other reason, to be better able to match wits with their customers. Organizations have to be ahead of the curve. All customers know what they want at the moment, but few truly understand what they need. It's up to organizations to provide evidence of need and to cater to it. That is the value-added that the best organizations bring to the fore.

The midi-skirt was resoundingly rejected, but the Walkman™ was warmly embraced. Snapple started a whole new trend in beverages, as had "designer" water before it. Range-fed chicken is not threatening Kentucky Fried.

Executives must develop the organizational abilities to determine which innovations make sense and which do not. One way to approach the issue is by using a model that segments potential customer interactions:

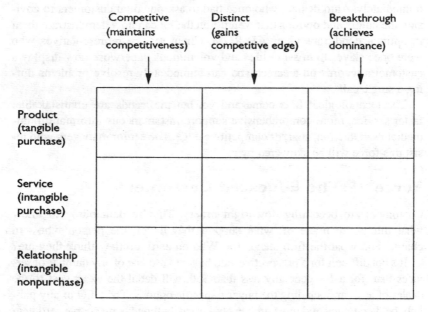

Figure 11.4. Strategic segmentation of customer interactions.

---

it spilled while precariously balanced between her legs in her son's moving sports car, but who am I to quibble with the justice system? The other case concerns two lovers, amorously engaged on an active New York City subway track—I kid you not, this is a true story—who were, surprise, run over by a train that was inexplicably using its right-of-way. They are suing the transit authority. Perhaps someone should start quibbling.

What is the profile that the company should seek and maintain to achieve its strategic goals? There are only three basic interactions with a customer: The organization provides (1) a tangible product (i.e., a car or a stove) that the customer pays for, (2) an intangible (i.e., advice or warranties) that the customer pays for, and (3) establishes a relationship (i.e., an 800 number, frequent flyer points) that the customer perceives as a benefit but not one that is purchased (even though it's built into the cost structure somewhere).

Southwest Air provides breakthrough service, while (I judge) Continental provides competitive service. Mercedes provides breakthrough product, while Buick provides competitive product. I believe that FedEx has a distinct relationship with customers, while UPS has a competitive one. But note that there are no value judgments here: The key is to meet business goals and financial plans. One can do this with strictly competitive products, services, and relationships, if there is a cogent plan to do so. Increasingly intelligent customers don't mind, for example, shopping at low-ambiance warehouses and outlets in return for rock-bottom prices. They will sacrifice service in return for fast food, and don't for a second expect the manager of a Burger King to come over and schmooze.

If senior people can create and apply the proper models and approaches to anticipate consumer needs and deliver viable fulfillment of them, they will be seen in the distinguished robes of the scholar. If they ignore these trends, and believe that they can dictate to intelligent, sophisticated consumers what they need is what's already on the shelves, they will be sent running naked through the streets.

Despite the stupidity of the past, there is the opportunity in these irresistible forces to respond with leadership, insight, and initiative. If that occurs, the organization will follow and past sins may be forgiven. But if not, the emperors will lose more than their clothes.

How to Clothe the Emperors, Part 11

1. Eschew fads.
2. Create an environment that synthesizes environmental and competitive information to identify trends.
3. Determine what emerging consumer needs will be, and generate alternatives to fulfill them, ready for launch as the need appears (or is created).
4. Create development and reward systems that encourage facilitators, catalysts, and consultants, not hierarchical control.
5. Develop coaching, counseling, and listening skills.
6. Embrace and celebrate diversity, not just in background and appearance but also in points of view and varying approaches to the work.
7. View your market as a world market.
8. Invest heavily in personal technological aids, which enhance the productivity of individual performers.
9. Create a market segmentation that is conscious and proactive, not dictated by competitors or environmental factors.
10. Empower customers. Invite them to comment, critique, and participate in some decisions. View them as interested partners, not adversaries to be overcome.

Chapter 12

Natural Selection
What Happens If We Do Nothing?

"If the misery of our poor be caused not by the laws of nature, but by our institutions, great is our sin."

—Charles Darwin
Voyage of the Beagle

"In matters of taste, swim with the current; in matters of principle, stand like a rock."

—Thomas Jefferson

What happens if even the irresistible forces of the previous chapter fail to clothe the emperors? What is our fate if they simply won't heed our advice? The weather will turn cold, and we will all freeze to death.

History, after all, is not on our side. There is great expense and effort required to eradicate stupid management. Perhaps if we simply allow things to run their course, future leaders will emerge—generations with different paradigms and values—who will improve things. Our organizations are resilient and have rebounded many times before, right? Don't take that bet.

If we do nothing, the United States will experience an increasing gap between the "haves" and "have nots." Menial jobs will grow dramatically, and sophisticated jobs, with their attendant challenge and opportunity, will stagnate and decline. We are beginning to see this even today, with hundreds of articles depicting former managers engaged in blue-collar work, and happy to have it. Or those describing university graduates with honors vying for a few fast-food jobs. It's become fashionable to point out that those who pursue degrees in philosophy, or literature, or history deserve what they get. Anyone can see that the opportunities in our society don't embrace such arcana. Yet we once were a culture that prized philosophers, respected the written word, and cherished our past.

Those who choose to put a positive spin on the decline of organizational opportunity emphasize the increasing numbers of professionals who have opted for entrepreneurship, small business, and independence in fields such as consulting, financial planning, and franchising. That positive spin is actually severe vertigo. There continue to be record levels of small business failures. Most "consultants," if you'll excuse an opinion from someone who really is one, are simply professionals in between jobs, like "actors" in between roles. They are too proud to acknowledge that they are involuntarily out of work, and too stunned to realize that calling yourself a surgeon does not mean that you can operate.

The true entrepreneurs in our society have declined to a few so precious that they make headlines, become the world's richest individuals, run for President, marry starlets, and revel in their idiosyncrasies. The pseudo-entrepreneurs are engaged in a feeding frenzy, swimming among the legions out of work and offering get-rich-quick schemes, "guaranteed" consulting leads, "unique" franchising opportunities, "immediate" lines of credit, and other nefarious deals. At least real sharks have principles: They'll eat you, but they don't deliberately torment you. And there's never been documented evidence of a great white demanding money and promising a 100-to-1 return on the investment.

What is positioned as a new independence and opportunity to be in charge of one's own destiny for displaced and poorly paid professionals is nothing other than an erosion of living standards and conditions in this country.

What follows in Part 4 is a prescription for improvement and innovation. But to guarantee that the medicine is seriously received, we're going to spend one final chapter on the repercussions of trying to live with the sickness.

Sports As a Metaphor

As I write this, in the fall of 1994, the baseball season had been canceled, and there was no World Series for only the second time in the history of the organized sport in this country. The first time was caused by criminality and avarice, as the infamous "Black Sox" accepted money to throw the games in order to retaliate against tyrannical management. This second time was caused by avarice and stupidity, as both wealthy players and wealthy owners fought to gain a larger piece of the others' pie. The players, if they were Rhodes Scholars, would cite the dynamic as *monopsony,* which is the power brought to bear by the single buyer of a resource: the owner.[1] The owners, if

---

[1] See *The Wall Street Journal,* July 5, 1994, Op-Ed page, "Poor Underpaid Millionaires," by Jack A. Chambless, for an impartial discussion of the players' perspective.

they were Rhodes Scholars, would call the situation *phantasmagorical,* since shortstops hitting .225 should be happy to be employed in the Big Leagues, never mind earn 800 large ones a year. The fans, who have been paying enough to fund Rhodes Scholars and deserve better, call it *unbelievable.*

As I write this, the National Hockey League season had not begun because of a strike. The National Football League was barely able to avoid a walkout of its officials. The National Basketball League averted a strike with a late bargaining agreement. The last time I looked, my kids' teams at Syracuse and Miami were still playing in the NCAA, but that's no lock, either.

Our society has become inured to the loss of values and the primacy of the buck. Sports were once games of diversion, which adults played for the love of it and watched for the pleasure of it. Paul Robeson didn't star in football at Rutgers because he envisioned a lucrative pro contract. Mickey Mantle didn't play center field in agonizing pain for all those years because he was in it for the money. Babe Didrickson Zaharias was not pursuing endorsements from equipment manufacturers. And high school athletes didn't view representing their school on the court, field, and track as the accelerated path to a full tuition at a college that would be proud if as many as 65% of its athletes eventually received degrees.

Stupid management began to destroy our games. They moved teams like nomads, seeking bigger returns in the short run, rather than investing for long-term loyalty and profit. They overpaid the employees who performed for the moment, preferring to focus on a few stars with box office appeal rather than building true teams that could stand the tests of turnover, injury, and time. They kept raising prices and seeking ancillary revenues from advertising and broadcasting to offset their spending and atone for a dearth of strategic thinking and consistently poor tactical decisions.

The result is an increasingly jaded public, watching professional basketball players continually break the rules by "walking" and "palming" the ball, encouraged by the coaches and ignored by the officials in the name of more "excitement" and higher scoring. Some NCAA African-American coaches demanded that college entry criteria be *lowered* so that more minority players could enter what have increasingly become professional farm teams, and decreasingly institutions of higher learning. We read of fights and threats against the officials—*among and from parents at the kids' little league games and soccer contests.*

Sports is a metaphor for our organizations. We have allowed unresponsive leadership to corrupt the games, lower the standards, plan for only the shortest term, and distort perspectives of pay and performance. Society has suffered, our values have eroded, and the standards we live by have declined.

If this can occur in what is essentially an area of recreation, what are the ramifications in the area of our economic well-being?

Rending the Fabric of Society

The dismal performance of our nonelected, often self-appointed organizational leaders has consequences far beyond the already serious concerns of the shareholders and employees. Our standards as a society are being battered by the ineptness of our organizational leadership, and our values are being undermined by the dismal performance and excuses of those enterprises.

Here are but a few examples:

1. Company loyalty is declining in the face of continued layoffs, down-sizing and cutbacks. Employees who once felt that they owed their employer the benefit of the doubt above and beyond a full day's work now seek ways to minimize their commitment. Top performers defect, not in fear for their jobs but simply because a slightly more attractive opportunity is detected. The reciprocity of trust has been lost, which means that no matter how good the employee's performance, there is no security, and no matter how well the organization treats the employee, there are no guarantees of the individual's remaining in the job. Our society reflects that diminution of trust. It's every person for himself and herself.

2. Organizations seek conformity and harmony, not diversity and candor. Senior management confuses affirmative action with multiculturalism. The former is a legislative mandate to prevent advertent discrimination. The latter is a willingness to embrace the legitimate differences of people, and the commensurate value they provide for the organization. Yet glass ceilings still exist; management judges its effectiveness in diversity merely by conducting racial and ethnic body counts; and employees are strongly encouraged to support their superiors—disharmony is frowned upon.

Similarly, our society has reverted into a kind of tribalism. The "melting pot" concept has become the pariah of metaphors. We encourage pockets of society in which English is not only unspoken, it is also unknown. We have insidiously acknowledged the hyphenated American, as though we are Balkan states attempting to form a confederation. The "Native American" appellation is reserved only for those who can claim aboriginal antecedents, although most of us are native-born Americans (and even those aboriginal ancestors came here across a land route from Asia). Attempts at rational discourse and open debate result in polarization and labels. You are Democratic or Republican, liberal or conservative, pro- or antiabortion, union or nonunion. The political arena, once the stump of orators and debaters, where Lincoln and Douglas contested the issues of the time, has been reduced to media sound bites, negative advertising, and salacious probes into intimate personal history. There is no more open debate, only harsh screams from opposing camps that seek only one outcome: their "win" at the expense of someone else's "loss."

3. Sound management, hard work, and ethical principles have been replaced with manipulation and legal remedies. Virtually every major organization, public and private, is contesting scores of lawsuits every day. General counsels are involved in business decisions, and the legal department's budget is often greater than the human resource training allocation. Insurance premiums are commensurately higher, and product innovation is much more conservative than necessary, not for lack of talent but for fear of litigation.

Our society has become one in which the lawyers enact the laws and then represent both parties in contesting them. Approximately 70% of the total of all awards in personal injury lawsuits is retained by the contingency lawyers representing the plaintiffs.[2] The response to perceived inequities, tough competition, unfair practices, and even petty annoyances isn't to work harder, turn the other cheek, or negotiate. The response is to get a lawyer. People sue when their significant other decides that marriage really doesn't make sense. They sue when their child is not selected to be the starting pitcher. They sue when their neighbors plant a hedge. They sue when they are hurt by the police who are apprehending them in the commission of a crime.

Anatole France observed long ago that "The law, in its majestic equality, forbids the rich as well as the poor to sleep under bridges, beg in the streets, and to steal bread." Legal remedies remove the need to exercise ethical principles. Lawsuits obviate the need for negotiation, compromise, and diplomacy. Legal opinions replace judgment. Legality replaces civility. Lawyers replace leaders.

De-Skilling the Labor Force

4. The focus of our enterprises has devolved to bottom-line, short-term payback. Leaders have not nurtured or developed people. They have mistaken high pay for "all stars" with the need to truly reward the qualities that provide for long-term stability and resilience. Tangential factors such as the bond market and a few Wall Street analysts, which should *react* to business decisions, have become the motive force *shaping* business decisions. Judgment has become less important than analysis. If issues can't be forced into templates, matrices, and models, they can't be dealt with at all. Don't think, just follow the operating procedures.

Our society is in the midst of trivializing education. Ironically, the country with the best institutions of higher learning in the world—and with

---

[2] Reported on the ABC television news program *The Blame Game: Are We a Country of Victims?* Oct. 26, 1994, reported by John Stossel.

greater access to higher education in the form of community colleges than is known anywhere else—is one of the poorest in its elementary and secondary educational systems. We are graduating generations of young people who cannot write a legible sentence, comprehend a paragraph containing abstract reasoning, or express themselves in more than rudimentary English. At a time when unions are diminishing in import in the private sector[3] teachers are heavily unionized and constantly in battle with local school boards.[4]

Organizations are reaping the whirlwind, in that they are forced to provide remedial training in basic English and math skills, not only at managerial levels but even for business school MBA graduates. We are de-skilling our labor force and our society concurrently. Rather than placing a premium on how to learn and how to transmit knowledge, we rely on technology to convey information and place the premium on command of facts. Consequently, we are rich in people who can analyze and poor in people who can communicate. We have an abundance of analysts and a dearth of counselors. We seek to describe the symptoms and remove the effects, rather than understand the reasons and prevent the causes. We are in the middle of two extremes: overanalysis and strict evaluation on the one side, and excursions into the occult, mystical, and metaphysical on the other. Few are standing in the midst of it all, trying to understand relationships, encourage debate, and appreciate that there are usually options.

5. We are lost in inputs and tasks, and ignore outputs and results. One report cites that 20% of executive time is spent on company politics and related internal concerns.[5] When I walk around organizations and ask people, "What's your job?" I'm likely to hear a salesperson say, "To make sales

---

[3] At this writing, Caterpillar Tractor is flourishing in the midst of a harsh strike by using office personnel, temporary workers eager to accept the $10-per-hour pay, and an increasing number of crossovers on the picket lines. The company has been well prepared for this, and parts for their equipment are being continually provided by union workers at suppliers' plants.

[4] The U.S. Bureau of Labor Statistics reports that private sector union membership continues to decline, while all gains are confined to the public sector, where it has actually increased for the first time in 14 years. Only 15.8% of the total U.S. workforce is unionized. See *HRMagazine,* Oct. 1994, p. 12: "Union Membership in U.S. Increases."

[5] Cited in *Management Review,* Sep. 1994, p. 7: "Tidbits: Time's a Wastin'."

calls," rather than "to bring in business." A receptionist often responds, "I answer the phone," rather than "I help customers." And a manager will usually say, "I provide this product or service," instead of "I develop people" or "I please customers." If you listen to idle talk at desks or in the halls, you'll hear a huge amount of comment on who received what promotion, why someone has been slighted, and how Joe is maneuvering to get Mary's people.

I once sat in the American Airlines Admirals Club at O'Hare Airport in Chicago, and observed a vice president (I spotted this on his luggage tag) from a major company call in to get his voice mail. Apparently, he was told by his assistant or secretary that another manager had not relinquished space that the VP had counted on for his staff. He then called the offender, and left a lengthy voice mail message threatening to go to "Don," whom I assumed was their mutual boss, and telling him on no uncertain terms that he was prepared to "go to the mat" over this office space. He then called his assistant's voice mail and left a verbatim, bragging description of what he had told his colleague, embroidering the commentary with observations about how important the VP's unit was to the organization and how Don would absolutely support him. The other manager was going to learn who was top dog. After that third call, he left to catch his plane.

The total time of that transaction, which began at 2:30 local time, was just over 50 minutes. Imagine—nearly an hour of company time spent on office space and who had the bigger, er, weapons, which would be exacerbated by his assistant's time, his competitor's time, more rebuttals, and, most probably, the august Don's time. My time wasn't wasted, of course, because I'm a consultant who knew that this was ripe material for a book some day. But what of this Fortune 500 organization, shooting tens of thousands of dollars of salary and time on floor space which should have been handled by someone's secretary? What if that time had been spent on clients?

Our society is no longer concerned with output; it is obsessed with input. Despite the fact that our organizations of any type only operate with 100% of their talents, and the focus of that talent is critical—the more oriented toward internal tasks and inputs, the less can be allocated toward external customers and results—we nonetheless concern ourselves with actions and not results. Figure 12.1 reiterates this dynamic.

Seven Ways in Which the Emperors Lose Their Clothes

There are seven habitual mistakes that most organizations make, all of which are caused, or at least controlled by, senior management. The decline inevitably begins at the top of the hierarchy, accelerated by a board's blind acceptance and often further misguided by consultants specially picked

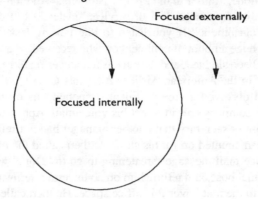

100% of the organization's
talent and energies

Focused externally

Focused internally

Figure 12.1. Talents can be applied externally or eroded internally.

because they are peddling the latest miracle cure. In 1989, Dun & Bradstreet was reporting 50,000 business failures in the United States. Three years later, the number had grown nearly 100%, to 97,000.[6] Here are the primary reasons for the massacre.

1. Multiple personalities. Ask most executives to explain, within 12 seconds, what they do and they'll quickly sputter to a stall. Few organizations have a central business concept around which all senior people can rally. The philosophy of "core competencies" is fine in the abstract, but when the reality is an organization believing it has double-digit core competencies it's like the multiple personality showing up at the therapist's office. The first question the counselor asks has to be "And whom am I speaking with today?" Is it Gloria the ballerina, Wolf the predator, or Rocky the flying squirrel?

Many senior people I talk to and observe haven't a clue as to what's propelled the organization to where it is today. Ironically, they may know what has caused some of their failures, *but they don't know what's caused their successes.* Forgetting history may cause you to repeat it, but I think that forgetting your victories causes you to lose them.

---

[6] See *Fortune,* Nov. 14, 1994, p. 52: "Why Companies Fail," by Kenneth Labich.

Daily decisions must revolve around a philosophical and pragmatic belief in what the business stands for, it's *raison d'être*—what Drucker calls its *contribution to the outside environment*. Otherwise, decisions are made independently, depending upon local issues, or turf, or the latest crisis. Sears is one of the prime examples of a company that lost its basic business concept and is still struggling to retrieve it. They could not compete with both K-Mart and Bergdorf's. Kodak moved away from its photography and film concept and strolled into pharmaceuticals and health products. During the stroll, it got mugged. Japanese automakers nearly engineered themselves right out of the U.S. market by inadvertently adopting a Mercedes mentality: They would incorporate every bit of technological whizbang into the vehicle that was possible, simply because they knew how to do it. To charge for all that technology, however, created a price range that quickly alienated their prime customers.

2. Lack of an exercise regimen. Most organizations do relatively little for their best people. Instead, they spend inordinate amounts on remedial training, re-skilling, probationary periods, and other efforts designed to raise a .220 hitter to .230. They should be spending that time, money, and effort trying to raise their existing .315 hitters to .320, since the payoff is so much better.[7]

Succession planning systems are seldom more than hastily thrown-together "depth charts" (I call them "depth charges") that indicate who could move into a position if the incumbent were hit by a beer truck tomorrow. But they don't provide means of developing those candidates, seldom provide increased responsibilities or challenges to test their mettle, and are usually ignored when the beer truck does occasionally strike someone. While organizations usually do a decent job of identifying and even compensating their higher performers, they virtually never do anything to maximize their development.

GE is a wonderful exception to this rule. They have so many talented people that they can regularly lose senior executives (i.e., the previously cited Lawrence Bossidy moving over to become a superb CEO of Allied Signal) and easily fill in behind them. This is no accident. Development of top people is a priority of Jack Welch, and he walks his talk: We've noted

---

[7] A little-noted fact in the midst of layoffs and downsizings is that organizations continue to support systems designed to support the poor performers. While people are thrown out the door daily in restructuring efforts, there are seldom efficient processes to methodically eliminate the poor performers.

above some of the intensive education GE provides for its management. In addition, it's a normal course of action for senior managers to be rotated among businesses and around the world, so that both the nature of the business and nature of the cultures vary. Someone from GE Capital might find herself or himself general manager of the locomotive operation, and staff from California might find themselves en route to Hong Kong. (My informal observations also note that most of the key managers assigned overseas are in their 40s, at the most. They are being developed and tested for more senior positions in which they'll be able to serve for many years.)

The Dodgers, once upon a time, invested huge amounts of money in their farm clubs, the minor league teams that fed players to the majors. It paid off in years of highly competitive teams with their share of championships. They also were the first team to integrate the roster, and have emphasized diversity at all levels ever since. Truly enlightened leadership created a model in which the best were sought out, developed, and given an opportunity to be stars. That's the kind of physical and mental regimen required to develop consistently winning teams. When was the last time the Red Sox won the series?

3. Power failure. Many organizations are stumbling around blindly in the dark. They have their strategies and their plans, and they can throw around terms such as *environmental scan* and *competitive analyses.* But the truth is that they think they know what to expect, and that is exactly what they are preparing for. *What derails companies are those things they are not prepared for.*

Is it reasonable that tobacco firms should have foreseen the changes coming in the perceptions about smoking? The stereotypical example in every case study is the Big Three automakers' blindness to the ramifications of fuel shortages and economic downturn, coupled with the Japanese initiatives.

But how does one prepare for the unexpected? How can one know the unknowable? Aren't there limits to anticipate disaster?

While it may be impossible to predict every content change that can afflict you, it's not that difficult to isolate the *process* areas that can do you in if signal changes occur. For example, every company I can think of should be carefully monitoring technology and assuming worse-case scenarios. We've noted that our language today is replete with "fax it," "cellular phone," "FedEx™," and "on-line." Today's laptop computer has changed many businesses. The question is: How will tomorrow's pocket computer (personal digital assistant?) change the business? Will video stores collapse under the options offered by interactive television? Several of my colleagues order contact lenses through the mail, which cost $100 for a 12-month supply that can be worn for 2 weeks, after which they're thrown out.

Besides technology, there are regulatory changes (Americans with Disabilities Act, Clean Air Act), demographic shifts (repopulation of the cities, Hispanic population growing to become the largest minority), changing geopolitical realities (Republicans taking over both houses of Congress, end of ethnic conflicts in Ireland), and similar process changes that must be monitored. No change can be dismissed as "not relevant to us." Every change is relevant, if management only removes the blinders, turns on the lights, and examines them for their ramifications.

4. Balkanization. Many of my clients can simultaneously report contradictory cultural events. Survey and focus group feedback will concurrently claim that the company is accommodating to diversity and hostile to diversity, decentralized in decision making and highly centralized in decision making, customer focused and not customer focused. One of the reasons for these contradictions is that the modern organization is allowed to become a set of microclimates—a set of countries that are rapidly abandoning diplomatic recognition of each other.

Specialties and "silos" create small cultures that begin to take on a life of their own. Within those cultures, there *are* differences in the perceptions of the organization. Local leadership becomes the equivalent of the benevolent dictator. Test this for yourself, but I've found many organizations in which benefits, perquisites, and even performance evaluation change according to these local interpretations. Some units have flex time while others don't; some allow employees to take a holiday on Martin Luther King Day and others don't; some sponsor holiday parties, others forbid them; some use a forced distribution for performance evaluation, and others measure performance against personal goals, period.

These deviations do not represent diversity, but rather discrimination. They tend to pit "us" against "them" and foster animosity toward either coworkers or one's own management. And, as in real Balkanization, the cause is poor leadership, and the result can lead to destruction.

I can't count the times I've encountered a field force that believes it has two battles to wage every day. The first is selling the customer; the second is selling the home office. The leader of this battle is the sales vice president, who sees the role not as one of being a member of the senior management team but as one of leading the sales force and protecting them against the evil forces of headquarters. At a major health products organization, the field force leaders told me that the home office was "without a clue" as to what it was like to try to please the customer. The leaders of the support functions told me that "it's a constant battle to try to support people who promise the customer something that doesn't yet exist to be delivered in an unmeetable time frame."

Leadership is about vision, but not in Fleet Bank's executive retreat at the Breakers for $600 per person a day. It's about *communicating* and *relating* that vision to the people who have to attain it. It's about melding a work force that has common objectives and common support for each other. Many organizations fail because they are torn apart from within.

5. Greed. I remember the speculation in land in California in the '70s and early '80s. I knew people who did nothing but buy and sell homes. (The problem was that they were also employed by an organization that believed they were working for it at the time.) Their downfall wasn't their speculation. Their downfall was that they believed the spiral would never stop.

Organizations fall into dire debt problems because they can't resist buying and selling one more house in a market that appears to be headed upward forever. Someone shows up to inform a seduced management team that their stellar abilities, the organization's positioning, and the market conditions are perfect for additional leveraging. Buy another operation (don't worry about the business concept), build a new plant, launch a new promotion, or, better still, restructure: The cash is magically there to alleviate the mundane albeit profitable conditions to which we've previously been subjected.

Just as the regulators descended on the thrifts in the late '80s and informed them that their real estate portfolio was worth exactly 50% of what it was worth 24 hours earlier—and, by the way, that puts them in default on capital reserve requirements, so we'll be here on Monday to take the place over—many organizations found that their forays into leveraged positions caused their bankers to reassess credit risk downward. A related aspect of this plunge is overpaying for acquisitions even when the money is solidly backed. There seems to be an "acquisition itch" that affects management which can't be scratched without buying something, usually something quite expensive.

In changing times, financial reserves, fiduciary prudence, and fiscal independence are invaluable assets, worth much more than a new facility or additional subsidiary. The failure of executives to resist the temptation of enlarging their company—and their own egos—at the expense of shareholders' long-term best interests is a prime contributor to organizational decline.

6. You can't get rich but you can't get fired. I was walking through a truly desultory operation in which I thought I spotted spiders stringing webs to people sitting at desks. "It's tough to get through the day," said my guide, "the place is such a bore." So why in heaven's name would anyone stay here? "You can't get rich," he admitted, "but you can't get fired. It's absolutely safe."

You might as well work for the government.

Our organizations become mired in "what has always worked." Complacency seems to be in direct correlation to size, not because the small are nimble and can change faster but because the large are arrogant and don't listen. After all, large organizations generally have far more resources for change than do small ones. They can absorb mistakes more easily, and invest in change more heavily. But they often don't, because they're trapped by past successes no less than the insects that will visit the webs of those spiders in Desultory, Inc.

Some of the huge winners of the past—GM, IBM, DEC—became seduced by their own successes. This is roughly akin to looking in the mirror, becoming overwhelmed by your good looks, and canceling your date because the other person can't possibly be as much fun to be with as you are. So let's stay home, because we've got all we need right here.

IBM wouldn't abandon the egomaniacal focus on mainframes simply because it was so adept at making and marketing them. DEC's Ken Olsen was a leader in the field, but stayed too long at the dance and was his own partner. He never stepped on his own feet, but neither did he learn any new steps. Roger Smith is one of the great organizational horror stories of all time, creating a bureaucracy whose seeming purpose in life was to thwart the very fine GM managers who had valid suggestions about desperately needed change. It is no accident that Akers, Olsen and Smith's replacement, Stemple, were all tossed out by their respective boards. They were placing the very survival of these huge enterprises in dire jeopardy.[8] The recovery of other giants, such as Sears, has taken much longer than necessary because this CEO jettisoning *wasn't* done.

In virtually every case like this, in which past arrogance overwhelms future needs, the only escape is with a new captain. In the examples we've used throughout the book thus far, from Apple to Kodak to IBM, the only antidote for arrogance is a firing squad.

7. The tail-fin factor. Incredibly, in an age of *customer*-driven, *customer*-focused, *customer*-led, and *customer*-ad nausea characteristics, many organizations continue to ignore the customer. The attitude is quite simple: If I tell you a tail fin is good for you, then a tail fin is good for you. There doesn't have to be any other rationale.

Not far from where I live resides an old-line family business called Cross Pen. The owners, with no small irony, are the Boss family. At one time not so long ago, a Cross Pen was considered *de rigueur* for the smart executive, college graduation present, or speech honorarium. The company made money hand over fist, and the two Boss brothers were seen by local society as one smart pair of executives.

---

[8] I cite Smith as such a disaster precisely because he escaped his own sinking ship and retired with full panoply, while Stemple took the hit for what were unequivocally Smith's screwups. Picture a naval tradition in which the crew makes sure that the captain is safe before looking to their own well-being.

Then some funny things happened. Cross quality began to dip. Although legendary for a lifetime guarantee and for taking back any damaged instrument—the hagiography is replete with people who ran over their pens with lawn mowers and returned them for a no-questions-asked replacement—Cross began *producing* damaged instruments. Their "very fine" point declined to a scratching, harsh implement which, when returned, brought another scratching, harsh instrument. My retailer advised me to got the medium point because "the very fine point they're now making is impossible to write with." It seemed to me that this was not a minor drawback for a pen manufacturer.

Then came the public's acceptance of a "fatter" pen, far removed from Cross's traditional, slim instrument. Enter Mont Blanc. Where Cross was considered expensive at $30 or $40, Mont Blanc was obscene at well over $100. But the latter seized the prestige pen market. The obese Mont Blancs have taken huge market share from Cross, which, in 1994, had to forego a dividend for the first time in its history. People are bemoaning the harsh twists of fate that befell the Boss family. However, there are at least two people the brothers can blame.

Understanding the customer is more than providing a reply card in each product package. One of our clients asked us to conduct a survey of customers who had left over the prior year. Was it more difficult and harder to execute? Absolutely. But the information was far more valuable than the traditional smile sheets from the current customers, who are usually rewarding their own sagacity, not the organization's, for buying a product they wanted at the moment. Tracking customers who are unhappy—who leave you—is an excellent tool to stay abreast of the market.

We can't sit back and allow natural forces to alleviate poor management practices. That's like saying that the next tornado should sweep away the wreckage from the last hurricane. It's time we started learning something and applying what we've learned. We don't have to build our houses in the path of every storm that comes up the coast, and we don't have to create organizations doomed to failure.

How to Clothe the Emperors, Part 12

1. Invest in star performers, even if it's at the expense of mediocre performers.
2. Provide a vision that transcends organizational microcultures and outposts.
3. Focus on and reward output, not input. Zealously crack down on activities that consume time for internal politics, turf battles, and internecine warfare.
4. Create, refine, articulate, and communicate a business concept that serves as a template for both strategic and tactical decision making. Define the business you are in and what it provides to the outside world.
5. If you've anticipated all that you think might happen to you, you've only just begun. Assign top talent to analyze the processes that might change, for better or for worse, and how you can mitigate or exploit them.
6. Avoid grabbing money for its own sake. Ensure that indebtedness does not threaten independence, risk taking, and creditworthiness.
7. Stop admiring yourself in the mirror. Find out what will cause your future success, and don't base plans on the causes of past success.
8. Find out what former customers and potential customers want, not just current customers. Why are people leaving you, and why are potential customers not buying from you?
9. Learn from the lessons of the giants who failed or stumbled. What approaches and processes did they fall victim to that you can eliminate or avoid? Are you inadvertently duplicating their weaknesses?
10. Do not be content with what customers want. Determine what they will need, demonstrate to them that need, and then fill it before the competition does.

Part Four

Prescription

" 'He has nothing on!' shouted everybody in the end. And the emperor
cringed inside himself, for it seemed to
him that they were right...."

Chapter 13

Educating
Nine Ways to Prevent Stupid Management

"Whatever resolves uncertainty is information. Power will accrue to the man who can handle information."

—R. Buckminster Fuller

"There are two equally dangerous extremes: to shut reason out and to let nothing else in."

—Blaise Pascal

The most effective cure for our dilemma is to prevent its occurrence. Our society and economy require a concordance between business and education. We have too often provided education in what the educators believe to be necessary, and too seldom in what our experience dictates is mandatory. If you don't believe that, simply consider the budgets for remedial training in corporate America, which often includes such skills as basic writing and grammar for college graduates.[1]

Architectural students in the better schools in this country often call their curriculum *architorture*. When the campus is dark and sleeping, there are usually lights to be found in the school of architecture. All-night sessions are known as *cherette* in the profession. Yet these students—who know everything about design that the schools can cram home in 5 years—are graduated with virtually no knowledge of business. They expect to go to work as a designer for

---

[1] According to the American Society for Training and Development in Alexandria, Virginia, the 1993 total budget for training in American private-sector organizations was approximately $32 billion.

197

one of the major firms, or to set up an independent practice and design in their atelier.

What they find, however, is a world in which there are more architects than there is demand for architecture. (During one of our projects, an architect in Duluth told me that the problem with the profession was simple: Stop any four people on a Duluth street, and three will be architects!) Consequently, the graduates will most probably take menial jobs in large or midsize firms and won't really design a thing for several years.

What's worse, among those who are successful in at least establishing their own businesses, there are paltry wages and long hours. When I found many architects taking on clients *at a loss* because they wanted so badly to design a particular project, I asked how in the world such a strategy can keep them in business in the long run. They usually reply, in all seriousness, "volume."

When I interviewed a success story, Art Gensler, founder and CEO of the hugely successful Gensler and Associates in San Francisco, and asked what his experiences have taught him about success in the profession, he replied immediately:

> This is a business. It happens to be a business whose technology is architecture, but it is a business nonetheless, and must be run that way. Look around. I have business people around me, business people on my board, and intimate involvement with other businesses. Just because architecture is an art form doesn't mean that it doesn't require business acumen.

Learning How to Learn

There are four basic requisites for success in any profession or occupation. Having observed thousands of business people in hundreds of environments over the past 20 years, I've tried to distinguish those who truly stand out from the legions of also-rans despite environment, despite content areas, despite organizational culture. That is, all things being equal, what accounts for excellence whether one is in an environment that stimulates achievement or one that is indifferent or antithetical to achievement? My analysis indicates that four qualities emerge every time. If an individual has three of the four, his or her chances for success are very strong. If all four are present, success is virtually assured.

Requisite #1: The ability to read with comprehension. Most people have difficulty comprehending what they read, whether it be a newspaper story, novel, biography, office memo, or set of directions. Pop psychology has entered the picture here, suggesting that some of us are "left-brained," and therefore highly analytic and sequential, or "right-brained," making us highly creative and nonlinear. (When I took one of these instruments, I emerged as "double dominant," meaning that I can use both hemispheres equally well. I asked the guru, who has built a name for himself with this stuff, what I should do with that attribute. "Use it," he said, and moved on to the next seeker of feedback.)

The claims of the pseudo-psychologists is that poor comprehension isn't our fault—it's biological or chemical or genetic—but it's nothing that can't be improved by focusing on how we take in information. To develop one's "right brain," it's suggested that one take up sculpting; to more easily read notes, it's suggested that we "mind-map" rather than write conventionally.

Take the anodyne of your choice, but I think the problem is that most of us are seldom taught to read critically. We understand the phonetics, perhaps, and may even comprehend the grammar, but we don't know how to "read between the lines." We're not seeking the author's intent, don't understand the tone, can't find the subtlety. We're not patient enough to read all of the author's statements, not disciplined enough to look at the totality, and not analytic enough to interpret the message. Those who have not actually read Shakespeare interpret Dick Butcher's famous quote—about "The first thing we do, let's kill all the lawyers"[2]—as an anti-attorney diatribe (and it's usually cited that way by those who know only the quote and have never read the context). Actually, Butcher was speaking in defense of lawyers. On the math side, few nonaccounting types are ever taught how to read a balance sheet, a profit-and-loss statement, or a budget.

The advent of the computer has made access to data easier, but it hasn't eased the need to create useful information. Only information, properly applied, can lead to knowledge, and only through the experience of applied knowledge do we begin to accumulate wisdom. We have a great deal of data but precious little wisdom in our organizations.

We must learn to comprehend what we read, whether it be in a book, in a memo, or on a computer screen. The vehicle delivering the material is irrelevant, because the common computer that is supposed to be processing it all is between our ears.

Requisite #2: The ability to write with expression. I am generally impressed with people who can fly airplanes, perform surgery, make a 20-foot jump shot, and repair an electrical outlet without getting singed. Yet I find that the real show-stopper occurs when someone finds out that I've written a book.

"You wrote a *book?!*"

"Well, actually I've written five."

---

[2] *Henry VI*, part II.

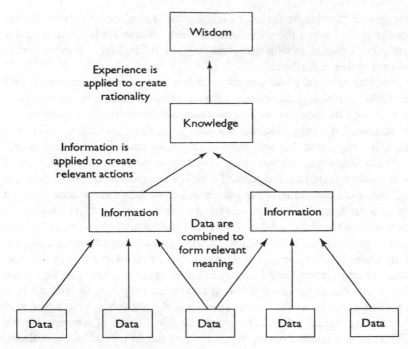

Figure 13.1. Creating wisdom.

"Five *books?!*"

"Yes."

"How did you do that?"

"On a computer keyboard."

"No—I mean how did you do that? I can't even write an office memo. . . . "

And, trust me, that person can't write an office memo. Writing has become a lost art. Just try to sort through the turgid, tendentious prose found in most offices. We don't express ourselves terribly well to our colleagues, customers, or suppliers. Here's an example:

"On Tuesday, the fifth of November, it is our intent for the senior management team of finance and the senior management team of marketing to convene for the purposes of clarifying fiscal accountabilities for the fiscal period ending December 31, 1996. The output of such a meeting should be directed to me immediately following for review and approval, along with any pertinent assumptions, graphs, charts, exhibits, or other documentation. This is a top-priority item for budgetary purposes, and I expect no other priorities to interfere with your meeting this directive."

Translation:

Next Tuesday the director of marketing and director of finance should conduct a meeting to determine next year's budget. Send the complete projection to me for approval by the next day.

The general manager of the Cincinnati Westin Hotel recently sent me a very kind, personal letter to encourage me to make her property my hotel of choice in that city. I was impressed at her taking the time to write me. I was less impressed by the fact that there were two egregious grammatical errors in the letter, which meant that her secretary, her computer spelling and grammar checker, and her own review of the letter before signing all failed to detect the problems (e.g, *percieved* for *perceived*). I'm hoping they're more attentive to their fire evacuation procedures.

Basic writing skills are not being conveyed well at any educational level and, what's worse, aren't being demanded. There was a time when college exams received two grades, one for how well the questions were answered, and one for how well *those answers were written*. Today, professors complain to me that they have to struggle with nearly unintelligible language in order to determine if the student answered the question. My response is that if you have to struggle, they didn't answer the question.

Here's a sure test for a poor writer: In American usage, a period and a comma always are placed inside quotation marks, despite the "rationale" of the sentence. A colon or semicolon is always placed outside. Question marks and exclamation points can go either way, depending on context. Poor writers invariably break these rules (and some even argue with the style books once they're shown the light).

"The comma always goes inside," he said.
"The period always goes inside, like this."
The article was "Making It Work"; it's by a local author.
"Was it always like this?" she asked.
Can it be that it was always "like this"?

We have to teach people to write with expression, clarity, and gusto. Ineffective writing, and the time needed to clarify and try to understand the intent of the writer, whether salesperson or CEO, consumes inordinate amounts of organizational time and energy. The converse speeds things along nicely. I remember one policyholder writing to me early in my career at Prudential Insurance. She opened her letter with, "I am writing to reiterate my discontent." I resolved her problem quickly.

Requisite #3: The ability to speak with persuasion. The last time I looked, public speaking was considered a graver threat by most people than a visit by the IRS. At least this is an egalitarian affliction, striking equally at all levels of the organization. There is, in fact, a booming business in "presentation skills" programs, which are designed to assist people in standing and speaking in front of colleagues without revisiting their last meal.

The language has been mangled, aided, and abetted by those whose philosophy is: "If it's in common use, then it's sanctioned." The "modern" dictionaries have capitulated to this trendiness and political correctness, apparently believing that it's easier to lower standards than to attempt to enforce them. Some of the worst offenses—committed by news anchors, public speakers, talk show hosts, and, generally, people who should know better—are:

- *Often* pronounced with a hard *t*. Sorry, the *t* is silent. The word is pronounced "off-in."
- "Between he and I" as an affected attempt at high tone. *Between* is a preposition that takes the objective case, which makes any such construction into "between him and me," "between you and me," "between you and them," etc.
- The confusion between *infer* and *imply*. A speaker implies, a listener infers. The former is active, the latter is passive. "Do I infer from your statement that you intend to cut the budget?" "You shouldn't. I meant to imply that the budget would be scrutinized carefully prior to such a decision." Many dictionaries are now letting this go either way. Those dictionaries are wrong.
- "Between the four of us. . . . " Here we encounter *between* again, but incorrectly so. Something can only be between two people. When there's more than two, then it's "among the four of us. . . . "

Our public (and even private) schools seldom provide courses in presentation skills. Yet many recommendations in business are accepted or rejected *not* on the basis of content and rationale but on the bases of the presentation and form used to present them. Sizzle is as important as steak in many contexts. The ability to make points or to rebut objections using compelling and captivating language is an invaluable talent. It is neither genetic nor situational. It is a pragmatic skill that can be learned and mastered and which, ironically, one gets better or worse at, respectively, the more times good habits or bad habits are employed. I've seen people speak who have been consistently bad for 10 years, because they keep repeating the same errors and bad habits to the extent that they've become "adept" at them.

One of the reasons that meetings invariably chew up so much time and productivity within organizational life is that very few people attending them—much less presenting at them—can communicate effectively. They simply don't have the tools of the language. The pity is that the tools are available to everyone, but most choose not to carry them around.

Requisite #4: The ability to listen with discernment. One of the great double whammies of life is that most of us don't listen well because we are too busy trying to speak incorrectly.

Active listening—or what we psychological types call reflective listening—is the act of becoming involved in a conversation from the recipient's standpoint. It means the following:

- Periodically summarizing the speaker's statements, such as, "In other words, you're saying that the competition has not taken our lost market share."
- Periodically paraphrasing the speaker's points, such as (Speaker) "No one has yet entered that market successfully." (Listener) "So that market is a prime opportunity at the moment."
- Indicating verbally and nonverbally that you are tracking the speaker, using head nods, hand gestures, and sounds such as "uh huh," or words such as, "yes" and "I see."
- Maintaining eye contact and refraining from nervous habits, such as tapping the table or doodling.
- Reacting appropriately and in context, by laughing or smiling at humor, showing concern over gravity, displaying surprise, etc.
- Subordinating ego to the extent that your own points can wait until the speaker is finished, no matter how reinforcing or contradicting they may be.

People tend not to listen well for the same reason they tend not to read well. They don't exhibit the patience and discipline necessary to comprehend what is actually being communicated. We are so eager to speak, to make our points, to exercise our egos, that we listen at only about 30% of our potential to do so.

We need to listen to the customer, the vendor, our colleagues, our subordinates, and our boss as though they all had something to say that was important. We often assume that what the boss says is important, without really listening, and assume that our subordinates have nothing to offer, without really listening. The result is that we implement policies that we can't understand, and ignore advice that could save us a great deal of trouble.

Remember Sherlock Holmes's fabulous observation? He had heard the *absence* of dogs barking. Now that's listening.

The Gladiator Mentality

The organizations that have emerged in the late 20th century, despite the aphorisms du jour about team work, servant leadership, and customer focus, are largely arenas of competition. If you dig below the surface—you'll need a toothpick, not a shovel—you find intense personal rivalries and decisions often based more on personal aggrandizement than organizational profit.

This shouldn't be surprising to anyone, due to these factors:

- The trend in the '80s to create heroes of sole contributors, best exemplified in the investment community, where traders made tens of millions and were glorified in the press for their greed[3] (Michael Milken, whom many still believe did the country a huge favor by exploiting "junk bonds") or their perspicacity (Elaine Garzarelli, whom no one ever heard of until she skillfully or luckily anticipated the stock crash several years ago).[4] For those of you who follow *The Wall Street Journal* regularly, you're familiar with the fact that random groups of "expert" traders have their hands full trying to outperform stocks chosen by darts randomly striking a dart board.
- The continual publication of huge salary, bonus, and stock option compensation to top executives, often in the face of—or actually because of—pay freezes and staff reductions affecting the rest of the company.
- Performance systems that, despite protestations to the contrary, mainly reward individual contribution rather than team contribution or corporate profitability. This is particularly true in the sales area, but it's also common throughout the organization for middle managers and above. One of my clients had a plan in place that rewarded the senior management team with an incentive pool of $900,000 for *missing* the annual plan by 10%.
- The massive layoffs and downsizings cited in earlier chapters have compelled the survivors (read: potential targets) to solidify their personal situations as best they can. Whether this means digging a fox hole and disappearing, or mounting a steed and visibly leading a bold product innovation, the result is the same. There is little time and less inclination to help colleagues, and major risk in seeing one's contribution diluted over a groups' involvement. Either I will remain a "hidden" outpost, emerging only to cash my check, or I will portray myself as the bold innovator, oblivious to the timid souls around me.

---

[3] Tom Wolfe's *Bonfire of the Vanities* (Farrar, Strauss & Giroux: 1987) was the best popularization of this phenomenon.

[4] Perhaps a small sign of the times is that she was fired from her long-time firm in Nov. 1994 for being too expensive an asset in a time of cutbacks. But what do you think this instills in the remaining traders: team work or self-preservation?

- Virtually all human development going on in organizations is in individual skills building. The "team work" that's going on is often peripheral or irrelevant, concerned with rappelling down mountains or trodding hot coals (no doubt useful if one is escaping a forest fire, but of less import if one is competing for market share). The "self-directed team" phenomenon we see publicized occasionally is of note precisely because it is written up occasionally. It is a relatively rare, often short-lived intervention that has yet to produce any documentation proving that it is either self-perpetuating beyond a senior manager's support or applicable to diverse organizations.
- The mantra of the '90s, "Do more with less," has been reified in many organizations. The result is that people work much harder, not at all smarter, and are so overwhelmed that there is little opportunity and less incentive to cooperate and collaborate. The old factory "piece-work" systems have come to modern management. How much can you get done today? That is your worth to me. The fact that you've helped someone else, trained an employee, engaged in planning, or just thought about the business is immaterial. How much more, quantitatively, have you done, and how much more are you capable of doing? Within this absurd philosophical construct, the ideal organization will eventually have one person doing everything. Welcome back to subsistence farming.

The result of these factors is that hostile workers are destroying organizations from within, with constant gunfights on main street at high noon, and with snipers popping from the rooftops.

At the old Eastern Airlines, one of the worst cases of management/labor conflict in the latter part of this century, employees were alienated and disenfranchised. Management often tried to pit mechanics against flight attendants and pilots against everyone. In turn, there were continual physical threats against management and the operation. At many organizations I enter today, there are tight security procedures that must be negotiated in order to reach the executive floor, and it's not unusual to find bullet proof glass and armed guards. Many CEOs are chauffeured by trained, antiterrorist personnel licensed to carry firearms.

We've noted that, at Caterpillar Tractor, a bitter strike by the once omnipotent Auto Workers Union has resulted in *increased* profitability for the company, largely through the hiring of nonunion personnel quickly trained (it's my survival against theirs) and office workers reassigned to plant work (do more with less). As for union unity and teamwork, Caterpillar is receiving an undisrupted supply of parts from vendors' plants staffed by—guess who?—union workers. Twenty years ago, under similar conditions, everyone would have walked out in sympathy. Ten years ago, Caterpillar would have suspended manufacturing. Today, it's running at a more profitable pace. Tomorrow it may be using these tactics as normal operating procedures.

Erosion as Deadly as Corrosion

The cowboy mentality and gunfights are obvious, but the *lack* of support and *lack* of commitment can tear a company apart just as easily. Erosion is as deadly as corrosion.

The best of the reengineering efforts, team-centered work, and organization renewal initiatives are often undercut by senior management for the sake of improving short-term profitability, which, of course, inflates current bonuses. One of my clients received a commitment from its huge parent company that it could reengineer the business—which everyone deemed a strategic necessity after 4 consecutive years of zero growth in a highly competitive market—and that the investment in so doing would include a $1-million stake and tolerance for a decline in profit during the reengineering year. That agreement was reached during the October planning cycle for the following calendar year. By the end of November, the parent was stipulating that profit had to at least equal the prior year. And by December, the divisional president, in a complete reversal of his commitment, was making it clear that the word from his superiors was to "be on plan by June, or else."

I have never seen a major structural renewal effort succeed concomitantly with pressure to reach a growth plan. This executive greed creates intense resentment at the employee level, which does not go unrequited.

We have cited Digital Equipment earlier as an example of a hugely successful organization that dismally failed, entirely due to executive malpractice. In 1990 it was #27 among the Fortune 500, with a stock price of $199. Its recent stock price is $28. When DEC realized—much too late—that it had missed the boat on workstations, it frantically reengineered, but only according to the gospel of its then-CEO, Ken Olsen. The result was a disaster that still plagues the business, long after his forced departure. Its current plans include a quarterly loss of $1.75 *billion,* a layoff of 20,000 employees, and the sale of its headquarters buildings.[5] What kind of teamwork and loyalty does this inspire? Perhaps enough to guarantee that employees won't spend more than 75% of their time seeking other employment, or agreeing not to cart away anything more than two of them can lift.

---

[5] All statistics from *Fortune,* Nov. 14, 1994, p. 68: "Why Companies Fail," by Kenneth Labich.

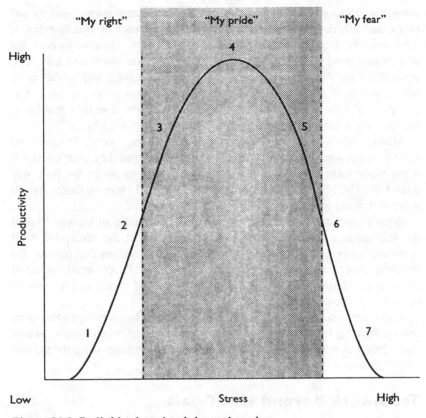

Figure 13.2. Individual productivity and anxiety.

In Figure 13.2, we repeat the normal bell curve distribution based on the effects of stress on productivity.[6] At the low end, employees see their jobs as entitlements that don't require any extra input or investment. In the middle, the stress level is appropriate to generate the adrenaline required to produce enthusiasm, risk-taking, and innovation. At the high end, people are paralyzed with fear for their basic security and are frozen into inaction.

In many American organizations, poor management belatedly awoke to the lousy results of its own inept strategies and found employees lazing about the low end of the curve. This was hardly a conceptual breakthrough,

---

[6] Adapted from work done by Judith M. Bardwick. See *Danger in the Comfort Zone: From Boardroom to Mailroom—How to Break the Entitlement Habit That's Killing American Business,* Amacom: 1991.

since those same employees saw their management reaping entitlements and perks, and felt that the least they could do for themselves was to relax in their own jobs. Now, however, in the face of a threat to executive income, senior management decided to downsize, reengineer, do more with less, and, generally, scare the hell out of people. A few mass layoffs will do this quite nicely. The result is that those folks hanging out at position #1 were driven at the speed of light to position #7—no more productive than they had been, but for quite a different reason: They were now scared speechless.

Management's reaction was that these employees were obviously no good to begin with (who on earth had hired them?) since they didn't perform when times were flush, and they weren't performing when the heat was turned up. The obvious answer: Let's get rid of still more of them, and do more with those who are left.

What's needed to break these vicious cycles is intelligent leadership with the realization that people perform best and support the enterprise most when they have manageable stress, pressure, and deadlines that provide for the right amount of dynamic tension in the operation. People need a sense of urgency, not desperation; a sense of importance, not panic; and a sense of control over stress, not helplessness.

Corrosion occurs when everyone is motivated to be an independent mercenary, fighting for personal fiefdoms. Erosion occurs when people quietly and subtly, but with no less deleterious effects, cease supporting the organization's goals and policies.

Teamwork Beyond Hot Coals

Prevention is always cheaper than cure, especially in management, where condign punishments prevail. Here's how to avoid another generation of stupid management from taking root.

1. Every business curriculum, at undergraduate and graduate levels, must include skill sets that go beyond reading the balance sheets. These should include:

- Coaching and counseling
- Problem solving and decision making on performance issues
- Implementing and ensuring positive change
- Communications skills and interpersonal relations
- Negotiating
- Resolving conflict
- Interviewing and recruiting
- Managing and developing diverse people

2. Every supervisory and managerial position should have a minimum of one-quarter of its success evaluated on people development. In other words,

I am rewarded based on my people's performance. (Imagine what would happen if teachers and professors were evaluated based on objective student performance?)

3. A 360-degree feedback and evaluation process is implemented, whereby managers receive feedback from subordinates, peers, customers, suppliers, and superiors. That feedback is used both as the basis for personal growth and as an input into the evaluation of performance.

4. Periodically, perhaps quarterly, managers spend a day interacting with customers in focus groups, mutual problem-solving sessions, and/or on-site visits. The same activity is performed with vendors.

5. Performance evaluations become disciplined, strict procedures, in which top performers are identified for more challenging developmental experiences, and weak performers are identified for improvement plans. If not successful in meeting those plans, the latter are terminated—no matter what their level, position, or tenure—as a normal course of improving the business.

6. Except for those performance-related causes, no layoffs are permitted without the approval of the board of directors, and under no circumstances can any manager benefit financially from any compensation plan affected by layoffs, no matter what profit is generated. Layoffs will not be approved without a comprehensive plan for changing the nature of the work itself, so that fewer people can be shown to handle more work through the intervention of new technologies, changes in processes, more efficient time use, etc.

7. All managerial employees are tied into team, unit, and/or corporate goals. Where individual goals may make sense, i.e., in the sales area, they are included as only a portion of the overall incentive compensation potential.

8. Annually, senior management evaluates all positions (regardless of the merit of the incumbent) to determine if those positions bring discrete value-added to the organization not found elsewhere. If positions fail this test, incumbents are reassigned to value-added positions. Commensurately, all individuals are assessed for contribution within the performance system, irrespective of the value-added of the position being filled. If they are not bringing value, and cannot be developed to bring value, they are replaced in that position and placed in another or outplaced.

9. Every organizational decision should be subject to the "why" test. "Why are we doing this?" demands responses superior to "We've always done it this way," or "Because we were told to do it this way." The "why" has to be justified in terms of usefulness to the customer, value-added, strategic need, market demand, etc. Anyone is empowered to apply the "why" test and receive a satisfactory answer.

Understanding the causes of our predicament is the key to preventing it from reoccurring. There is no reason to expect that we must always live with stupid management. The next chapter will explain why we don't even have to tolerate it now.

How to Clothe the Emperors, Part 13

1. Reform school curricula to reflect the current realities about jobs, management, and skills required.
2. Teach people to read with comprehension.
3. Teach people to write with expression.
4. Teach people to speak with persuasion.
5. Teach people to listen with discernment.
6. Abandon the "feel good" team experiences (or use them for what they are: pleasant socialization and physical challenge) and create real incentives for teams to operate as cohesive units on the job.
7. Discourage the cowboy mentality by reducing incentive and recognition based solely on individual contribution.
8. Reward managers directly for developing others. Assess a manager's performance by assessing his or her people's performance.
9. Do not tolerate an "entitlement" mentality, but do not frighten people into paralysis, either. Intelligently manage anxiety levels so that they produce optimum motivation and a sense of reasonable urgency.
10. Use the performance system for what it's intended to provide: Identify top performers and challenge them still further, and identify poor performers and either develop them or remove them.

Chapter 14

Correcting
How to Eliminate Stupid Management

"To free oneself is only the beginning. The real problem is to live in freedom."

—André Gide

The fact remains that there is too much stupid management in place, too much in the "pipeline." If we wait for attrition to reduce the ranks, the attrition might include us. It doesn't take an act of God or an act of Congress to remove stupid management. It does, however, require an act of volition.

Human resource professionals, board members, customers, shareholders, consultants, trade associations, vendors, and civic institutions can all participate in the eradication of stupid management. There are discrete actions that interested parties can undertake. It's usually uncomfortable for the public to see a "leader" removed, just as it's sad to see the removal of the captain from a ship. (Even Queeg had his empathizers by the time the Caine Mutiny court martial was concluded.) But it's far sadder to see the ship sink with all hands due to the captain's ineptness, particularly while that officer is viewing the tragedy from the safety of a departing dingy.

When organizations talk about the need for "execution," it is the noun, not the verb, which they should obtain. In the long run, we all get the kind of government—civic or organizational—that we deserve.

Not long ago, we had a series of 800 toll-free numbers installed at one of our sites to handle client "hotlines." These are generally opportunities for employees to call in on an anonymous basis and voice their concerns about a policy change, acquisition, restructuring effort, or other organizational initiative that is causing discomfort or alarm. The calls are sorted by category and demography and provided to the organization's management so that key issues can be addressed rapidly, enabling people to return their focus to the job and its output. We've done this hundreds of times over a decade.

We remarked earlier that, on this particular installation, the local phone company—Nynex—installed the system and then "handed off" the process to MCI, our long-distance carrier. Although Nynex checked to see that the system was working locally, *they never verified with MCI that the latter had received and processed the request to "turn on" the service on an interstate basis*. MCI claims they never received the advisory, and I know that Nynex never bothered to check on the final product, because the 800 number failed to work on the first day outside of our own state.

We fixed the problem by the end of the first day, thanks largely to MCI's eventual response to our frenzied calls. The client was understanding, but we had lost a day for them, and suffered some embarrassment. As a gesture of good will, we waived 3 days of charges to the client for the 1-day mishap, a gesture warmly received. Then I wrote the president of Nynex.

More than 2 weeks later, I received a call from a customer service manager, whom I will call Margerie. Here is the verbatim conversation, including the annoying fact that she felt it appropriate to address me by my first name right from the outset.

Margerie: Alan, I'm calling about the letter you wrote to our president. You claim that you lost revenue because of a problem.

Me: That's correct. We lost a day's revenue, plus the salaries of the operators hired who could not work.

Margerie: And you're asking us to make good on that loss?

Me: Yes.

Margerie: Well, all I can advise is that you'll have to get a lawyer and sue us.

Me: You're advising me to sue you?! A lawyer and a lawsuit would cost more than the amount at stake. That means I'm simply out of the money due to your error, and you're protected by the system.

Margerie: If that's how you want to look at it. But there's nothing else we can do.

Me: Don't you feel, ethically, that this is inappropriate? Don't you think you should do something as a responsible organization? Don't you think that you at least owe me an apology, which, candidly, I haven't heard in your words or your tone?

Margerie: Frankly, I don't know why you think this is such a big deal. If it's that important to you, I'd be willing to bump this up to my boss.

This midlevel manager was acting according to her corporate culture, her exemplars, and her formal and informal directives about how to act. Note that there was no apology ever offered nor an acknowledgment of culpability.

One reason attrition won't work in the elimination of poor management is that cultures are being created that continue to promulgate and perpetuate behaviors that support arrogance: the idea that you can walk the halls with no clothes and demand that people compliment you on your attire. "Only the good die young," and it's time we realize that nature will not take care of this problem by itself. We have to start putting poor managers out of their misery.

Who's in Charge Here?

We've previously established that "culture" is simply that set of beliefs which governs behavior. Behaviors are manifestations of what people believe, what values they hold dear. "Turn the other cheek" reflects one set of beliefs, while "an eye for an eye" reflects quite another. It's no accident that virtually every aphorism has an antipodal adage; i.e., "haste makes waste," and "time waits for no man."

Sets of beliefs, or culture, establish defining behaviors that strive for self-consistency. Individuals seek to maintain what psychologists call *self-efficacy,* the ability to behave in a consistent manner, compatible with self-image. If I see myself as a patient, loving individual, it's stressful for me to act in an aggressive, vengeful manner. If I see myself as assertive and innovative, it's equally difficult to act in a passive and risk-averse manner. The more I have to "shift" my behaviors from my norm, the more uncomfortable I become. My impetus is to return to that "home base" of my self-image, where I am most comfortable acting in conformance with how I view myself.

Organizations foster cultures that maintain their self-consistency as well. The cultures are determined by the people who control reward and consequences. Take a close look at the true reward systems of any organization—financial and nonfinancial—and you should be able to determine its defining set of values. Nordstrom's will accept virtually any item as a return, while Nynex isn't prepared to even admit it has made an error. The former's employees are given wide latitude to accept such returns and are rewarded for that kind of customer consideration, while Nynex does not delegate the ability to spend money on resolving customer problems.

It's time that we held senior managers accountable for a simple set of relationships: values, vision, consequences, performance.

In Figure 14.1, we see the relationship among values, vision, and strategy. Values determine what a company stands for, why it's in existence. Two elements emerge from an organization's values: (1) What it should look like in the future if it is to conform to those values and maximize its contribution to

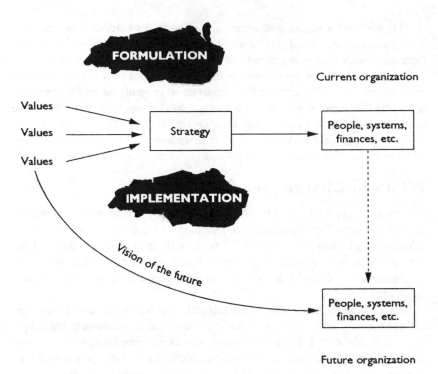

Figure 14.1. Values and strategy.

the environment; (2), what strategies are required to manage the current organization so that it constantly heads for that future state. (The vision is consistently unfolding, so one has never "arrived." The goal is to continue in the right direction, and it's the journey, not the destination, that's important.)

The "formulation" stage, in which management develops strategies with Gnostic awareness and minute precision, is only the beginning of this process. Formulation seldom "fails" because it's done on paper and in perfect conditions. A document, even one in a three-ring binder, isn't going to fail. It's the implementation phase that's critical, and the one that often proves the undoing of strategy, since it deals with present realities and variables.

Senior executives have to be held accountable for the following:

- Articulating the values of the organization in a manner that allows for every stakeholder, employee, shareholder, and customer to understand and identify with the *raison d'être* of the enterprise

- Exemplifying the values, so that executive decision-making, behavior, and policies are consistent with and reinforce those values
- Providing for reward systems that encourage the behaviors that fulfill the values and discourage the behaviors that undercut the values
- Establishing and defining a clear, concise, and relevant vision of the future state of the organization, so that everyone associated with it knows the direction of the organization and his or her role in helping to guide it
- Defining the performance of all key managers which will constitute successful contributions in meeting the business objectives
- Evaluating performance of individuals, teams, and the organization to determine the interventions necessary to make "midcourse corrections" as the current organization evolves into the future organization

I suspect that six areas of performance appraisal are too many for high-priced executives to handle, yet I doubt that many are continually held accountable for even three of them. But these accountabilities can only be those of the people at the top. Otherwise, "Who's in charge here?" is no idle question.

Take Us to Your Leader

The only way to eliminate present-day stupid management is to create performance standards that are clear and realistic, and hold top managers accountable for them. In that case, talent will "out." At the moment, without these clear criteria, too many executives can slip through the cracks: The strategy formulation may be beautiful, but the implementation fails "because of the people below." The organization's productivity can be improved by firing all those extra people in middle management, but who hired them in the first place?

In Figure 14.2, we can see three possible failure points in our dynamic:

1. A coherent future isn't defined, meaning that the organization has no consistent destination to pursue.
2. Values aren't articulated or aren't translated into strategic goals, preventing a relevant strategy from being formulated.
3. Strategy isn't translated into pragmatic implementation steps, preventing intelligent management of the current organization.

The result of these failures is a current organization that makes progress toward an unknown and, probably, undesirable goal. It is not headed toward a future consistent with values and vision, but one that is created by short-term developments, the competition, the government, the local leadership, and/or situational demands. Every organization has a motive power, a driving force.

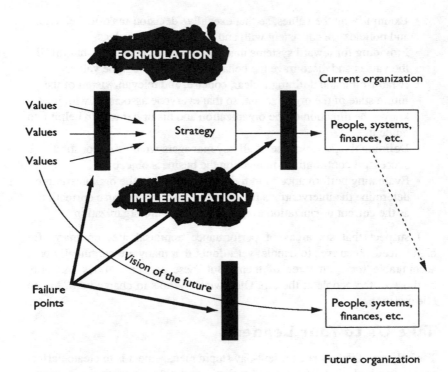

Figure 14.2. Failure points.

It will default to this force if a managed one is not superimposed. Sears failed in defining its future, believing it competed with everyone for everything. Kodak failed in its formulation of strategy, allowing for pharmaceuticals to somehow take a place alongside its photo business. And GM has failed in its implementation, unable to wrestle its existing organization into one that could expeditiously move toward a renewed vision.

If a UFO on a trade mission landed in front of the company gates and said "Take us to your leader," that leader had better be doing the six things listed above. And someone or some group had better be charged with enforcing that accountability. Here's one list of those responsible:

The shareholders. Shareholders, especially those with clout, such as institutional investors, should refuse to pass board resolutions by proxy and by indifference, particularly compensation resolutions. Investors need to know what the board is doing to hold the senior officers accountable, what the measurements are, and how the evaluations will take place. Under no circumstances should reciprocal board membership be allowed, much less such membership that involves serving on each other's compensation committees.[1]

The board of directors. The board must create specific criteria and processes for establishing senior management performance goals, measuring the progress toward those goals, and awarding appropriate compensation and incentive. Boards should have more outside directors than internal directors, and no internal director should ever serve as a committee chair. An internal auditor from the organization's financial area should be directly responsible to the chair of the board's finance committee on demand. No multiyear contracts should be signed for officers without a provision allowing dismissal for cause, and that cause should include performance that does not meet the goals established. Under no circumstances should the board reward profit performance that has been based on cost cutting of people and operations, both of whom and which current management hired and implemented to begin with.

Customers. Every one of us, in our capacity as consumers and service users, should complain every time we receive shoddy service, poor products, and rude behavior. Make no allowances and take no prisoners. Whenever we are placed on "hold" for 15 minutes, receive merchandise 3 weeks late, ignore the fact that a repair wasn't made to our full satisfaction, or tolerate consistently late transportation, we are aiding and abetting stupid management.

My complaint to the Nynex president was followed up with a complaint to the public utilities commission and the inclusion of that example in this book. What have you done, as a customer, when the hotel missed your wakeup call, the airline canceled your flight, the department store overcharged your account, and the charity kept besieging you with requests for contributions? Do you accept the sloth as part of a world in which quality has gone to hell, or do you take action?

Employees. Employees must stop accepting "necessary evils." While I've consistently heard how hard it is to "speak up" and endure a threat to one's

---

[1] In other words, if an officer from American Airlines serves on the board of Bank of America, no officer from Bank of America should be allowed to serve on the board of American Airlines. At the moment, we often have "back scratching" to the extent that I'm on your compensation committee, determining your pay, and you're on mine.

job, I've also observed how much more horrible it is to live in fear and adverse conditions than to lose an abusive job. If an employee hasn't received a performance evaluation—or isn't apprised of its content—the employee should demand it. If policies are implemented which interfere with the relationships shown above, employees should point them out. If "doing more with less" is creating workloads that threaten service, quality, and profitability, then employees have to demonstrate this. While there is fear over jobs and threat to security, these dangers are sometimes overly exaggerated and used as excuses not to act.

I once worked with a newspaper editor who told me that the job was 80 hours a week, with old equipment, poor management support, inadequate resources, and a generally ungrateful advertiser and reader base. I asked him why he didn't go into another business, since he was in his mid-30s. "What!" he said, "I love this work!"

George Ade remarked that we shouldn't pity the martyrs, since they love the work. We'll never get rid of stupid management if employees endure it, are martyrs to it and, inadvertently, make it look brilliant by their own sacrifices. The Emperor allowed himself to be fitted with invisible raiment because his advisors were afraid to tell him the truth—that he was being swindled by some fast talkers playing on his arrogance. He paraded around naked because the populace didn't dare state what was right before their eyes.

Ultimately, a child exposed the Emperor's lack of clothes and the subjects' lack of courage.

When the Subjects Have No Clothes

One of the primary causes of stupid management's longevity is stupid employees. Some organizations are chock-full of court jesters, and little else.

There are movements constantly afoot to improve *empowerment,* once upon a time known as *delegation.* But "empowerees" have to want to be empowered. There is an immutable, inverse law of gravity at work in all organizations:

Decisions will invariably rise to a level at which someone either constantly dares to make them or constantly dares to refuse to make them.

As people refuse to make decisions, for whatever reasons, those decisions that beg for outcomes will rise, because people "upstairs" are being made uncomfortable. ("Where's that report?" "Why haven't we launched the new program?" "When will the figures be ready?") The decision will finally arrive at someone's desk who will either:

1. Make the decision himself or herself, on the logical grounds that it's not going to get done otherwise

2. Refuse to make the decision and assign someone below direct accountability for making it, on the logical grounds that otherwise a precedent is established that will place every decision on the superior's desk

The only exception to this rule is in the case of those decisions that are truly unimportant, in which case they won't get decided and no one will care. But either of the two conditions above produces great waste, excess time, and considerable confusion. Yet they are indicative of an organization in which employees, as well as managers, aren't performing well.

Here are the conditions in which we usually see evidence of stupid employees. These people blame management, but they are their own worst enemies.

Decision-making. Decisions are not made because people are busy trying to figure out "what the boss wants to hear" (when, often enough, what the boss wants to hear is the truth). This is an extension of the "yes-man" mentality, in which rationality and legitimate goals are sacrificed in terms of political correctness.

At a meeting with a division president, his staff, and the group vice president from the parent company, the president had presented a plan number—based on his staff's inputs—which he believed was entirely reachable. In reality it was based on what his staff thought he wanted to hear, rather than on their own best estimates. The group vice president was skeptical when he heard the number which, of course, he would be responsible for to his superiors.

"I want every one of you in this room to tell me you can make this number," he said. "Now's the time to say you can't if you don't think it's reachable, and there will be no penalty or second-guessing. But I need to know now, looking each one of you in the eye."

Every staff member told him the number was reasonable and achievable. "There will be no second chances," said the VP, "because I will hold you to this number." The president felt quite comfortable, now having received the number from his people *and* hearing them vouch for it in the presence of his boss.

The company missed the number by a light-year. But the ending isn't what you might envision. The group vice president was fired. The parent believed that the accountability was with him. The following year, the president having been shaken by past events, asked me to interview privately each member of the team who set the number for the new plan. In one-on-one interviews in January, 12 of 24 people believed their newest plan could not be reached, and 6 were uncertain. Only 6 felt the plan was achievable. And this was in January, with more than 11 months to go!

It's easy for the Emperor to go naked when everyone's telling him how good he looks.

Collaboration. Turf issues are fought more fiercely around fox holes than in headquarters. That is, it's hard to have hand-to-hand combat using models and matrices, but easy when you're creating your own enemies face-to-face every day.

Earlier, we described the vice president who spent valuable time battling a colleague for office space and bragging to others of his tactics. I doubt that the reader found the story far-fetched. There is too little cooperation, collaboration, and collegiality at the soldier level. Emperors used to divide and conquer. It's seldom necessary in most modern organizations. One health products organization's field force is fond of citing the two sales they make for any single purchase: one to the customer, and one to their home office, to convince them to deliver. "I have to call with enticements, hoping my own support people will return my calls," commented one salesperson.

The lack of collaboration—internal, eroding friction that keeps the focus inside our circle, reproduced from Chapter 12 in Figure 14.3—is primarily caused by combinations of the following cultural artifacts:

- The cowboy mentality, which holds that the individualistic, ego-centered approaches work the best and are most favored by the organization. This value puts women at a particular disadvantage, since most organizations continue to maintain that what is assertive for a man is "bitch" for a woman.
- Reward and incentive systems that emphasize individual performance *even at the expense of* team and organizational performance. Awards that are reserved for the top three producers or use forced distributions automatically disenfranchise everyone else. Unless incentive systems are carefully devised, they tend to be divisive rather than collaborative in their effect.
- Distrust of others "not like us." There is a new diversity in our organizations that has nothing to do with political correctness and everything to do with evolving demographics. The first major shift was caused by large numbers of women entering previously all-male positions, which has created an awkwardness in how to act and in whom to trust. (This has been exacerbated by the avalanche of sexual discrimination and harassment lawsuits in an increasing litigious society.) The second major shift was caused by ethnic groups participating at all levels of the workforce *no longer willing to hide their ethnicity and cultural traits*. There are more people for whom English is a second—or third or fourth—language, more turbans and dashikis. We have become moral strangers, no longer trusting each other because our frames of reference and roots are unrecognizable to each other.

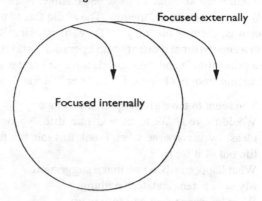

100% of the organization's
talent and energies

Focused externally

Focused internally

Figure 14.3. Lack of collaboration.

- Communication is seldom face-to-face anymore. At Hewlett-Packard, people commonly ask whether you'd like to receive information by paper, desk, or voice, meaning a paper memo, e-mail, or voice messages. At most organizations, you are as prone to get a coworker's message system as to reach him or her personally. (Many executives have abandoned voice mail after finding that they can't reach their own people. Imagine how the customers feel?)
- Insecurity caused by downsizing and layoffs has created islands of retreat. Sometimes these fortresses are inhabited by hermits who feel guilty that they remain while friends and coworkers were arbitrarily dismissed. Sometimes they are the reserves of those who intend to be the last ones to go, come hell or high water. In either case, these are basically noncommunicative, isolated people for whom collaboration provides no benefits and no motivation.

Helplessness. Due to a variety of factors discussed throughout this book—which include threats of technology, instant communication, changing values, economic uncertainty, and radically changing organizational structures—I've noticed a growing sense of despair, helplessness, anomie, and declining self-esteem among employee groups. I'm confronted with reactions such as, "Whatever they want is fine—I don't care"; "What's the use, I have no power here"; "I'm just trying to put in my time until I can get out"; and "There's no place for people like me here anymore."

221

The fundamental driver behind this "surrender" is the society-at-large drift toward victimization. None of us is responsible. None of us can be accountable. We are all victims of "them." "They" did this to us.

The problem is, there is no "they." "They" is us. Here's a conversation recorded with a supervisor at a distribution operation, who is a marginal performer with a poor attitude and who spends most of her day doing as little as possible and hiding from her bosses. I'll call her "Gloria."

Me: You seem to have given up on the company.

Gloria: Wouldn't you? We're treated like dirt. No one listens to our ideas. I was enthused when I took this job, but they've taken the life out of it for me.

Me: What happens when you make suggestions?

Gloria: My boss listens and does nothing.

Me: What happens when you follow up?

Gloria: I don't follow up. It's up to him to do something . . . get back to me . . . take some action.

Me: But how do you know unless you ask him?

Gloria: Look, I know what's going on. The only people who are listened to and promoted are the ones with bachelor's degrees. I didn't need one when I started here, but it seems that times have changed. My associate's degree used to be good enough.

Me: Doesn't the company have a tuition-refund program?

Gloria: Yes.

Me: Why don't you go back to get your bachelor's part-time? Even the act of doing it might carry some weight in combination with your experience.

Gloria: Why should I have to take the time out of my life to go back to school? I know everything that the others know, and more. It's the job that's important, not what you learn in some classroom.

Me: Have you gone to Personnel to explore what it would take to get promoted? Maybe they could recommend a series of performance reviews, developmental experiences, and internal goals that don't require more school?

Gloria: I don't trust Personnel. Besides, what would they do? They're only there as supporters of the management line. . . .

And so it went. Gloria couldn't advance or change her status because of all the people and procedures making her a victim. There *are* many factors that tend to disempower employees, factors over which they have no control. But these adverse conditions are no worse than what others have faced during depression, societal upheaval, war, and mergers. A friend and colleague on the speaking circuit, W. Mitchell, tells his audiences, "It's not what happens to you. It's what you do about it." Employees are totally immersed in "what happens to them," and mostly unprepared and unwilling "to do something about it."

We are victims because we allow ourselves to be victimized. We are helpless because we refuse to help ourselves or accept help from others.

Tolerating the Intolerable

We have to eliminate stupid management, because natural selection won't take care of it. In fact, natural selection has produced the exact opposite result.

The elimination of poor management has to begin with our own discontent expressed honestly and openly, whether consumer, supplier, shareholder, or employee. The more we tolerate shoddiness, the more we'll have to endure it. John Gardner made this observation:

> We must learn to honor excellence in every socially acceptable human activity—and to scorn shoddiness, however exalted the activity. An excellent plumber is infinitely more admirable than an incompetent philosopher. The society which scorns excellence in plumbing because plumbing is a humble activity—and tolerates shoddiness in philosophy because it is an exalted activity—will have neither good plumbing nor good philosophy. Neither its pipes nor its theories will hold water.

Our Emperors have to be told when they have no clothes. The subjects have to be willing to tell them. We are not victims of the system; we are its architects. Winston Churchill observed once, "We make our houses; then they make us." He was referring to Parliament, but the insight holds true for all of our organizational constructs.

Each of us who tolerates late deliveries, broken promises, canceled meetings, poor-performing equipment, misleading advertising, poor returns on investments, late payments, and rude behavior contributes to the perpetuation of those weaknesses. Each of us who rises to complain, suggests new ideas, innovates, demands proper treatment, and rejects poor quality is contributing to a positive change in the status quo.

The decision is ours every day. It can't be delegated, avoided, or passed up the ladder. It can, of course, be ignored.

How to Clothe the Emperors, Part 14

1. Send out clear messages about values and beliefs that reinforce appropriate behaviors. Senior managers must exemplify those behaviors personally and visibly.
2. Establish and maintain reward systems that encourage teamwork, not isolationism.
3. Establish and maintain reward systems that encourage desired behaviors, and discourage undesired behaviors.
4. Evaluate managers at all levels for their support and enforcement of the desired values.
5. Create clear, concise performance standards that support the direction of the organization and provide for clear measures of success.
6. Push decisions downward. Managers should refuse to make decisions that are properly made at lower levels.
7. Establish collaboration based on trust, in an increasingly diverse workplace.
8. Do not tolerate victimization. We are accountable for our conditions and should take action based on that reality.
9. Accept dissent and disagreement as positive and desirable behaviors, when they are voiced in a manner consistent with reaching corporate goals.
10. Don't tolerate poor performance and unacceptable behaviors that simultaneously endorse and perpetuate stupid management.

Chapter 15

Leadership
Moving into the Future

"In seasons of pestilence, some of us will have a secret attraction to the disease—a terrible passing inclination to die of it."
—Charles Dickens
A Tale of Two Cities

We have allowed ourselves to become a nation of victims. We have allowed standards to be lowered rather than attempt to raise performance. We have wallowed in our problems rather than recognize the challenges that can propel us forward. We have tried to participate in the spoils of a corrupt system, rather than fight to change the system. The enemy, indeed, is us.

Worst of all, perhaps, is that when we have attempted to affix blame, assign cause, and correct our organizational dilemmas, we have focused on the wrong place and the wrong people. The American worker, in the vast majority of situations of organizational malaise, is not the problem.

We've discussed earlier the precipitous decline in unionization in the private sector. Workers have eschewed the safety and adversarial positions of organized labor over the latter part of the 20th century. They have accepted wage freezes, layoffs, larger shares of their health care costs, productivity demands, longer hours, and harsher conditions. They have persevered through forced relocations, less time with their families, sacrificed vacations, and continual reorganizations.

In fact, American workers are among the busiest and most productive in the world, second only to the Japanese in total hours worked. This trend is likely to continue, since 33% of workers responding to surveys indicate that they would voluntarily work still more hours in order to earn more money, while only 6% indicate they would not.[1] (The average American worker puts in 130 more hours annually than the average among industrialized countries, while Germans, for example, put in 131 hours *less*.)

Rocket Science

The criminal aspect of stupid management is that workers at all levels are being hurt no matter how hard they work, how many hours they invest, and how loyal their efforts on behalf of the organization. The system has created a safety zone at the top, in which executives are not held strictly accountable for their actions and, when they are, golden parachutes and "soft landings" create the kind of affluent departure that lower levels couldn't achieve after 40 years of hard work and full vesting in their retirement plans. Even the most egregiously stupid behavior is condoned in the executive suite, reaching an apotheosis when top management is rewarded by the board for terminating the thousands of people they hired to begin with. Their reward comes for brutally responding to their own ineptness in failing to manage head counts, missing key market trends, belatedly responding to competitive activities, and allowing poor performance to continue far longer than it should have.

It's the equivalent of an admiral being surprised by the enemy because he blindly sailed into harm's way, had no scouts, was not at battle stations, and provided for no training or discipline on his ships. When attacked and destroyed by the enemy, he orders the ships abandoned and scuttled, loses the entire fleet, and is rewarded by his government with either another fleet or a fat pension and the accolades of a grateful nation.

We are rewarding our admirals for salvaging the wreckage of their own stupidity. The employees have become the flotsam and jetsam.

Businesses of one type or another have been in existence for a couple of millennia. There are some constants that we should have mastered by now which—despite computerization, communication, globalization, and procrastination—can be relied on for stability in organizational life. Leading people in pursuit of business goals is not rocket science, although our business schools, consultants, and fad-of-the-month clubs would have us believe it is an arcane and complex alchemy.

Recently, I was a guest lecturer at St. John's University in New York. While working on my notes in a faculty office, I overheard a conversation in the next cubicle between a middle-aged woman who was pursuing her doctorate in

---

[1] See *Management Review,* Dec. 1994: "Lazy American Workers? No More," by Catherine Romano.

business and the professor who was her advisor. The conversation went like this:

"Professor, I was thinking about Lonberg's thesis and his alternative reciprocal communities of informal power."

"Hmm, Lonberg has always interested me, although you'd have to be careful with your measurement devices."

"I wanted to examine the role of missionary driving force intruding upon a professionally bureaucratic organization."

"Then you should also consider Green's work on the 12 organizational subtypical mentalities."

"Actually, I intend to prove that there are only 10 permanent types, and that the other two can only be transitory."

"All right, let's talk about your instrumentation...."

Why don't we talk about a stiff drink for innocent bystanders? Or warning whomever these two come in contact with to run for their lives? The last time I looked, tuition at St. John's was hovering around $12,000 a year.

We could create a list of "good" companies and "poor" companies right now, and most of you might agree that these candidates would be representative in a current snapshot:

Good Performers	Poor Performers
• Chrysler	• General Motors
• FedEx	• Kodak
• Wal-Mart	• K-Mart
• Hewlett-Packard	• Digital Equipment
• Southwest Airlines	• Continental Airlines
• Rubbermaid	• McDonnell Douglas
• Microsoft	• IBM

As I write this, Orange County, California, has declared bankruptcy. Ironically, Orange County is home to some of the greatest wealth in this country and was once considered the most glowing part of a once-golden state. "Excellent" and "poor" at any given moment are irrelevant. It's the long-term that's important.

Over a decade ago, Tom Peters and Bob Waterman wrote of superb companies in their wildly popular work, *In Search of Excellence*. [2] Guru Warren Bennis called it a "landmark" book, *The Wall Street Journal* called it "rare," and *Savvy* commented that it ought to become "a text in every graduate school of business

---

[2] *In Search of Excellence: Lessons from America's Best-Run Companies,* by Thomas J. Peters and Robert H. Waterman, Jr., Harper & Row, 1982.

in the country." Yet, over the ensuing years, critics have lambasted the work as being ephemeral and short-sighted. After all, among their "winners" they had cited Digital Equipment, IBM, Delta, and Caterpillar. In the intervening years, these organizations had major difficulties, and some haven't yet recovered. The authors also made some inaccurate observations about resiliency, remarking for example that "GM ... will likely survive [auto industry] troubles better than the rest of the American auto industry."

However, zealots and critics both missed the point by a country mile. Peters and Waterman were discussing attributes of successful companies (i.e., their famous buzzwords about "sticking close to the knitting," "a bias for action," and "simultaneous loose-tight properties"). There is no guarantee that any organization, no matter how it may embody those attributes (and assuming they are the "right" ones to begin with), will continue to embrace them. Just because a company represented those qualities at the moment didn't mean that it always would.

The reason for that is twofold, in my view:

1. Leaders change, and the new people bring in different attributes.
2. Conditions change, and the existing leaders do not.

Anyone can lead through good times, particularly when business is growing and external conditions tend to be stable. My dog could sit in the president's office munching on one of its bones and, on 9 days out of 10, the business would get along just fine. When times are bad and external conditions are stable, it is tougher to run the organization, but not critically so, because old paradigms should still apply. Working harder, sacrificing more, and paying closer attention to details might well see you through a downturn if the environment is unchanged. But when times *are* tough and the external conditions are rapidly changing, leadership is hard-pressed. This is the moment when supreme skill, innovation, risk taking, and pure "follow me" leadership are desperately needed. My dog couldn't do that. Neither can many of our corporate leaders. The difference is that my dog doesn't blame anyone else, and doesn't try to downsize the family.

The reason that *In Search of Excellence* couldn't provide a crystal ball for future success is that leaders change, and leadership, *not corporate attributes,* is the key variable. Bill Gates is providing superb leadership at Microsoft at the moment. Will that continue if he retires next year to see if it's possible to spend one of the world's great fortunes in one lifetime? Will it continue if he stays in place but the government demands significant divestiture because of unfair competition, or a new technology knocks the stuffing out of Windows™?

Corporate attributes are the results of what our leadership exemplifies, supports, and rewards. Strong organizations can tolerate ineffective leadership for a while, but they will inevitably decline (IBM). Weaker organizations will decline precipitously (USAir). Strong leaders, however, can take weak organizations and build competitive operations (Chrysler), and can make strong organizations into world champions (Coca-Cola).

A Model for Strategic Leadership

There is no perfect model to provide for strong leadership, but there are ways to view the dynamics and interrelationships in a cogent manner. The simpler we can make this, the easier it is to evaluate whether leadership is up to the task.

The model in Figure 15.1 is meant to illustrate what strategic leadership is all about.

Business Goals. Organizations succeed or fail based on their ability to meet legitimate and well-thought-out business goals. These goals may include customer retention, market share, contributions to society, reinvestment in organization growth, profit and return metrics, and other pursuits of the business. The role of leadership is to:

1. Formulate the correct goals for the business
2. Articulate and instantiate the goals so that they are understood
3. Monitor progress toward the goals
4. Reward or "punish" behaviors that support or impede progress
5. Exemplify the values that support the goals
6. Reassess the goals periodically for additions, deletions, and changes

Team Performance. Teams will operate as both "family groups," which are homogeneous teams pursuing departmental goals (i.e., the sales force working toward its revenue quotas), and "stranger groups," which are heterogeneous teams pursuing organizational goals (i.e., a new product launch that involves research, sales, marketing, distribution, etc.). Cross-functional teams were once exceedingly uncommon, with everyone consumed by their "silo." Today, such cooperative endeavors are all the rage, with accents on "boundarylessness," "crossing turf," and "pulling down walls." There is no guarantee that this rage will be with us tomorrow, when organizations just might return to "focus on your specialty," "create areas of accountability," or "build walls to contain problems."

Nonetheless, teams will continue to operate in support of business goals, because minimum levels of cooperation are required when people work together in common pursuits. And within those teams, management is responsible for:

1. Providing incentives that support collaboration toward goals
2. Delegating (empowering) accountability and authority
3. Providing interpersonal skills building to enhance collaboration

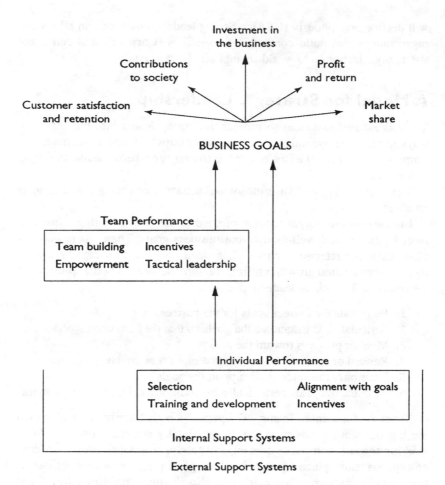

Figure 15.1. Strategic leadership model.

4. Identifying and assigning local leadership for greatest synergy
5. Enhancing communication among and between teams

Individual Performance. Some individuals directly support the business goals on a singular basis. These people can range from a corporate attorney, to an assembly line worker, to a client service representative on the telephone, to a hotel desk clerk. They might occasionally serve on teams and may be excellent collaborators, but their primary roles are as individual contributors. That is, they perform their tasks and are responsible for their outcomes in isolation. They can make a difference without the immediate support or involvement of others. (The hotel doorman brings your bags promptly to the front desk; the operator politely takes your order; the repair person suggests how to prevent a future breakdown.)

So, whether as the contributors to team efforts or as direct supporters of the organization's business goals, individuals require the following from their leadership:

1. Careful selection and assignment in appropriate jobs
2. Alignment of individual goals with the organizational goals
3. Incentives/disincentives that support appropriate behaviors
4. Training and development in relevant skills
5. Equal opportunity and freedom from discriminatory practices
6. Working conditions that maximize time "out of the circle"[3]

Support Systems. Finally, strategic leadership provides for a combination of internal support (i.e., finance, human resources) properly apportioned throughout the organization, and external support (i.e., consultants, employee assistance programs, alliances) available to the organization, so that the individual and team development can continue to evolve and thrive. Internal support structures are vital for rapid response, knowledge of the culture, and replecatable processes. External support is important for objectivity, fresh insights, confidentiality, and cost-effective, short-term focus.

Leadership in this area should ensure that support is:

1. Interwoven in the organization, and not in "silos"
2. Painless and nonpunishing
3. Proactive and innovative, not reactive and restrictive
4. Aligned with business goals, not in opposition to them
5. Relevant and individualized, not "an end in itself" and generic

There is nothing sacred or magical about this model. You might feel that R&D superiority is a business goal; team performance should include international assignments; and individual performance should embrace succession planning. The details are at the reader's discretion. It's the overview that's important. Enlightened leadership must provide a holistic system in which business goals are directly supported by team and individual efforts, which are in turn supported by relevant internal and external mechanisms. That systemwide view and influence can only be taken and provided from the top. Only top leadership can establish those interactions in a manner consistent with the business goals of the enterprise.

---

[3] See Chapter 14.

How to Clothe the Emperors, Part 15

We are not doomed to repeat the mistakes of the past. While we won't create a world in which all organizations are brilliantly led and all employees are superb contributors, we can create a business environment in which leadership at the top creates accountabilities throughout the organization and all people, top to bottom, are evaluated on their performance. We are not doomed to repeat the mistakes of the past *but we will if we don't change the systems and behaviors that have created and sustained them.*

Our emperors have paraded around with no clothes because of their own arrogance, the charlatans who have designed the wardrobe, the incompetents who don't know the difference, the timid who are afraid to speak out, and the indifference of the subjects. But the metaphor is too gracious—and the problem with most of the management fantasies and fairy tales on the shelves is that they tend to gloss over the abject nature of the harm being done. By allowing our senior managers to endure without tough performance standards and with lifetime financial guarantees, we have been party to the massive misery of hundreds of thousands of employees whose quality of life has been seriously eroded. We are not idle observers of a morality play but active participants in one of the most appalling changes in our social fabric of this century.

We'll conclude this chapter and this book with an in-depth view of our final recommendations. It's our intent that these and the other recommendations that close each chapter can serve as a template for boards, shareholders, employees, customers, and—most of all—managers themselves, against which their strategies, tactics, and behaviors can be compared. Some are subtle and not being addressed; some are obvious, but go unheeded. All are intended for organizations large and small, private and public, manufacturing or service. They apply to the departmental manager of a Fortune 500 firm, and to the sole proprietor of a family-owned business employing 100 people.

I. The organization has become the primary conveyor of standards, values, and proper behaviors, like it or not

By default, our organizations have become the graduate schools of social mores for our population. Their dynamics influence not only the interactions of their employees but also the behaviors with customers, suppliers, government, competition, and the community. Because of the decline of the traditional sources of ethical development and moral growth, the modern organization has become a replacement for the family, school, and religious institution. This wasn't intended and it's not the best manner in which to inculcate values, but it is, for now, the only one we've got.

Executives must understand and exploit that role. Newly hired employees, whether off the street, from another company, or from the campus, are entering the organization with vastly different belief systems and work ethics. The organization must provide for the orientation, training, and role models that clearly convey what it stands for. I'm not referring to the core values of the annual report, in which we are all acting for the good of humanity. I'm talking about our daily conduct and discourse, and how we are to interact.

One of the primary roles of executives is to articulate and convey values. Those values may be to win at any cost, or they may be to make a reasonable profit while contributing to society. They may be to avoid risk and never appear to differ from the company position, or to take initiative and speak out when something isn't right. These daily operating beliefs never occur in a vacuum. They are always the result of the real or perceived behaviors of the top people. The chronic complaint about "not walking the talk" emanates from this dynamic.

If leaders don't state their positions, people will assume a position from the actions they see. If they don't see any actions, they will make unfounded assumptions about them. If they hear one thing but see another, they will always emulate what they see. Employees must hear and see congruent values and behaviors if organizational cognitive dissonance is to be avoided.

"Management by wandering around" is an empty, silly tactic by itself. Most managers get in the way when they wander around without objectives, and can undermine their subordinates when they mindlessly meddle. However, being visible in the organization at all levels, clearly demonstrating the behaviors that fulfill the company's vision, and reinforcing the behavior of employees that support that vision, are mandatory in today's environment. Just a couple of hours a week dedicated to this exemplar role will make a tremendous impact over the course of a year.

In many organizations people tell us that they speak to vice presidential-level executives perhaps once a year, and may lay eyes on them only two or three times. Executives spend far too much of their time talking to each other, and not nearly enough talking to their own employees.

2. Productivity improvement is not a rationale for mass layoffs, and mass layoffs are not the holy grail of productivity

"Doing more with less" is another vacuous, delusional contemporary aphorism that compares favorably to the famous "blivet" of the Army, which is roughly defined as trying to put 10 pounds of something into a 5-pound bag.

Every organization should have a performance evaluation system that accurately provides feedback for management and the employees about quality and quantity of work being performed. It's incumbent upon every executive to ensure that every year, no matter what the financial condition of the enterprise, poor performers who cannot be developed are removed. A company having a good year is seriously negligent if it uses the excuse of a profit to tolerate poor performers in its midst. Executives who condone—or who don't try to identify—poor performance are malfeasant. If, every day, poor performers are identified, developed, or terminated, organizational performance would continually improve.

Conversely, poor organizational performance should not trigger scrutiny from the bottom of the organization, *but from the top of the organization.* Any board that contents itself with top management's promise to "do more with less" or to resolve current problems solely through layoffs deserves what it gets. Unfortunately, the employees don't deserve what they get.

Someone was responsible for allowing the organization to get fat, or for missing the environmental signs that the current organization was headed in the wrong direction, or for making incorrect assumptions about the economy, or for allowing poor performance to continue until drastic measures are required. Those responsible must be held accountable. *No executive should receive any incentive compensation in a year in which mass layoffs (i.e., more than X% of the workforce) are implemented.* Rather than luxuriant executive golden parachutes and guarantees, organizations should allocate severance pay packages based on seniority and performance evaluations over an employee's tenure.

The justification for substantial executive protection is in the risks attendant to the position. But that's like saying that generals are in more danger than privates in battle. The risk these days is with the employee, and some modicum of protection is required. Boards should force executives to stop worrying about their own survival and worry about the organization's survival. What is senior management doing to protect the largest investment of all, that made in talented and productive people?

People who were fired were doing something. The people who are left will either have to ignore what they are currently doing to pick up the load or try to do both jobs at a lower level of quality and quantity. You can't simply get two jobs done by one person by saying "do more with less," any more than you can get a goat to fly by telling it to take off. Reengineering and restructuring programs are too often management's way of justifying the termination of large numbers of people, in an attempt to show that the work will be more efficient.

Productivity improvement is an ongoing, preventive, proactive endeavor in good times and bad, not a knee-jerk, reactive, one-time event when things are headed south.

3. A diverse workplace directly contributes to organizational results

We have to avoid the emotionalism of the word *diversity* and the bizarre nature of today's "political correctness," because we refer here to an essential ingredient of organizational health. As we use the word, *diversity* means more than multiculturalism and gender issues, although it certainly embraces those factors. It also refers to the ability to speak one's mind, to look and speak as an individual and not as a regimented soldier, and to convey differing viewpoints and perspectives. White males are as much a part of a diverse workplace as is anyone else. Unfortunately, those white males have often been denied their own uniqueness through conformance with dress codes, presentation styles, and political behaviors.

We're working with several of our clients to gather longitudinal data that demonstrate that a diverse workplace is one with greater productivity, higher retention rates, and more innovation. We've noted that anecdotal studies have begun to emerge which show that diverse, heterogeneous teams reach project goals more quickly and with better results than do homogeneous teams. The problem is that a dip in productivity can occur if the organization resists diversity in its halls and decides that its senior people are paying lip service to the effort or are only interested in keeping the government away from the door.

"Silos" are created by power structures perpetuating themselves, and this is done most efficaciously and most devastatingly when similar people blindly support each other. Senior management is uniquely able to cross organizational boundaries, invade silos, and create diverse work groups. They are also uniquely able to crush such intents.

Many leaders continue to support a white-male power structure in organizational America. This is a dangerous phrase to even suggest at most conferences and meetings, because the faces are mostly white male, and those that aren't are uncomfortable rocking the boat. The position is too often transmogrified to "it's either us or them." In fact, it should be both. The key words are *opportunity* and *access*. If diverse people and viewpoints have equal opportunity and access, then the most competent may rise to the top. But if, by dint of diverse appearance, background, or viewpoints, such opportunity and access is denied or restricted, then senior management is at fault.

"Allowing" women or minorities to rise to the top in narrow disciplines (i.e., human resources, legal, finance) is woefully insufficient and increasingly transparent. We'll know we've made progress when a woman is vice president of sales or a minority is in charge of operations, and those people aren't obvious because of their rarity. Similarly, those who are unafraid to speak out at meetings, to dress in something other than the organizational uniform, and who may make formal presentations with some flair and controversy should be seen in key roles as well.

Every board deserves a wide variety of choices as it considers successors to key posts and nominations to new positions. Are the current executives providing for an environment in which those choices are developed, or are they simply carefully nurturing clones of themselves?

4. Eschew the fads and myths, and never let anyone borrow your watch

There is an old adage in my profession that says, "A consultant is anyone with a briefcase more than 50 miles from home." Sometimes I think that neither the distance nor the luggage is demanded anymore.

Consulting is a noble profession, and there have been counselors and advice-givers from the time of the pharaohs. But for every Machiavelli, there's also been a Rasputin; for every Peter Drucker, there's been a Werner Erhard; and for every legitimate management development system, there have been people rappelling down the sides of elephants.

My apologies for poking fun at some of your favorites (particularly members of the Rasputin Society), but shouldn't we demand the same performance and guarantees from our advisors that the boards should be demanding from their executives? External consulting and training shouldn't be a "hit or miss" blind toss at a dart board. Consultants should be accredited;[4] training programs should be codified; and test instruments should be validated. Why on earth would a firm that must clear its products with the Food and Drug Administration, gain approval for its distribution from the Interstate Commerce Commission, and meet the tax standards set by the Internal Revenue Service hire a consultant without so much as a reference check, evidence of the results of the intervention proposed, a guarantee of some outcomes, and/or documentation of malpractice insurance?[5,6]

In all of my years in consulting—and being accredited by the Institute of Management Consultants—I have only been asked once if I carry malpractice insurance. In addition, about 50% of the time no one bothers to check my references, and about 75% of the time, no one asks for details of my speeches.

---

[4] This applies to all of those moonlighting college professors, as well. Merely by holding tenure at a recognized university does not make one a consultant with valid approaches. I've seen professorial consultants with designs and schemes so unrelated to the real world that ET would wince.

[5] Ironically, the government is the most notorious for hiring schlock, since its decisions about external help are based bureaucratically on "requests for proposals" that are evaluated on quantitative but not qualitative measures.

[6] With the exception of the large consulting firms, most consultants do not bother to carry errors and omissions insurance, because of the expense. Incredibly, clients seldom require it.

My bookshelf is overflowing with works that contain blueprints, grids, matrices, steps, models, aphorisms, and programs for organizational success. There are tens of thousands of seminars on the market, scores of "outward bound" experiences (and probably some out-of-body experiences), and another hundred thousand or so video- and audiocassettes. And they are not without their effects: Walk around many organizations and you'll hear management espousing "breaking the paradigm," discussing how to "empower" employees, searching for "total quality," and priding themselves on being "customer driven." Yawn.

Who cares? Results are what count, and the results are seldom there, except for the firms selling all this stuff.[7] *Nothing replaces inspired leadership. And nothing can compensate for inept leadership*—not seminars, not excursions, not aroma therapy.

5. Focus on the result and the output, not the task and the input

Finally, we must overcome our fixation on what is easy to measure but often meaningless, and be bold enough to focus on what is vital but sometimes difficult to measure. We are inclined to rely on what we can measure, rather than what we should measure.

Recently, I helped an organization decide on how best to use another consultant—I was actually the mediator, a consultant helping in the process of engaging the consultant—by demanding that both parties focus solely on two issues: desired outcomes and their measurement. Every time a task was raised, we would delegate it to a list of deliverables or interventions. By the end of the 3-hour session, three fascinating developments had occurred:

1. The client has decided to *raise* the fee originally in his mind, because it was clear that so much more *value* was being delivered.
2. The consultant, in his third year with the client, stated that this was the most accountable he had ever been held by the client, and thought his contribution was much more structured and visible than before.
3. Both agreed that not one executive in the organization had performance measures as tangible and measurable as the consultant now had.

---

[7] Am I the only one bothered by the fact that many, if not most of, the training and consulting firms in this country are struggling? How is it that the advice-givers can't use their own? The Big Ten accounting firms are now down to six, and publishers like Times Mirror, Prentice Hall, McGraw-Hill, and John Wiley, which purchased training firms as cash cows, have been unpleasantly surprised by their lack of profitability.

The value that any of us brings to an organization must be expressed in terms of some contribution to the business goals. Salespeople aren't paid to make sales calls—although that activity is usually mandatory—they are paid to bring in business. (If they could bring in the business without the sales calls, so much the better.) It's not enough for executives to ensure that their contributions are outputs in support of the business goals (although that is no small accomplishment). They must provide for everyone's contributions being so directed and so measured.

Many of us have asked how it came to pass that organizations plummeted so precipitously from their heights. It's as though IBM fell into a hole, or someone mugged Delta Airlines. The pundits report that they "became victims of their own arrogance" (i.e., "mainframes are forever") or "made key strategic market errors" (i.e., buying Pan Am's European route structure).[8] What often happens, however, is that organizations are lulled into a false sense of confidence because they are tracking all the wrong things. The tasks are, indeed, being performed. But the results aren't in the offing. IBM continued to build quality mainframes, continued to attract and retain high-caliber salespeople, and carefully monitored things like dress code. The problem, of course, was it didn't appreciate the permanent nature of its sales decline relative to those of work stations and client server networks. Delta prided itself on its arrival and departure times but didn't take its passenger capacity as seriously as it should have. It gained Pan Am's structure, but also gained ancient, poorly maintained Airbus jets, which eventually would have to be replaced at great expense.

Everyone in every organization, from CEO to receptionist, should understand what outputs he or she is accountable for generating, and how success in so doing will be measured. Sometimes it's hard to do that, but it's never as difficult as trying to recover from an economic landslide during which everyone has received splendid performance ratings.

Failure is seldom fatal, and success is never final. It's wisdom that counts. We can learn from the stupid management mistakes we've endured, from the patchwork, jerry-rigged, smoke-and-mirrors solutions that have made matters worse over the years. As a manager in Fleet's downsizing (see Chapter 6) told me, "We have only two options here nowadays: to laugh and improve, or to cry and despair. To me, that's a no-brainer."

---

[8] Sometimes the pundits can score points. When Pan Am sold its famed Manhattan building to raise cash for the airline, someone suggested that they sell the airline and keep the building. In retrospect, it would have been a better investment for all concerned.

We can apply what we've learned to our schools, our relationships, and our future. We are not a nation of underachievers and scant resources desperately scrambling to eke out an existence. At least, not yet. We have succeeded in many cases despite ourselves. Our opportunity is to apply our great energy and resources in the pursuit of enlightened leadership and intelligent management.

There are, happily, sufficient examples around us of organizations and leadership which are exemplars of what the future can be—with unremittingly high standards and a bright future for the enterprise and its employees. We should be able to look back on an era of stupid management and be thankful for the lessons learned, for the chance to profit by them, and for the fact that the era is behind us and not awaiting us.

In writing this book, I've tried to focus not on the task of creating paragraphs, chapters, and checklists, but on the result of readers who are better able to change their organizations and their lives through a renewed sense of purpose and common sense. The measurement depends on you. I hope you'll let me know if we've both succeeded.

About the Author

Alan Weiss is the founder and president of Summit Consulting Group, Inc., a firm specializing in management and organization development. Summit's clients include organizations such as Merck & Co., Hewlett-Packard, GE, National Westminster Bank, *The New York Times,* Mercedes-Benz, the American Press Institute, the American Institute of Architects, and more than 90 other organizations in four countries.

Weiss has published more than 300 articles in the fields of strategy, innovation, leadership, ethics, diversity, and interpersonal relations, in publications ranging from *Management Review* to *The New York Times.* He is the co-author of *The Innovation Formula,* and author of *Managing for Peak Performance, Making It Work* and *Million Dollar Consulting.*

He frequently appears on radio and television interview programs to discuss productivity and quality. He is a member of the American Counseling Association and the American Management Association, and is the past president of the New England Speakers Association. He is one of only seven people who hold both the designations "Certified Management Consultant" from the Institute of Management Consultants, and "Certified Speaking Professional" from the National Speakers Association.

Weiss is the former president of the Kepner-Tregoe Continuing Education Division, and vice president of Kepner-Tregoe, Inc., an international training firm, and the former CEO of Walter V. Clarke Associates, a behavioral consulting firm. He holds a bachelor's degree in political science, a master's degree in political science and psychology, and a doctorate in psychology. He has traveled to 49 countries and 48 states in the course of his career. He has been a guest lecturer at the University of Georgia Graduate School of Business, the University of Illinois, St. John's University, Case Western Reserve University and the Institute of Management Studies. *Success Magazine* has cited him in an editorial devoted to his work as "a worldwide expert in executive education."

Index

An asterisk (*) after a name identifies a present or past CEO or senior manager.